Motherless America: Confronting Welfare's Fatherhood Custody Program

Doreen Ludwig

Copyright © 2015 Doreen Ludwig

All rights reserved.

ISBN 10: 1515-256-219
ISBN-13: 978-1515-256-212

DEDICATION

To Elizabeth and Kathleen, may they know the truth,
To David Miller for his loving support,
To all the women and children whose suffering has been caused by
the fatherhood,
To those who work to correct the problem,
I wholeheartedly thank you and dedicate this book

ACKNOWLEDGEMENT

I wish to thank Leora N. Rosen, author of "The Hostage Child: Sex Abuse Allegations in Custody Disputes" (Indiana University Press, 1996) and "Beyond the Hostage Child: Towards Empowering Protective Parents" (Createspace, 2014), for her patient advice and support, and for the legislative history and ideas for reform contained in Beyond the Hostage Child, a must-read for mothers, advocates, legislators and custody practitioners.

Doreen Ludwig

CONTENTS

INTRODUCTION

PART ONE – PERSONAL STORY

    Prologue

1	Leaving	Pg 17
2	The Trial	Pg 45
3	The Vagina Claim	Pg 61
4	Jail for Mothers	Pg 77
5	Working to Correct, Looking for Help	Pg 91
6	Rebuilding	Pg 111

PART.TWO   THE RESEARCH

7	Abuse	Pg 131
8	War on Women	Pg 173
9	Best Interests of Father	Pg 201
10	The Players and Their Methods	Pg 247

PART THREE – A BETTER WAY   Pg 283

INTRODUCTION

The 1996 passage of the Personal Responsibility and Work Opportunity Reconciliation Act (PRWORA), reformed welfare from funding basic needs to funding family courts, mental health and legal practitioners, to favor fatherhood over motherhood without any consideration of abuse. The outcome is a family court system that forces fatherhood and eliminates mothers who leave abuse from the lives of their children. Welfare Fatherhood Initiatives have resulted in increasing numbers of motherless children living with abusive dads.

In 1995, David Blankenhorn published "Fatherless America: Confronting Our Most Urgent Social Problem" a book credited with keeping the fatherhood issue in the public's consciousness, thereby making fatherhood government policy. Blankenhorn claims the sexual revolution diminished fathers, leading to a decline in child well-being and a rise in social problems such as crime, domestic violence, and child abuse. Blankenhorn blames society's ills on women's increased rights and autonomy. Poverty, minimum wage pay, substandard education, unsafe neighborhoods, are not a problem: only fatherlessness.

The conservative movement against women's freedom to raise children without males with bad character traits and negative behaviors resulted in increasing amounts of welfare money being apportioned to Fatherhood Initiative Programs; away from cash assistance and other measures that help impoverished women and children, towards an industry run out of family court geared to giving custody to dad regardless of his financial need.

Motherless America confronts the hidden outcome of government funding an industry that hides abuse and endorses preferential treatment for fathers, creating what I call "forced fatherhood" operating by way of "fatherhood courts."

Part One of Motherless America's six memoir chapters let the reader feel the problem by revealing events that occurred when I divorced an abusive man and entered Pennsylvania's fatherhood court.

Part Two contains four research chapters. "Abuse" defines abuse and explains how it is processed by the industry. "War on Women" informs the reader of the groups that invented and carry-out the fatherhood custody agenda. "Best Interests of Father" details Fatherhood Initiative programs and funding sources. "The Players and Their Methods" takes a hard look at practitioners and how they operate in fatherhood courts.

Part Three, "A Better Way," proposes a new, computer-based method of custody determination. "A Better Way" recommends shifting welfare funding towards the whole family, by turning the focus of the Office of Child Support Enforcement towards elevating financial stability for both genders.

Motherless America has two purposes. First, to publicize the methods used by judges, mental health practitioners, lawyers and court administrators, to hide and cover-up their intentional case rigging. Second, to begin a movement for accountability, oversight and reform using the vehicle of a non-profit called Mothers Against Court Custody Abuse, www.MACCAbuse.org.

Motherless America cites research using a journalistic format. Referenced research is posted at www.MACCAbuse.org.

PART ONE

Personal Story

PROLOGUE

This personal story was written and included as an exhibit for my custody trial because I felt the court did not understand the abuse. Judge Keller refused to permit it to be a part of the record.

His anger and resentment really kicked in when I stopped working to stay home and care for the children. I believe some part of it was his want to be the stay-at-home mom. He felt he knew just how I should be doing my job and he and the family he wanted to emulate never failed to remind me that they knew better then I, and if they were in charge there would be no crying baby. Meanwhile, I was the one doing the work while he sat on the sofa with the TV or slept through the night. When he wasn't staring at the TV he watched me constantly, ready to criticize over the smallest of things. When the first girl was four weeks old, she woke up from a short nap and he screamed at me that the baby "had no respect" as if a four week old knows respect. I cared for her constantly.

With the first child I still tried to please him. His real resentment began when I became pregnant within a year. I remember his berating me at Home Depot because I couldn't walk due to the sciatic pain in my back and legs, hollering at me from the back of the store all the way to the car and throughout the drive home. He never noticed my tears.

I remember the pain I felt when, nine months pregnant, I tried to nap anticipating a long night delivery. I left him downstairs with the one and a half year old and listened to his complaining and yelling at her. I finally slept and met with his anger when waking. That may have been the first time I yelled back.

When the second, more intense baby was born, his attitude was set. He'd yell that I was a "psycho" and he'd cry and complain about losing sleep due to her crying even though he had spent the summer collecting his cherished unemployment, not enough to pay the property taxes. One time that summer, he came in from cutting the grass and took a shower. We did not have air-conditioning, he was too cheap. We all spent the summer sweating, the children in plastic diapers, no wonder the baby was miserable, and me nursing. I went to shower to get the humidity off my skin and left him with the children. The baby started crying. He brought her up and placed her on the floor of the bathroom where the sound would reverberate. I, in my post pregnant body didn't feel like being assessed by his critical scowling eyes, told him "Take the baby downstairs." When I pulled back the shower curtain his hand connected with the right side of my head, making my ear ring for a day. It was then the terror set in. The incidents start slowly, with little bits of anger over things they can't control. At first they hit objects. Then they move to you. You make a quick outlet for their frustration. If you are lucky like me he keeps his venom controlled and satisfies himself with one hit or act of containment. Most of the time he is satisfied with verbal lashings and open hostility.

I tell him he needs to work. His mother dies and I have nothing to give. He spends his time on the phone with his family or visiting his dad. I am left with the kids. I put up with it. He gives me a sweatshirt for Christmas, the one the company he works for gave him. For my birthday in April, he comes home from work and starts spraying weed killer on the front lawn. The two year old runs out and he yells at her and me. I cry "How can you yell on my birthday?" He gives me three lottery tickets. I hate the lottery. I feel it takes advantage of under-privileged people looking for an easy way out. He makes me scratch. I go upstairs and sit on the toilet and cry. I vow to leave by the time I turn forty. I hate this man. My sister calls and says "How was your birthday?" I say "Typical." Nothing more needs to be said.

For his birthday in June I stay home with the kids making him a handprint card. He goes to an auction and spends $4,500 on a '54 Chrysler. He feels he worked hard this year and that's how he wants to spend the money. The car smells like the old horse hair that was used to stuff the upholstery. He insists we go for a ride even though there are no safety belts. I perch in the back holding on to the children.

I start taking the kids to playgrounds. I find friends with children similar ages who stay home too. He is angry when he comes home from work and finds them there. I am glad when they leave before he arrives. I clean-up the toys, and the food and vacuum and mop least he find one crumb to get angry over. My family comes for a fourth of July picnic, leaving after dark. He makes me clean every surface in the house because Robin's kids may have touched poison ivy even though it was after ten at night, I had worked all day and the children would be waking up during the night. I cry the whole time I clean.

I get angry. My friends have loving husbands. They don't cower and obey. They seem happy and content. I'm not. I'm always on edge, never capable of doing anything right although I do nothing wrong. He yells at the meals. He is angry all the time. He walks in the door and yells about the traffic he endured.

One day I blow. I've had enough. I scream at him "You don't even say hello when you walk in the door. You start yelling about traffic and work." Eventually he stops saying anything. He sits in a chair and stares at me, scowling while I make dinner, waiting to be served. He waits til the food's on the table. He never gets up to help. He eats and leaves his plate where it sits. On a good day he'll mutter "Thanks that was good." On a bad day, he'll yell at the kids. I tell him he's not allowed to yell at a dinner that I've prepared. That gives him justification for his hatred and he'll spend the night sulking in front of the TV, saying nothing.

I spend his money. I give the kids dance and swimming lessons. We go to McDonalds and the public pool. He hates me for this but I joke it's part of the "business arrangement." He has no sense of humor.

After three and a half years of abstinence he decides he has interest again. Four weeks go by and he has no more interest. After visiting friends at Christmas I say "I want to have sex, I looked nice tonight and you didn't say anything." He says he is tired. Months go by. He wants it only when he feels the urge which isn't often. If questioned he says "You yell at me" "I'm tired" "I work hard"

"Everyone goes through this, we have to suffer together."

I know what he is doing to me and I am a prisoner. My mind can't grasp my alternatives. The children are young. We'd be forced into poverty, something I'm deathly afraid of. So I stay and console myself with their happiness. But my anger builds. He is in what seems like a constant state of hatred and anger directed at me. He wakes up on the weekend and spends the morning laying on the floor. He watches my every move. He is critical of the smallest of things. He blames me for his forgetting to brush his teeth before a family gathering and all other sorts of ridiculous nonsense. I call him an asshole. I tell him I hate him. I say he's pathetic. He tries to get me to listen by digging his hands into my shoulders, I scratch the sides of his arms. I spit water at him when he is belittling me.

I tell him I'm leaving. One time, after hours and a box of tissues, he promises to change but never does.

The system blames me for leaving. They make every effort to protect him. He cries to them that I have taken advantage; he loves me and only wants the best. They believe him because I am guarded, I have reason to be.

He gets a lawyer who is full of tricks. They both walk away from every encounter grinning. It's been almost a year. He lives in the home and I've received nothing. But I'm glad to be gone. I'm a person again.

Chapter One

Leaving

Fall, 2004

    I take action. I attend a support group for abused women run by the Lancaster County DV group held at a church in the town of Ephrata. I go every other Tuesday afternoon, while the girls are in school. I know he is abusive. The teacher, a young graduate student, tells me "Don't let volunteering for the Kerry v. Bush election stop you from doing what you need to do." We both know I need to leave him. Looking back, I realize she had no idea that when women leave abusive men, welfare fatherhood programs help dads continue their abuse through family court.

    I visit a lawyer to make sure I can financially take care of myself and my kids. We live in a log cabin on 2 acres, with a spring-fed pond, located a mile outside of French Creek State Park, 50 miles from Philadelphia. We own both our new model cars. We have $40,000 in a bank account, $10,000 in certificates of deposits, a large union pension, and an annuity of $150,000. The lawyer tells me I am entitled to a divorce settlement of over $200,000, enough to buy a house and aid me on my way to financial independence. My plan is to complete a bachelor's degree, so I can find a job that will pay enough to support the three of us. The lawyer assures me there will be no problem. Chet has the house and accounts in his name only, but we have been together since 1983; living together for ten years, legally married since 1993. Like many abusers, Chet keeps the financial assets under his sole control, in his name only. Chet doesn't care what will happen to me and the kids if he suddenly dies. It doesn't concern Chet that I will have to litigate with his family because his father is as controlling as him and would not want me to receive the assets.

`Our fighting increases. I tell Chet what I don't like about him, vehemently and often. I hate him because I hate the way he treats me. I sleep on the sofa. One afternoon when he isn't working and the kids are in school, a couple come to the house to purchase the antique car Chet owns. They all leave for the notary public located in Churchtown, a twenty minute drive away. After a while, Chet telephones and orders me "Pick me up." I say "I'm making dinner. Why don't the people who bought the car drive you home?" He grumbles "They wanted to head home. I'll walk." I irritably answer "You can't walk home all the way from there." I feel he doesn't consider me when making his plans; that I always do for him. In a normal relationship no one would feel slighted, but in an abusive one, every slight is large.

I turn off dinner and drive to pick him up from the side of the road where he is walking. After a few minutes of silence, I tell him "I am filing for divorce and I want you to move out until the kids are finished the school year."

I want him to have the house so that the kids can live in it when they are with him. It will not be sold. There are enough assets to permit this. For the short-term, I want him to move out so the kid's environment doesn't change immediately. Instead of moving out, he increases his hatred and sulking. I continue to cook meals and take care of the kids.

One weekend morning I take a shower in the downstairs bathroom. The pipe leaks. Chet walks into the room and yells "Turn off the water!" I continue to rinse soap from my body. Chet yells louder "What are you crazy, turn off the water now, you are ruining everything!" He never tells me water is on the floor, there is a leak. I say to him "In your house, when something went wrong, was it always your mother's fault?" I leave with Elizabeth and Kathleen. We stop for lunch at a crowded Friendlies and wait for a table. While we are waiting another family plays a hook the stuff animal vending game. Beth and Kathy whine "We want to play." I answer "No." Kathy cries louder, the hostess calls our table. As we sit, Kathy trips over my foot and screams. A mother with two small boys hatefully stares. We all have frayed nerves.

The following weekend we leave Chet to visit Pop and Aunt Carole to celebrate Elizabeth's 8th birthday.

I take the girls to my sister Robin's house in Maryland for the next weekend. Sunday night is Halloween. Chet is going to take the girls to his brothers' housing development for trick or treating. As I drive home, Chet calls "Where are you? When will you be home?" I say "Traffic is stopped at the bridge." He continues to telephone, each time asking "Where are you? You better get home." I arrive home before dark. Chet furiously takes the kids to his brothers.

The next weekend, I tell him "It's your turn to leave." He doesn't leave. He sits and angrily watches.

I write a $2,000 check to the lawyer, David Campbell, to file for divorce. Two weeks pass before he files the paperwork.

I don't know it, but in the meantime, Chet has retained his own lawyer, Jacqueline Rae Marks (JR). Before my divorce petition had been filed and served, JR is busy typing up paperwork claiming I am crazy so Chet should get sole custody. JR tells Chet to get a protective order against me. Abusers love to claim their prey is the abuser. It is a common legal strategy and very easy to do. The men cry that women are filing for protection from abuse in order to get a legal advantage and that these women are not really abused. In reality, abusive men use this tactic more frequently than women.

One November day, the girls have a school holiday. Kathy's friend Ana is over our house playing. Chet comes home early from work. He sulks and stalks, making us all uncomfortable. I don't know it, but, that was the day he unsuccessfully tried to get a protective order against me. Chet was told his accusation that I was taking the children away from the home on the weekends was a custody concern, not abuse.

Two nights later, I ask Chet "When are you leaving? We are getting a divorce." He calls the local police and claims I am abusing him. Me and the girls cower in the upstairs bathroom. He isn't able to manipulate the police to take his side. Instead they convince him to leave and tell me "Go to court in the morning and get a protective order. You can get one even if he is emotionally abusive."

I'm incredibly relieved Chet is gone. The next day, the girls go to school and I go to court. Maria, a domestic violence employee stationed at the courthouse can tell I am upset and unsure. She provides comfort and help, walking with me from the PFA office to that day's assigned PFA Judge who refuses to sign because Chet has been given a hearing for Monday. But Chet never paid the fee to put the case on the court docket (schedule). Maria tells me to come to the hearing on Monday and file for a PFA after that.

I expect Chet to stay away, but that afternoon, he comes home. I ask "What are you doing here?" He says "I will just stay in the bedroom and go to sleep." I don't want him there. My fear is too great, although I will never let him know I am afraid. In our relationship, if he tried anything violent I would fight back. Violence didn't work for him, because he wanted me to stay. When he choked me, he would stop before he went too far or I would dig my nails into his arms. This type of abuse provokes fear because there is no guarantee he will stop next time or that my defense will be enough to protect myself.

I feel adrenaline and panic. I feel threatened, in danger at all times. Chet's domination is fearful to me and the kids. His threat of violence is palpable. It oozes from him. It's in his body language, how he holds himself, ready to strike, his eyes full of hate. When he is gone, the threat is gone. I want him gone!

But he has shown up again; five minutes before the kids get off the school bus. He makes it clear, he is not leaving. I call Aunt Carole and Pop and ask "Can we come stay with you?" Pop says "Yes." The girls walk in the house. Chet stands in the kitchen. I am upstairs looking over the loft railing. I tell the girls "We are leaving to stay with Aunt Carole and Pop." Chet cries and grabs the girls while I pack a few things. We leave.

At Pop's, we stay upstairs, there is a sitting loft, a bathroom and two bedrooms. It is Wednesday night. I have to wait 'til Monday to go back to court. I spend the next few days in a fog of nerves; it's an enormous effort to function. I buy toys and craft supplies so the girls have something to play with. I only packed a few clothes, so we wear the same ones. Beth and Kathy love Aunt Carole and Pop, Jeff, their disabled son, and Iggy, their West Highland White Terrier. They know the house and are comfortable there. Aunt Carole and Pop have acted like loving Grandparents since their birth.

Aunt Carole and Pop, my Uncle John, want us to move close to them so they can be near to help. They want us to see the local school so we go on a tour. It's a much bigger school. It has a pool and lockers for elementary kids. During the tour, I'm polite while inside I'm in a panic, scared of how a change would affect my girls; I don't want to put them through a change of school. This one feels so big and institutional. It frightens me.

We leave the school and tour the neighborhood. Even the townhomes look dark and dirty, scary. This area is closer to Philly. It's more suburban than rural Morgantown, where we live. The main route has a large mall, strip malls, and mini-malls covering miles. I know I will get in a car accident because of the sheer volume of traffic.

On Saturday, I drive the girls to my sister Debbie's house in Philadelphia. It gets late. Debbie says "Sleep here." I forgot to pack the items the girls sleep with, baby and blankie . I lay with Kathy for an hour while she cries over not having her blanket. I feel sick but there is nothing I can do but try to get her to sleep. Now that I write this, I think she must have been just as distraught when she lost me in August, 2006.

Debbie's grown son, Chris, my nephew, has a new girlfriend, Jennifer. Once my children are sleeping, Chris and Jen want me to go with them to the corner bar to sing Karaoke. Because I wore them all day, I have to take my contacts out; my eyesight is very blurry. I'm good at pretending to see; I anticipate the environment, what and where things should be. I need the bathroom which is just behind the bar where we are sitting. I go in the room and shut the door and I'm in the dark. I don't know where the light switch is and I can't see. Jennifer opens the door and turns on the light. Her son is blind, so she understands my limits. I'm touched, no one has ever been so instinctively thoughtful of my needs.

Back at Pop's on Sunday, we go to my cousin Anne's house for dinner. While we are there, Pop gets a call from the woman who is at their house caring for Jeff. She tells Pop Chet called yelling and screaming that I had better get back home with his children.

On Monday Pop and I drop the girls at school and he drives

me to the courthouse. There is no hearing, Chet does not show up. Now I can file a PFA. It is given. I have to pay a fee for the sheriffs to serve Chet with the notice to leave the house, stay away from us and come to a hearing in a week. Pop and I pick up the girls at school and drop off the paperwork at the local county police station. We buy candy and snacks for the girls for the ride back to Pop's. We get stuck in traffic and Pop remains cool. I say "Thank you" because if I was with Chet his anger would have filled the air and we all would have been panicked and tense. We spend the time calling out numbers as they change on the dash thermometer. Kathy eats Swedish red fish, dropping some and grinding them into the leather interior which we don't find out until we get out of the car. Pop calmly gets the Carbona and cleans the spot; no one gets yelled at or blamed.

The Sheriff calls and tells Pop "Chet was served with the PFA, he is out of the house, they can go home." We go home the next day and the girls say "Thank you Mom." They need the same routine: school, home and surroundings, friends. They understand.

This is not how I wanted things to happen. Some women dream that they can leave the abuser and he will suddenly be involved with the children and a cooperative parenting arrangement will flourish. The divorce will be better than the marriage. They want the children to have a kind, loving father. But that is not what happens. The abuse escalates. He actually gets worse. He puts you down to keep you with him, under his control. He thinks by working on keeping your self-esteem low, making you unlovable, claiming he is the only one who will have anything to do with you, he will be able to keep you tied to him. When you leave, he is losing. The abuse didn't pay off by keeping you under his control.

The day after I return to the house, Debbie calls "You need protection. I am giving you Anna." Debbie has several generations of cocker spaniels. The next day, while the kids are in school, I drive to pick up Anna, a six-year-old black cocker spaniel. Beth and Kathy love her! We all enjoy Anna, who is excited and happy to be living in the country, away from the crowded, cement city house. We buy Anna a bed, food bowl, and toys. The girls like to hold me down while she licks my face. I cry "Yuck, yuck!" Sometimes I hold Anna and we all dance.

A week passes. The kids go to school. Things are calm. I have to go back to court about the PFA. I have been out of the abuse for ten days and I'm feeling more comfortable.

What is not understood by women leaving abusers, is that once they hire a lawyer, they lose their voice. The lawyer does the speaking and agreeing. By writing a check, you have given away your right to speak the truth of the abuse. Lawyers don't understand abuse. They don't understand your psychological state; they don't understand the threats lingering against you and the children. Judges do not want to hear it. Judges want agreements to be made quickly, without having to hear long stories, or hear evidence, or be required to make complex decisions.

So, as is often the norm, my lawyer negotiates for me. That means, I have no idea what is occurring. I agree Chet can see the kids and someone decides that he would have them for an overnight visit right then and there. They are at school and nobody has told them that they will be spending the night wherever their father is staying! I am upset because I like the kids to know what is happening to them. No one else cares. JR walks past me with a gleam in her eye and a smirk on her face. At that moment, I realize JR doesn't care about my kids. David

Campbell, my lawyer, doesn't comprehend that the terms he agreed to meant Beth and Kathy would have to sleep somewhere without any of their stuff.

All these agreements are made in Judge Keller's backroom with Campbell occasionally running out to apprise me. Without me being aware, because it went on in the backroom, JR files that I am mentally ill and unfit to parent. Later, Campbell tells me "JR's petition sounded like it was written right out of a textbook. Judge Keller told JR to go back to her office and rewrite it." We went to lunch while she did this, costing me more money in legal fees: $200/hr. X 5 hours equals $1,000 for one hearing.

After the backroom dealing, Campbell informs me "Judge Keller ordered a custody evaluation by Dr. Timothy Ring." I hesitate and ask "Can I trust him?" Campbell replies "He's good." What I know now is that Dr. Ring is a big, important man in Berks County. He is the courts favorite psychologist. He gets judicial orders for counseling at his for-profit business, Berkshire Psychiatric, where he bills two insurance companies for the same session charging, in 2005, mother's insurance $75 and father's insurance $75 for a total of $150 per counseling session, when the market rate is half. Mother and father can't have the same insurance or the double billing doesn't work. Ring is running a fatherhood court counseling scam. Ring can do and say anything. He is paid to show up in court with fraudulent reports and opinions. If you are charged with a crime, Ring will make up a psychological condition to get you off. If you need a witness in family court, Ring will make up a psychological condition to use against mother. In 2005, he charged Chet $3,200 for this service.

During the same hearing, I agree Chet can return to the house on June 2nd, the last day of school. At this point, I think this is all that is needed for Chet to "behave" himself. Campbell tells me our finances will get settled. Little do I know, Chet and JR have their own plans. They are claiming that I am mentally unstable to care for the kids. This claim was never made before I filed for divorce and it was completely false. I am the one who takes care of the kids. But, JR and Chet know Ring will submit a false report and give Chet custody in order to remain in control and not pay support. Prolonging resolution of finances will destabilize me emotionally and aid in awarding custody to father.

At home with the kids, things settle into the holiday routine. We get a computer for Christmas. My friend, Lisa, her husband and son, come over and set it up. During a visit at their home, they helped me place an on-line order of the Dell computer. They are excited to put the new model together. Beth and Kathy play happily with daughter Julie, while Lisa assembles the fiber optic tree. The next morning, I go through the motions of decorating. When I pull out the stockings, Kathy says, "Hey, we can give Anna daddy's stocking!"

Even though it is my weekend, I meet him at McDonalds so he can take the kids to the Union Christmas party which they attend every year.

At night, when the kids are asleep, I sit and stare at a book. I can't focus enough to read. I don't sleep well. I don't know it, but this is PTSD.

At first, when Beth and Kathy return from his weekend, I scrutinize them, looking for changes. They have always been with me. Before I filed for divorce, the kids were never alone with him. Slowly, I learn to enjoy the free time because I can work on me.

I have committed to running the school's Santa Shop with another mom, Crystal. I have been shopping since school began. I call the man who plays Santa and ask "Will you be our Santa this year?" We store gifts in the school supply closet. We ask for volunteer Elves and wrappers. Friday night we set up. Beth and Kathy help until Chet picks them up for his weekend. Saturday, the day of the Santa Shop, I work all morning and afternoon. Chet brings Beth and Kathy to shop. What a day! Exhausting but fun! We did it!

I continue to volunteer in each girl's class. As homeroom mom for Elizabeth, I get to arrange parties with another mom and spend Tuesday mornings in class grading math papers. On Thursdays, I copy for Kathy's teacher.

I feel light, free, happy. No one is looking over my shoulder, bearing down on me, ready to criticize. What a feeling! I sing! I dance! I'm elated. I'm shining and others notice. I exercise every morning. I feel good. Energized!

In September, when I first told Chet I was filing for divorce, he went to see a counselor referred by the Union whose office is located in West Chester. The counselor gave Chet a book which blamed the wife for a bad marriage, it was her fault for being "hysterical" and not communicating. Chet told me "You can go see him" so I made an appointment. Just before my 1:00 appointment, I pull into a parking spot and a red Porsche zooms by, nearly hitting my car. I walk into the office waiting room and hear the counselor enter from a back door. The male counselor looks flustered and rushed as he sticks his head out to say "Come on in." His next statement is "So why do you want a divorce?" I answer "Because Chet is abusive." The counselor responds "He's just middle class." I spend the session defending myself while the counselor makes excuses for Chet. He ends the session by saying "Well, I can't treat both of you."

The next time I attend the abuse support group meeting, I tell the facilitator about the experience, I conclude "I felt abused by the counselor." The facilitator says "I know a psychologist who understands abuse, Dr. Susan Atkins. Her office is in Lancaster." I contact Susan to arrange an appointment. She schedules a day and says "I will mail you a multiple page questionnaire, so I can understand your background and concerns. Mail it back to me before our first meeting." I stop attending the support group and visit Dr. Atkins instead, hoping to address the reasons I stayed with Chet for so long.

One day, while sitting in Dr. Atkins waiting room, I notice a pamphlet advertising writing classes. The workshops are called "Write From the Heart" and I decide to sign-up for the daytime beginner session.

Campbell told me Ring would call to schedule an appointment. It is mid-January and no one from his office, Berkshire Psychatric, has called, so I call and schedule a 10 o'clock appointment. At 10:10 Ring enters the waiting room and escorts me to the rear corner office. As we walk through the halls of Ring's jointly-owned, counseling firm, he remarks "People magazine says Ben and Jen are getting divorced." As I sit in a chair, I answer "I don't read People. I read Vanity Fair." Ring spends our first meeting informing me about his liability. He asks "What is your level of education? Do you have a college degree?" I answer "I have some credits from community college, but I got my education on the street." He says "Fill out these forms and mail them back and schedule another appointment on your way out." Later, I complete the forms which ask for the name of the children's school and teachers. I am disturbed by the question "Have you ever had an abortion?" I answer "No" while thinking "This is not Ring's concern, and has nothing to do with determining who is the better parent." No question asks "Did you breastfeed? How long?" When I learn more about Ring, I'll realize he was looking for things to use against me. Ring doesn't ask if I breastfed because he knows I am the type who breastfed exclusively for the first year because it was best for the children.

Ring never contacts school employees. My resume disappears; in his final report Ring implies "Doreen never worked." I give Ring a letter written by Dr. Siviglia, my kerataconus specialist, because I'm afraid Ring will claim my poor eyesight makes me unfit to care for my children. In the letter, Dr. Siviglia writes "I have observed Doreen being loving and kind to her children on many occasions, even when they had to wait long periods of time, and the children responded in kind. Doreen's Kerataconus does not affect her ability to parent." This letter disappears, and is never mentioned in Ring's final report.

I give Ring Dr. Atkins name and address. His final report lambasts her! He writes an entire conclusion inferring Atkins doesn't know anything. Admitting that I have been seeing Dr. Atkins since November 30, 2004, Ring states:

> "Atkins diagnosed her with PTSD which she believes was precipitated by physical and emotional abuse sustained in her marriage. Dr. Atkins says Doreen's description of her marital relationship was consistent with dynamics of abuse, including frequent minimization and protection of the relationship. She indicates that Doreen clearly devised a presentation that protected her husband's behavior from family members and friends. Dr. Atkins has seen Doreen five times prior to producing this case

summary. She reports Doreen indicating significant progress in a short period of time. Dr. Atkins believes Doreen has good coping skills and is a devoted parent, despite never having observed her interacting with the children or evaluating the parent-child relationship. She further indicates that Doreen appears to provide a stable base for the children."

In reality, I had taken the children with me to appointments. In Dr. Atkins' 12-page letter refuting Ring's evaluation, presented to the court at trial and in appeals, which Keller refused to admit as evidence and the appeals courts ignored, Dr. Atkins retorts:

"This letter summarizes my impressions of her emotional issues and will counter many of the claims made by Dr. Ring as a result of the custody evaluation performed in his office. Contrary to what Dr. Ring stated in his report, I have observed Doreen with her children. I observed her to be responsive, warm, and appropriately authoritative in her interactions. I also observed that the children were not overly needy and they responded well to her directives. Unlike an artificially derived observation setting, the interactions, I observed were in a natural, everyday setting. Neither the children, nor the mother had any reason to be nervous or preoccupied about being observed."

When the fatherhood is providing false evidence against you, truth is ignored.

I develop a crush on my lawyer, Campbell; my first nice guy. I like the gentle way he talks and his non-threatening body language. He is ten years older and heavy, which I think makes him a teddy bear. He has nice eyes. He sends me an email

"Have a happy and peaceful Christmas." I feel warm and special. I like when he tells me "It is good weather for hanging Christmas lights." Chet never wanted to decorate because he is miserable about work and holidays. Campbell tells me he has a 14 year old son and cooks. I respond to the family image.

I like writing. I write a long story about my teenage years and my parents. I give a copy to my lawyer and Dr. Ring. Writing is helping me come to terms with myself. I ask "Why did I put up with the abuse for so long?" I know some of the answers: I wanted the stability of a long-term relationship, since my parents treated me poorly. I didn't have a strong sense of self-worth, nor did I have high needs or expectations. I am happy cooking and cleaning, so I'm slow to see when someone takes it for granted and expects it so much that they feel they can be critical and mean.

When I go to Lititz for weekly writing class, I buy coffee at the coffee shop, and chocolate at Wilbur's chocolate factory. The other writers and I sometimes go to lunch together. In class, we take turns reading what we have written. I love hearing what everyone writes. One woman has an Eastern European accent. When she raises her voice while reading, I get tense and nervous. I associate the accent with Chet's loud, abusive, Polish father. Melissa Greene, our teacher, reads American Contemporary Literature during class. She turns me on to Raymond Carver and I purchase "What We Talk About When We Talk About Love." I respond to his use of simplicity to represent complexity.

Dr. Atkins' waiting room has a library. I borrow "Letting Go of Shame." I think I need to stop feeling embarrassed about things that happened when I was young, but instead the book talks about families who "shame" you. They criticize and make you feel worthless. There are exercises to help you deal with having been shamed, to help you realize that you are loveable. Sometimes I cry, but this book moves me forward in a big way. I order two copies and give one to my cousin, writing in the front of the book "This is our family."

"Letting Go of Shame" highlights a second type of shaming family: those that lie. Families with an alcoholic parent hide the drinking problem. The alcohol abuse, and the need to hide that abuse creates dysfunctional children. Chet's father is a loud, overbearing parent who came to America after World War II, having been put in a Polish work camp and then joining the Nazi's and ending up in France. Chet and his siblings were taught to lie and distrust others.

I take "Letting Go of Shame" to my next meeting with Ring. I tell Ring "I think this is Chet's problem. I want him to get counseling." Ring replies "Don't worry, there will definitely be counseling." I want Chet to heal. I just don't want to be a party to his problem anymore. I leave thinking Ring will help, not understanding Ring runs a counseling racket, profiting from abusive divorce.

All assets are in Chet's name. I file for support to pay bills. I take advantage of credit card offers with 9-month 0% interest rates. I use cash advance to give Campbell more money. Abusers are controllers and financial control is a typical tactic which puts their prey at a severe disadvantage, often being the sole cause of her not leaving. My plan is to get my divorce settlement, buy a small house, go to school for a bachelor's degree and be able to support myself within two years. Again, what I don't know is that Chet and JR are planning to use the fatherhood strategy outlined in books like "Divorce Poison" to ensure I get nothing.

My younger sister, Robin, calls me "Come visit this weekend." I leave Anna at Stephanie's house. Stephanie is my friend Patti's sister-in-law. Stephanie is a veterinary nurse and she operates a grooming, boarding, dog walking business in her basement. I drive to Robin's house in Bel Aire, Maryland. I chat with her husband, Joe. Robin says "We are going to go out tonight with my neighbor whose husband just left and a friend of hers who is divorced." We go to a restaurant that Robin heard was the new cool, downtown spot. Robin doesn't like the restaurant. It is not fancy, has a blue collar feel, like a pub. While we are talking, Robin tells us her relationship theory "He must love you more than you love him." She rules her house; everyone revolves around her. Me, Robin's neighbor and friend hit it off and talk about how much better we feel since losing the man. The friend pulls out an old driver's license and says "See how much better I look now!" I remember that I made Chet's lunch every day, three sandwiches, and that I actually lined up soda's in the fridge for him to take! I laugh at the absurdity of doing this for twenty years. He never once got his own lunch!

Robin is getting grumpier by the minute. We leave and she is not talking much. When we enter her house at ten at night, the lights are off, Joe and the kids are already in bed! They are going to sunday school and church in the morning. I think they are leaving at 10, but at 7 everyone is up showering, dressing and fixing hair. I know I cannot be ready on time so I say I will stay home and read my book on patience. I'm sitting in the living room and in walk Robin and Joe. I say "I thought you would be gone longer." They say "We didn't go to church, we will go pick up the girls later." After a few minutes, Robin yells "You're a sinner." I say "Robin, I could tell that you were making fun of me last night." She yells "Get out of my house!" I say "You are my sister." I go upstairs and pack and leave. As I'm driving home, I yell to myself "You are a sinner!" I laugh and yell louder "You are a sinner!" This is a big moment for me. I finally realize it isn't me. I'm not a sinner. I'm actually a nice person who tries to do my best. I don't intentionally hurt anyone. From that day on, I stop letting other people make me feel bad about myself.

As I drive home, I stop at a discount bookstore and purchase "50 Ways to Meet Men" and "Creative Divorce."

I tell Dr. Atkins about this incident and she tells me that the church can attract people like that (abusive in their own right, controlling). When I tell my sister Debbie what Robin did to me, she is mute. That is my family. What I now know is that you can say something small and kind. Debbie should have said something like "Robin was wrong to do that." But, I'm the one on the self-improvement program. That's why I'm getting divorced: to improve myself.

"Creative Divorce," the book I bought on my drive home from Robin's, is about using the divorce as a chance to examine and improve yourself. It advises waiting to get into another relationship, work on yourself instead so that you can avoid repeating the relationship problem. I like the advice so I give a copy of the book to Chet.

My last meeting with Ring is a joint meeting between me, Chet, Ring and Sandhya Shephard, the unpaid intern. Ring begins the meeting by asking "Is there any chance you two can get back together?" Chet begins "Well, she filed against me..." I interrupt with an emphatic "No." Ring then asks Chet "Did you ever hit her?" Chet describes three instances which are times I wrote about and gave to my lawyer. (I am having a hard time confronting Chet's physical violence, because his other acts of abuse were much more pervasive. But, because everyone else only thinks of abuse as hitting, I have to recant the violent episodes.) Chet concludes "But she deserved it." Ring quickly says "Well, we are finished because we are getting nowhere here." I walk out thinking there should be no problem because Chet just told Ring that he hit me because I deserved it. Does it get more abusive then that?

Funny though, the admittance of unprovoked violence disappears and never shows up in Ring's report. If we had been in a court of law, where we should have been, there would have been a record since a court stenographer would have written every word. It is my right to have the admittance in the record and not have Ring cover up evidence or testimony. But this is part of the scam and the reason why we are taken to Ring in the first place – in order for Ring to change and make-up evidence and to keep real evidence out of the record.

Spring arrives. I tell Campbell "I need to move. Chet can return to the house on June 2nd. I want to buy a house and need money. How will this be handled?" Campbell has no answer, so I ask Chet "When are you going to give me money?" Chet yells back "What am I supposed to live on?"

Back support is owed. Campbell tells me "They will take it from the tax return." Instead, the return comes in the mail. I take the check to Campbell and ask "Can you have Chet sign it?" A week passes, I need to pay for college, so I phone Campbell "Do you have the signed tax return?" Campbell answers "No. Just pick it up at my office and get Chet to sign it." The girls play softball. I take them to games and practice when it is my day. Chet likes to be involved in the team so he is there. I ask Chet "Can you sign the check?" Chet walks away yelling, frantically pressing his phone, calling JR. Two days later he signs the check when he picks up the kids. Later, when I'm at the support office, the clerk tells me Chet called and reported I stole the rebate.

I tell Dr. Atkins "I'm starting to notice the threat in Chet's body language; the way he comes at me as if he is going to hit me and the uncontrolled anger which hints of barely contained violence."

Beth and Kathy have taken dance lessons since they were two, when the local library started offering KinderDance. I took them for the social and physical activity. For years, I drove them to different locations while the program changed and grew. They both loved dancing, ballet and jazz. I wanted them to continue as long as they loved it; I wanted them to be comfortable with their bodies. They had progressed from KinderDance, to studying at a Dance Studio which had a half-day recital that Spring. I sat with the other kids moms. Chet sat by himself. I didn't realize this would be their last recital, because I would have no money and Chet would never pay and take them to weekly class himself. Their activities and enrichment were my priorities, not his.

Ideally, I would have had a house to move into. But I have to start looking for something to rent because Chet can move back into the house on June 2, the last day of school. My friend tells me of a place being offered by a mennonite couple. I go and it is not fancy but I think the landlords seem nice. I have no job and no income which makes it difficult to rent, so I explain about the divorce, that I am entitled to a sizeable divorce settlement. I explain that I am going to college. I ask if I can have the dog and they agree. I give them two months' rent up front and I take a month to move in, organizing and giving the girls time to adjust to the move. I use credit cards to buy furniture and mattresses.

On June 1st, movers come to the house. Campbell tells me "Take whatever you want." I try to be fair and split our belongings. I write a list of what I take and what I leave for Chet. The next day, Chet returns to the house. I have to pick up the girls and while I sit in the car in the driveway, Chet stalks out of the house yelling "You took furniture. I am calling the police that you stole." He stands on the front porch screaming and waving the phone. The kids get in my car and say "He is really mad." We pull away and drive an hour to Pop's house, looking in the rearview mirror for police the whole way.

I sign up for summer classes at West Chester University. I take philosophy and Intro to Journalism. Four days a week, three hours each. I sign the girls up for a summer camp run by a local day care center. The women owners promise swimming and day trips which never materialize. Instead, the kids use a hose outside on a two foot stretch of lawn which means they stomp around in a pile of mud. Beth and Kathy are used to being with me all summer. They have taken dance, swim, and Spanish lessons, visited a friend weekly, gone to the state park pool, had regular playgroup get-togethers, and visited family. I kept them busy, away from TV, learning and exploring.

They hate the day care. I feel bad because their life is changing. I'm paying over $300 a week for something they hate! I take them as little as possible. Towards the end of summer, we arrive at 9:30 and the director comes out and yells at me "They cannot be here today. The other kids are on a bus trip." I answer "I was not told. I have something to do. I have paid you." The director yells "They cannot stay here. I'll write you a check." She reimburses me for the last few days and we all drive to the University for my career center appointment to review my resume. When we are finished, I drive the girls home and Chet picks them up for his "time." I drive to Dr. Atkins for a counseling session. I pick-up the girls at 8.

I ask Campbell "How will I pay for summer child care?" He answers "Go back to support and file. He has to pay." I don't realize Chet can argue. But Chet refuses to agree to pay for daycare. He shouts "What am I supposed to do, live in a box!" I pay $300/week daycare, $800 rent, utilities, and food using credit cards and $1,500 a month taken from Chet's paycheck.

I get A's in my summer classes and I sign up for fall, taking journalism and writing classes on the nights he has the kids.

We got through the summer. The kids start another year of school. Four days in, I get a call from Campbell asking "Are you going to be in court tomorrow?" I answer "*What?*" Campbell replies "There is a hearing tomorrow morning. By the way, is your psychologist prescribing you any medication because you are schizophrenic?" I answer "*No.*" Campbell says "Dr. Ring thinks you need to be on medication. I will talk to Dr. Atkins."

So, at the last minute, I have to be at court before the kids get on the bus. In the morning, I leave Beth and Kathy to get themselves on the bus. When I get to court, I call the school to make sure they made it to school. Campbell has talked to Dr. Atkins. Because of Ring's report, the hearing master, Pam Ullman, wants to give Chet primary custody. Even though Ring knows Chet is abusive, Ring has written a report that loves Chet and makes me out to be a never-worked-deserve-to-be-beaten mental case. Campbell tells me "You are not allowed to see the report, but I will send it to Dr. Atkins for her input."

Because Dr. Atkins doesn't agree with Ring, custody isn't changed and we are told to come back to court in two months. Of course, I don't really know what was said since all the talking occurs behind my back, in a so-called "conciliation hearing" held between the lawyer-acting-as-judge, Pam Ullman, Campbell, and JR, while I sit in the elevator area and Chet sits in the waiting room.

In the meantime, we have a support hearing over paying for summer day care. I get to attend that hearing. Ullman seems belligerent towards me. She reminds me of the woman who stared me down at Friendly's on the day we escaped Chet's yelling about broken plumbing. Her first question is "How old are you?" Then she berates me "Why are you not working?" I answer "I want to get a degree because that would be the best way for me to care for the kids in the long term. I am looking for a job and have a possibility. I used to do secretarial work, but don't have current computer skills and would only get paid about nine dollars an hour in this area. I also have a corneal disease, I'm blind without corrective contacts, which I can only wear about 8 hours a day, so a full-time job would be impossible for me. I worked part-time before staying home with the children. Since the day I first filed for support, I have been assessed as having a minimum wage income. He controls all the marital assets." As I am on the witness stand, JR asks "Didn't you get $7,000?" I answer "No." JR gets ready to argue but Chet leans to her and whispers. Later I say to Campbell "Find out what they meant about me getting $7,000." Campbell replies "I don't know what you are talking about. I didn't hear her say it.

In the end, Pam Ullman, lowers the amount Chet is paying me, instead of adding child care expenses. Chet is living in the paid-for house which is in his name only and I have to pay rent. Chet controls all the money accounts and is refusing to settle the divorce. It is now one year since I filed for divorce and my credit card interest rates are set to increase. I tell Campbell "I am like someone without a bank account." Campbell answers "I will appeal the decision."

I am hired as an organizing specialist by The Perfect Plan, a moving company specializing in moving seniors. I am paid $10 an hour for part-time work.

I visit Pop on the weekend and we talk and he suggests I get a better lawyer. I see the point. He suggests a big firm, Wolf, Block, Schorr and Solis-Cohen. I know the firm because fifteen years previously I was a billing clerk in their Philadelphia office. I call David Campbell because I want him to improve. As usual, he never returns my call. Pop and I meet with the high priced lawyer and he loans me $5,000 to retain Gerry Shoemaker.

I finally reach David Campbell. He sounds hurt when he says "Jackie told me you got a new lawyer." I am upset when I answer "I'll pick up my file in the morning." The file contains Ring's report. I stop and make myself a copy at Staples on the way to Gerry's office.

Gerry tells me "Write down what is wrong with Ring's report." I take the report home and read it. I identify four to five factual mistakes on each page. No wonder they were hiding this! I type up all the problems, stopping to cry when I become overwhelmed at the nasty lies printed about me. I end up with a thirty-page document.

Dr. Atkins suggests I research battering men and custody. I use West Chester University's access to find professional articles explaining how battering men are able to use the court system to continue their abuse by fighting for control of the children through custody litigation. There is a lot of professional work confirming that custody evaluators like Ring skew their reports and have little knowledge of abuse and its detrimental effect on children.

Using my home and school computers, I print over 40 articles. I give all the articles to Gerry along with my list of what is wrong in Ring's report. Gerry gets angry. It is my fault there are so many mistakes in Ring's report! Gerry yells "I can't give this to Pam Ullman. Pick two or three."

Pam Ullman has scheduled another "conciliation" custody hearing. Ironically again, I never get to conciliate because I never see Pam. I sit in the waiting room for three hours. When Ring walks in he loudly proclaims "Hey Chet, how are you doing!" My out-of-town lawyer, Gerry, hobnobs with his lawyer friend. The two of them verbally embrace Ring. "You have a great tan!" "Ohhhhh, you just got back from Tuscany!"

Remember: I've read the nasty lies Ring has written about me. He doesn't know I've got a copy of the report.

I leave the waiting room, enter the hall and sit on a window sill. Gerry comes out and yells at me "You have to say hello to Dr. Ring." I answer "He is unethical. I've read what he wrote about me. I am not saying hello." Gerry tells me "I asked Dr. Ring if Chet admitted hitting you and Dr. Ring said "Yes." "You have to go back to see Dr. Ring and let him write another report." I answer "I am not going back. He lied the first time." Gerry yells at me "You can't say anything about Dr. Ring. He is in this court every day."

Friday night a month later, just before our second Christmas, the mail contains Pam's decision handing the kids to Chet. The decision is based solely on Ring's report. In Pennsylvania, Masters like Pam cannot change primary custody, but Berks County has created its own rule that Masters have to do what the evaluators decide. They are not allowed to do this, but it doesn't matter.

I am devastated. I go to the bathroom and sit on the floor and call Gerry. He tells me "If you appeal the decision, custody does not change." The kids go to Chet's for the weekend and I go to the emergency room where they give me pills and recommend I attend their Partial Program, an outpatient mental health treatment program.

For our second Christmas alone, I buy gifts using a credit card, spending as little as possible, less than $100. On Christmas day, Chet brings the girls home at noon. They open gifts and play. I take the pills the hospital gave me. We spend Christmas vacation together. I don't have to work because no one moves during the holidays. After Ullman so readily held up Rings credibility, I take Dr. Atkins advice that I file an ethical complaint against him. I spend a lot of time researching the process and writing the complaint while the girls play. I mail the complaint in early January. The appealed custody trial is scheduled for March.

We do not have cable since there is no extra money. The girls watch video's like Bratz Movie, Recess, and Barbie Rapunzel. They love Anna, the dog. She provides lots of entertainment. They make her kiss me while I cry "Ew, Yuck" or I pick her up and we all dance. Beth and Kathy play with Bratz and American Girl dolls given to them by Aunt Carole and Pop. There are craft supplies and tape because they like making things. Kathy is the cutting and taping queen. They have computer games like Barbie Pony, and they use sites like Littlest Pet Shop to print out pictures. There is model magic and they make miniature dogs and dog dishes. We visit friends. Julie and Ana come over to play.

One night during the holiday they want to go to Chuckie Cheese. I tell them I don't have money so they use their own. We take refillable cups purchased at an earlier visit.

In January, Beth and Kathy go back to school; I go to the partial program because I feel I'm losing my hold. I'm given Lexapro, an antidepressant. I have insurance so attending is no problem. I drop the kids off at the Y's morning daycare and head to Reading Hospital for the 5 hour, daily program. The day begins with an hour group therapy where patients talk about their problems and counselors give input. The other participants talk of problems like losing jobs due to an affair with the boss's wife, seizures causing embarrassment because of loss of bowel control, and one girl cries that her mother isn't a real mother because she doesn't cook meals when she goes over. After an hour of this we get a lesson and then lunch. We play games after lunch. Sometimes we take walks. There may be an afternoon lesson.

I attend the first week. I think the routine helps. The second week, I miss one day because of a Perfect Plan training. I tell the counselors I am going to miss another, consecutive day to visit Dr. Atkins. They get angry, they don't want to lose the insurance payment. I get upset and cry "Dr. Atkins is helping me." Atkins had trained at the partial program and the staff respected her. When I return to the program after two days away, the other participants have changed. There are a lot of males with a new bunch of problems. There are no woman that I can identify with, which I need because I am still not comfortable with men.

The counselor reprimands me "When you give tissues to someone who is crying, you don't let them experience their emotion." While we are sitting in a circle discussing our problems, another counselor turns to me "Are you sure you are not the reason for your problem?" I keep my feelings to myself, unlike many members of the group who seem to love the opportunity to go on about their problems and feelings. I finally do speak up "My husband was abusive and he is taking my children." The group solution is "You need to go to legal aid. Why won't you go to legal aid?" I answer "I will."

At our next session Dr. Atkins asks "How was the partial program?" I answer "Some of the people go on about themselves. One girl listed everyone she ever slept with and a teenager was complaining because his parents bought him too many material gifts." Dr. Atkins responded "I didn't think it would work because of your high intellectualism." The partial program was my first experience with our countries institutional mental health system.

Chapter Two

The Trial

January, 2006

Gerry calls and tells me the custody trial is set for the last week of March. He adds "You need to get more money from your Uncle." I answer "I am not asking for more money. You need to file for Interim Disbursement." That means a payment from the marital accounts before the divorce is settled. Gerry types up a motion and a hearing is set for late January. Gerry is asking for $10,000 to cover the costs of legal fees for the upcoming custody trial.

I tell Gerry "I have filed an ethical complaint against Ring." Gerry is furious! "You cannot say anything about Dr. Ring. He is in there every day!" I say to Gerry "Did you ask Susan (Dr. Atkins) about an incident at the day care during the custody hearing in front of Ullman? Why didn't you ask me about it?" (Gerry telephoned Dr. Atkins to testify at that hearing and JR started accusing me of having an incident with the day care. During our session, Susan told me, saying she "didn't understand what that was about.")

I tell Gerry "I want to be present at all times, there is to be no discussion without me." He angrily answers "You want to go in the Judge's office?" I say "I want to hear everything that is said." Gerry answers "You can't!" I say "Then you are fired." This makes both of us happy. I can't stand Gerry, he is not like Campbell, the nice lawyer. Gerry is glad because he wants to be friends with Keller and Ring. Defending me means going against the fatherhood court.

On the day of the hearing for Interim Disbursement, Gerry hands Keller a motion withdrawing from my case. The hearing continues with me representing myself. Keller assesses if there are marital assets to give me. I provide a bank statement proving Chet withdrew over $39,000 from a savings account in the first three months after the divorce was filed. Chet sits in the witness stand claiming "I don't know what happened to the money." I tell Keller "I have bills to pay and credit cards are now accruing at 31%." Chet and JR claim they offered a settlement to both of my lawyers. I ask "Where is that settlement? What was it for?" Chet cannot answer. In the end, Keller yells at me "You are not entitled to that much money. It is not like you own businesses. It really is not all that much money. I want this settled." Then he refuses to give me any marital assets to pay bills or to prepare for the custody trial.

I fill out the form for legal aid. I'm broke so getting income-approved is not a problem, but getting an answer is. It takes a month for the director, Val West, to tell me I qualify but they will not help me. Val agrees to meet me for lunch in her office and she gives advice and lends me a legal book and a sample trial memo which I must file for the March custody trial. I am going to have to represent myself.

While I research battering men and custody, I find a judges group (NCJFCJ) that compiled packets of academic articles which they call a Domestic Violence Custody Information packet. They send me three copies of the packet. I write a letter and mail a packet to Pam Ullman, Keller and the court administrator. I call the local domestic violence group, Berks Woman in Crisis, and they tell me Ullman attended a training given by Lundy Bancroft the author of "Men Who Batter" and "Understanding the Batterer in Custody Disputes." The DV counselor tells me there is a local group called RAISE that offers a battering man program. (During our trial, I ask Keller to order Chet to the program. Chet attends one session. When I call, the counselor, Lou Vetri, tells me "I can't treat Chet because he doesn't own his behavior.")

I research Ring's credentials. Ring claims he is a member of the Professional Academy of Custody Evaluators (PACE), headed by Dr. Barry Bricklin. I mail Rings evaluation to Bricklin and ask for his review. He telephones and says "I am so busy, I was away treating a really bad case of alienation." Then Brickllin tells me Ring "made his report look like he did a lot" and "he graded the child scales incorrectly." I send a letter informing the State Department, to be included with my ethical complaint against Ring. (At this point, I don't know about Bricklin's organization, and I don't know that his wife is the head of Pennsylvania's Psychological Association.)

I am taking three more classes at West Chester University and working moving seniors into retirement centers. I spend days with 93 year old Grace who is blind. I take her possessions out of closets and bureaus, describing, I place them in her lap so she can decide what to pack and what to throw away. She tells me amusing stories like how one night her husband said "I'm bringing a male associate for dinner, but don't arrange a date for him, because he isn't that way." Grace tells me "In those days, you didn't talk about men who liked men." I'm in charge on moving day. I make sure Grace is driven to the retirement center while I supervise the movers and settle her in as I unpack her apartment. I make sure she knows where to find light switches and the pantyhose she still wears every day.

I prepare to defend myself at the March, 2006 custody trial where Keller, the Judge, will determine who shall be primary caretaker of the children. Although I have been their full-time mother since their birth, once I file for divorce, this stops to mean anything. Until I filed for divorce, Chet never spent any extended time alone with the kids because when Kathy was 1 ½ years old, I left to take an exercise class and when I returned, Kathy was in her room screaming. Chet made her drink hot sauce when she cried and he refused to give her milk. I never left him in charge after that.

Even though I think it would be best if as little as possible changed for the girls, and that any changes would be taken slowly with little disruption, the goal of the court is to force fatherhood, without regard to the children's habits, familiarities, or needs.

I prepare a memo outlining my case including a list of witnesses and evidence. I ask friends and family to come to court and witness. I subpoena Ring's intern, Sandhya, because she administered the tests and heard Chet say he hit me. At first, I think Sandhya is part of the problem, but when I telephone, she tells me "Dr. Ring did this to four other women. I will not go into forensics because of my time there. I did not get paid."

I ask my boss to testify by telephone. She agrees and during the trial says "Doreen is a good employee. The job has very mother friendly hours."

I ask my first lawyer, David Campbell, to testify. He testifies "Doreen was not expecting anything out of the ordinary, she was not asking for more than would be expected."

I make a list of questions for each witness. I've read the borrowed book and I've researched how to question a custody evaluation. I subpoena Ring and receive a letter from his lawyer. I scream when I see the masthead "Ullman and Ullman." I telephone and ask if Pam Ullman works there. The receptionist answers "She's his wife." I can't believe this huge conflict of interest.

For evidence, I focus on proving the abuse because there is no mention of it in Ring's report. I'm still trying to justify why I am leaving Chet, even though Pennsylvania has a no-fault divorce law which means I don't need a reason.

I write a personal abuse story thinking this will make them understand. I use the same story for a school writing assignment. The teacher comments "This man killed his grandmother!"

I make lists of each time I gave Chet the kids without being ordered by the court; extra time. I list every time I stayed home with the children during school holidays and when they were sick.

I make copies of telephone bills proving Chet made continuous calls to my family; harassing and threatening, abusive behaviors.

I get copies of the transcript where Chet and JR claimed they had offered a settlement to my two lawyers. I get emails from those lawyers stating that they never received these claimed offers. That means Chet and JR perjured (lied) under oath. Perjury will prove to be a common strategy of Chet and JR. In fact, the fatherhood advises perjury in books like "Fathers' Rights: Hard-Hitting and Fair Advice for Every Father Involved in a Custody Dispute," by Jeffery Leving and Ken Dachman.

I assemble research articles including Lundy Bancrofts "The Batterer as Parent" and a comprehensive compendium of research entitled "Are Good Enough Parents Losing Custody to Abusive Ex-Partners?"

I subpoena Twin Valley School District employees because I had been employed at the school before giving birth as the special education secretary, and I had been a volunteer in many capacities since the children started attending. I had also spoken to the counselor concerning a student who was making school difficult for Elizabeth. In the custody evaluation, Ring brags about how Chet handled this situation while never asking what I did. Chet went to school demanding school employees make the new student stop clinging to Beth. I quietly spoke with the counselor and teacher and taught Beth to move away and say "I don't want to sit with you right now." I thought it was a good chance for her to learn to protect herself against people who would take advantage of her kindness and caring, not realizing her father was using this tactic extensively.

I subpoena the school assistant superintendent, Bob Cunningham, because I wanted to ask him questions about child development. He also has a doctorate in childhood education, the same degree Ring uses to claim he is qualified to determine what is best for my kids. Since Ring's report was full of lies about me and my parenting, I had every right to have all these school employees testify. Ring never contacted any of them! They were the most common people in my children's lives besides me; yes, even more than their father!

However, Judge Keller decides I am not allowed to have any of these people refute the claims made by Ring. Surely, if a criminal has a trial, the judge would not stop witnesses who could prove innocence from testifying, but quashal of witnesses, (a legal term meaning stopping) is common in custody cases where the mother is being railroaded in favor of the father.

The biggest witness and evidence at my trial is Dr. Atkins. She writes a 12-page letter in response to Ring's report. She contests Ring's absurd assertions and cites much of the research. For this she charged me: nothing. During the trial Dr. Atkins drove over thirty miles and sat on the witness stand for several hours including waiting out a lunch break. For this she charged me: nothing. Ring charges $350 an hour for his appearance in court.

Of course, it is Chet and welfare that pay his salary.

On the day of the custody trial, I go to court dressed in my Jones New York brown suit. My hair is straightened because the court does not like curly hair, according to Gerry, they deem it confirmation of craziness.

My uncle, Pop, comes with me, again, for emotional support and to be a witness about how I took care of the house and kids. While witnessing, Pop mentions "Doreen was the one who set-up an educational toy area in the house." I am touched, I did not know he noticed.

On the day of the trial, I sit in front, alone at the table reserved for lawyers and their clients. What happens is truly amazing: a B rate movie! Everything has been planned out in advance between Keller and JR. (If you don't believe me, I have the transcript.)

The first thing that happens is Keller goes through my list of witnesses and exhibits and refuses to allow me to present <u>any</u> of my evidence. JR typed why she thinks each piece of evidence should not be permitted. Keller agrees or decides to "hold in abeyance" which means he'll decide later, but that never happens, so I am permitted <u>no evidence</u>. (Remember, Keller denied half my witnesses before the trial began.)

At a break, I run out in the stairwell and call legal aid and leave a message "They are not allowing me to have any evidence, what should I do?" Of course I get no answer, but I find out later that denying witnesses and evidence is typical when a case is being rigged for father.

The second amazing thing that happens is that Ring shows up with his lawyer, Ullman, the brother-in-law of Pam Ullman, the lawyer who has been making rulings in my support and custody case, including changing primary custody to Chet because of

Ring's report. Pam's husband is a partner in Ring's retained law firm, Ullman & Ullman, so her family income is heavily tied to Ring's credibility. Because of her family dependence on Ring's business, she will never rule against him, even when she knows his reports are fraudulent and missing important facts like Chet hitting me.

Ullman is there to protect Ring because I have filed an ethical complaint. Ullman tells Keller that Ring must be protected and cannot be put on the witness stand or submit to cross-examination because he could incriminate himself. Keller yells at me "You have set a precedent!" Keller is furious that I have filed an ethical complaint. I say " Then Ring shouldn't submit his report until the ethical investigation is complete, especially since he refuses cross-examination." JR wants the report and its findings for father submitted as evidence anyway, after all, that is what they paid for and what the welfare fatherhood goal is all about: getting dad the children, no support payments, the child tax exemption, and, best of all, ordering mom to pay dad support.

Sandhya Shephard, the intern who did the testing, (Ring's report is based solely on testing), is an important witness to the falseness of Ring's report. Sandhya is there to witness that Chet admitted hitting me and that Ring did this to four other people. (Several weeks before the trial, after working a moving job in the area, I stopped by Immaculata College and found Sandhya in order to serve her with a subpoena. School security was calling my cell phone, trying to track me down and remove me from school property before I located her. I evaded them, but, I was still worried that she wouldn't honor the subpoena.)

Ullman also doesn't want Sandhya to witness because she will incriminate Ring. Suddenly, my trial and my kids future has become about protecting Ring!

Keller says "I am going to allow Ring to submit his report as evidence, but there will be no cross-examination of him or Sandhya. Dr. Ring, do you verify that this is your report?" It is against due process law, the fifth amendment of the Constitution, but we are not following the Rule of Law, we are adhering to the welfare fatherhood program and this trial is merely to achieve the goal of giving father control.

My friend, family, and boss witness that I am a good mother, but the biggest witness is Dr. Atkins. Keller will not allow as evidence Dr. Atkins 12-page report refuting Ring's accusations of me, which also points out the many fallacies of psychological protocol, omissions of valid research, and distortions of test results. As an excuse, Keller and JR claim, it is invalid because it was faxed to my lawyer, Gerry Shoemaker. Keller tells me to call Atkins and make her come to court to testify. I go out in the hall and call her to come to court. She cancels her appointments for the day. When she arrives, Keller grills her for several hours and tries to get her to say I am crazy. She stands her ground. Keller has a habit of yelling, basically bullying, trying to force answers he wants. He knows how to set up the transcript in case there are appeals. At one point he says to Dr. Atkins "Dr. Ring claims here that she (me) has a constellation of mental illness" as he waves his hand across the room. "Look at her!" Susan sticks up for me, saying "It is difficult to represent yourself." She says about Ring's report "That is not even a DSM diagnosis" and "I diagnosed her as having PTSD, Adjustment Disorder with Mixed Emotions, and ADD." Of course, Keller hears none of this because the purpose of this hearing is to use Ring's false report to give Chet the children, to eliminate mother.

Keller yells "Get the children" so during lunch my Uncle and I drive half hour away, take the kids out of school and drive them back to Reading. The children are taken into Keller's secret chamber without any other adult except the transcriptionist. To seven-year old Kathy, Keller says "If I gave – if I said that you were to stay with your dad a little bit more than you are now. Would that be okay with you?" and "I'm going to decide if you stay with your dad more than you have been now or you stay the same with your dad and your mom or – that's what I'm going to decide, just a matter of how much time you're going to spend with both your parents. You're going to see your parents, no question about that. Okay?" To nine-year-old Beth, Keller says "Not that you're never going to see any one of them again because you are going to see both of them. It is just where – how often you are going to see one or the other okay? Do you understand that?" Fourteen weeks later, mother was eliminated.

David Campbell, my first lawyer, shows up to testify. Keller yells "What is he doing here?"

As part of my evidence, I subpoenaed Chet's timesheets. He was going to work three hours late every other Monday because he dropped the girls at school in the morning when they slept over on the weekend. He was leaving work two hours early when he took them during the week, picking them up at school at three. Meanwhile he signed his timesheets that he was at work every day from 7 to 4.

JR was so angry that I got this evidence that she had Keller sign an order telling me that I was not able to contact Chet's work or I would go to jail. That was my first jailing threat. Jailing is used frequently by judges who want to force fatherhood and eliminate mothers. If mom is not cooperating, or is attempting to advocate for the children, she will be jailed. Fatherhood court Judges will also threaten mothers lawyer with jailing for contempt if they represent her too well. Trade association and welfare reports term jailing and monetary fines "punitive measures."

Because I am my own lawyer, I get to ask Chet questions. I ask him why he is claiming to be at work when he is dropping off and picking up the kids at school. He has no answer. Keller yells at me "Forget it," then Chet says "I work at home" and Keller yells "He has an answer." I say "He is a mechanic and can't take his work home."

Keller asks JR if they have more witnesses. She says "No, we just have Dr. Ring and the children." Ring is supposed to be independent, but, as JR admits, he is working for father. The transcript lists their only witnesses as Dr. Ring and the children. The bottom of each page of Ring's report says "copy of defendant's exhibit no. 1."

(A month later when the completed transcript arrives in my mail, my friend Kathy looks at it and says "Why is this underlined?" Ring's report was added to the transcript and it is underlined at parts that are positive to Chet. This is actually tampering with evidence, but it is obvious that JR underlined parts for Keller – Keller doesn't actually read Rings report – just the underlines – he already knows that the report is there to give the children to father.)

At the end of the day, Keller claims "I think I was fair. I gave you an entire day of my time." Then he says "but Dr. Ring after all" and he orders that Chet will become the primary caretaker for the children and they will now spend one overnight with me and one with Chet, and we will each get a weekend. Pop had taken the kids back to my rental. I leave alone and start walking. I forget where I am going. I forget I have my car. Eventually, I remember to get my car and I drive home.

The next day Chet gets the kids after school and I go to West Chester for class. When I get home it is after 8 o'clock. Elizabeth calls "Can you bring baby and blankie?" I had just taken my contacts out and I can't drive without them because I am legally blind. I can only wear them for eight hours a day or I have pain and can't tolerate them at all. So I tell Elizabeth "Have your father come and get them." The log cabin is five minutes away. He refuses. I tell her to insist. She says "That's ok. We don't need them." I hear him grumbling in the background. I insist that she tell him to come get them and eventually he drives out and she picks them up. After that every day, the girls have to take their baby and blankie with them in their bookbags to school.

One day as we drive home from school the kids cry "We don't have a home anymore." The constant changing of houses and sleeping places is making them neurotic and unhappy. They were happy when they came home at 8 at night and slept in their beds and got up with me in the morning. They had a routine. Because the school bus doesn't go to his house, he has to forge his time cards when he drops them off and picks them up on his "day."

A month later, in April, another hearing is scheduled. Ring still doesn't have to testify. I have called the State Department to find out when I will know about the ethical complaint and I get told they have a lot of work, thousands. My uncle again attends the hearing with me. JR says "Your honor, it has come to our attention that mother has been drinking in front of the children." I say "I had two beers while we were at a friend's house. It's better than his pot." The stenographers eyes and mouth gape open, JR immediately shuts up, Chet looks guilty, Keller pretends not to hear. Keller writes in his order "Plaintiff is not permitted to have more than two drinks." My uncle says "What, you are not allowed to drink?"

During this hearing, I ask Keller to award money so the girls can attend a summer program. JR says "He is not working because he needs hernia surgery." Keller orders me to drop the girls at Chet's instead. "Why should he pay for summer camp when he is home." So the kids start the summer in June staying in the isolated cabin with no stimulation but each other and the TV.

Seniors are selling their homes for record prices, so I am working almost every day. I often work until 3, and then drive to the courthouse to file something before they close.

One Saturday I come home from work and receive a telephone call from the Wyomissing police. JR is claiming I am stalking and harassing her. During an hour long talk, the policeman reads me the statute for harassment. I say "That is what she is doing to me." He agrees I am not harassing JR. He tells me "Come to the office, I'll give you a copy of her claim."

After a while I notice Beth and Kathy are stressed and bored. They are too involved in their parent's problems and they are not getting to see friends. So I use the little money I have to sign them up for a two week summer camp run by the YMCA at the home of local veterinarians. The property has a pool, a lake with boats, a barn made up for crafts and eating. There are lots of structured activities. On my court ordered days I take them to camp. Chet could take them on his court ordered days, but he doesn't and so they again sit at the cabin. Chet tells them they don't like camp, yet the girls wind up in a promotional brochure smiling.

I "file something" to try to get the kids some activity for the summer. I am also trying to get money to pay the premium on a $50,000 life insurance policy and get work done on the car. It has been a year and a half since I filed for divorce and one year since I moved out of the paid-for home, and he still controls all the assets.

I get a date for a hearing. JR gets the date changed. I have already changed my work schedule so I type up an emergency motion not to change the date and I go to court with the kids on Friday morning when I am not working. You can present emergency motions at the same time you file them. The clerk in the filing office tells me to go on up to Keller's courtroom even though he is listed as having a custody trial scheduled for that day.

I enter and sit on a bench waiting for Keller to hear my petition. I look around and realize that JR is sitting there. There is another woman at the opposing table. I can't figure out if she is a lawyer because she sounds very confident and familiar with legal terminology. Her name is Melissa Dietrick. She is a mother like me, representing herself.

JR gets angry when she notices me. I look around and comprehend that JR and Keller are setting up Melissa too. I quickly write "We need to talk" on a small piece of paper. Keller calls a break. He is furious that I am there. As Melissa passes me I shove the note in her hand.

Outside the courtroom, Melissa asks "Who is that woman?" The guard tells Melissa "They are doing the same thing to her that they are doing to you" so Melissa waits until I am finished, sitting with my girls who are working on activity books while they wait for me.

I am inside the courtroom while Keller is yelling at me "What are you doing here?" I make my case for having my hearing on the day originally scheduled explaining that I have to work and already scheduled that day off.

When I'm finished I go out in the hall and Melissa and I bat facts back and forth. I tell her JR is my husband's attorney too. I tell her I filed an ethical complaint against Ring. She tells me she was advised not to go to Ring. She tells me how JR set her up by claiming she kidnapped her children when she left her husband. We both say that we are representing ourselves. We quickly become friends and we frequently telephone and talk about law and our cases.

In order to settle the money side of the divorce, Chet and I have to pay another lawyer pretending he is a judge, appointed by the court, working under a contract with the court. Meyers is extremely verbose. He writes me a letter instructing me that I must conduct myself with proper decorum. The first day of the hearing, JR yells at me "Go to hell you bitch and get off my ass." I raise my eyebrows and say to Meyers "It seems Ms. Mark is not acting with proper decorum." Meyers tells her to stop.

I have all my financial proof but the pension needs to be assessed by an actuary which requires payment. JR submits a letter claiming the pension is valued at $40,000. JR represents this to be an actuarial assessment even though I object. I telephone that person and they inform me that they are a financial representative, not an actuary. They are upset that they are being misrepresented. Meyers refuses to order a proper actuarial valuation.

JR submits a copy of Chet's legal fees-to-date, hoping Meyers will order me to reimburse him out of my divorce settlement. In a year and a half, she has billed $25,000. The case will continue for years, including appeals. During the marriage, Chet would complain about every dollar spent, yet he has no problem giving tens of thousands to JR. There are other interesting facts contained in the bill: On July 24, 2006 JR billed for 1 ½ hours with client and children. That was the day she attempted to use the children for "The Vagina Claim." In January and February of 2005, the bill lists amounts "transferred from Trust" then it says "this entry has been deleted."

Chet and JR try to submit a letter from a realtor as a home appraisal, but I have a real appraisal. They claim bank accounts belong to Chet's father without any proof. We spend two days with JR and Chet making false claims and me providing proof to the contrary, while the kids go to camp. One day takes too long and I have to call my friend and ask her to pick up the girls from camp. Of course it is me who makes the arrangements, not Chet.

On the second day, I tell Chet that I will be taking my week of vacation with the girls the following week. He gets mad but JR whispers to him "Just wait.

Chapter Three

The Vagina Claim

Dialogue in this chapter is quoted directly from transcripts.

Summer, 2006

My divorce was filed in November, 2004. Chet moved out. Beth and Kathy were happy about the breakup because they were aware of the disharmony. The children were doing well, adjusting to a new routine, sleeping at my rental during the week, being with him after school two days a week and every other weekend, until March, 2006 when the trial changed their lives so that they had to spend every other night at a different home. So, I petition for a hearing, hoping to create a more stable home life for my daughters, one where they will have more time for enrichment activities and friends and less time devoted to making their father happy, having to be his only friends.

The weekend before the hearing, I take Beth and Kathy to Melissa's house. Her children are a boy and two girls close in age to my girls. The kids play badminton in the backyard and we all take a walk through the local park to the school where we walk around the track field. When we get home, I say to Beth "You have to start to tell me what they are doing so that we can fight them." She is put in the middle and she is exhausted.

That night the lights are out, the girls lie in their beds. I sit on Beth's bed while Anna lays with Kathy. Beth says "Daddy took us to Jackie's and she told us to say you are mean. She was asking about you being naked." I laugh it off, it seems absurd to me at the time, but in an attempt to make me pay his legal fees, JR submits a copy of her bill to date, showing the 8 & 9 year-old girls were with JR for an hour and a half getting probed and prepped. JR was hounding Beth for anything that could be distorted, events later prove. Beth was only nine and not real sophisticated against a manipulative psychopath like JR.

Our rental house is an old two story farmhouse. The upstairs has a landing where I put a desk, bookshelves and a chair. The front bedroom has a door connecting the second bedroom, where the girls sleep, which leads into the bathroom. Each space has two doors. We are all the same sex so sometimes the girls see me showering, like one time when Elizabeth was pooping and I was in the shower. I sleep under the covers without clothes but I keep pajamas at the top corner of the bed. I have always wanted my girls to feel good about their bodies, which is why they went to dance class. I did not make a fuss if they saw me without clothes. I just acted normal. I did not flash myself or parade around. Somehow, in the hour plus of grilling Elizabeth about life at our home, JR found out that the girls saw me without clothes. Since then, I have learned that the fatherhood accuses mothers of the actions that they are doing. For instance, they accuse mothers of sexual abuse when they are actually perpetrators; they accuse mom of turning the children against them when they are the ones trying to isolate the children. Abusers believe they are the victim, this mindset is what permits them to victimize others. Fatherhood courts help the abuser become the victim through the acceptance of false reports, enabling MHPs, the creation and admittance of false evidence and the suppression of truth.

Our rental house is located on a small country road that had recently been oiled and stoned. This is what they do in the country instead of laying asphalt. It is rather messy until enough cars trample the small rocks into the street. Our landlord, Elsie, is an older woman who loves to bike ride. She has a personal goal to bike 30 miles each day. When me and the girls were outside talking to Elsie about how they treated the road, Elsie remarked "I don't like riding on the gravel."

These two innocent events turned up in JRs twisted petition. In actuality, JR just needed to present something to Keller so that they could behave as if the elimination of mother was justified. For Beth and Kathy it took three hearings to eliminate mother.

When I arrive at the courtroom for the hearing on the afternoon of July 26th, another custody hearing is occurring. Meyers is representing the mother in this case. A female lawyer is representing a father who is not there because he now lives in Ireland. Ring is sitting in the witness box testifying what a great mother Meyers client is. Ring says "We can tell what a great mother she is by the good behavior of the 3 year old." Ring concludes by saying "This child should not have long visits with the father and will require steady counseling."

When they are finished, I stand up and say to Keller "I request that Dr. Ring testify and be cross-examined as was promised in my case at this time." Keller answers "Is that ethical thing still not resolved?" Ring replies "My lawyer advised me not to be cross-examined because I could be liable in the ethical complaint and any civil suit she files." I say "Then Dr. Ring should withdraw his evaluation." Keller yells "I am the one who gets to say if an evaluation is accepted. Dr. Ring you may leave."

I have petitioned for another Interim Disbursement because the credit card companies call every day and the children hear. I say "I am going to lose a $50,000 whole life insurance policy because I cannot pay the premium." Keller asks Meyers "Are there any liquidable assets?" Meyers answers "I'll look." In the end, Keller allows Chet to control all the assets and I forfeit my whole life insurance policy.

Next, we address my motion to require JR to act ethically and stop filing false reports to the police and cursing at me. I say "Mr. Meyers can witness to Ms. Marks foul language." Meyers states "I can attest to that." I present the fraudulent police report which an officer unofficially gave to me. JR sits with her attorney, Kauffman, whose firm JR later joins and leaves within a year. Kauffman and JR have filed a counter-petition making a myriad of false claims. Kauffman stands in front of Keller blustering "Ms. Ludwig is threatening, stalking and harassing Ms. Mark." I keep repeating "They are completely making up everything." Kauffman asks Keller "We request you order Ms. Ludwig to pay $1,000 for Ms. Marks legal fees." In the end, Keller orders JR to act professionally and treat me as a pro se litigant.

I think that settles the problem of JRs malicious, lying behavior. Hah! I believe we are getting on to a hearing about the children. I sit in the witness stand and say "The children are doing poorly, they panic and are anxious. Beth is sick to her stomach and regressed to using a baby voice with adults, a problem she overcame years ago. The children said they were happier a year ago and this court has gone on too long."

I tell Keller "I drop the children off every day at Chet's where they are isolated because of the rural property. They have no activities or enrichment during this summer when they are used to having Spanish classes at school, art lessons at the library, dance camp weekly, and visiting a special friend once a week. I signed them up for two weeks of camp and on father's days, he does not take them. They need to be with friends their own age, not their parents. If we were co-parenting we would work these things out, but he continues to be angry and threatening."

I continue "The custody arrangement should be changed because the children are not happy. They will be going to another year of school and I have been approved to receive paid-for morning day care at the YMCA through the Berks County Intermediate Unit which would be good for the children and I believe I need every weekday custody in order to receive this subsidy. The Y program will help both parents work and give the children a safe, enriching environment. It will even be located at the elementary school."

Keller cries "I don't know what that is and what you are talking about." Suddenly, a judge is making determinations about the children's schedule when he has no idea about the realities of child care. Remember: Keller is pretending Chet can arrange his work to be at school at 9 am and 3 pm for drop-off and pick-up. Chet is still forging his timesheets in order to drop off and pick-up the kids from school.

While I sit at the witness stand, I state "As an exhibit I have documents from the partial program affirming my diagnosis doesn't agree with Ring's "constellation" diagnosis and that I am not mentally ill."

I say "I believe that I am better able to make choices that would benefit the children. I don't see that a parent who is keeping them in their house and not arranging any activities, even though low cost activities are available - that's certainly not a better parent. You know, he has used his custody – and it's really just a matter of an overnight visit twice a week – to cut my support in half. And I know that is his intent to begin with. And so I think that that in itself proves what his real motivation is and not the interest of the children."

When I am finished talking, JR says "We have filed a counter petition." I answer "I never got a copy." (She is supposed to serve me when she files something but I never get any documents so that I cannot prepare a defense against the made-up accusations.) Kauffman says "We'll give you a copy now. It was filed two days ago." I say to Keller "I have not had time to read this." I am begging and pleading for the children; Keller, JR and Chet are setting me up for elimination.

JR gets to ask me questions. She starts by saying "You bring the dog to Chet's house when you pick up the kids. You make sure the dog relieves itself in the yard during those exchanges; is that correct?" I answer "I don't control the dog's defecation."

After a few more dog questions, I say "I understand that my husband puts undue stress on the children because of the dog which they love and that he is very negative about the dog. And he has even told them that mommy got the dog so you would like them better when indeed I was given the dog as protection because my family was concerned for my safety. And I am very sorry that Mr. Stepien has been replaced by a dog, but we find her more loving."

JR then asks "Mrs. Ludwig, you've taken up stretching on your bed in the evenings. The children talk about your stretching?"

ME: "Do they?"

JR: Are you aware of that?

ME: "I have something to say. The children were not allowed to go to camp yesterday and apparently they were in Ms. Mark's office and she was trying to get them to say things that seemed a little ridiculous to me. And she was trying to put ideas in their heads, and my children told me they said maybe, maybe, maybe. But apparently one of the allegations that Ms. Mark said was that I lay in the bed naked with my legs spread. My children are very open to me and that's actually very humorous to me that anybody would even come up with something like that. So I was well aware that you were going to bring that up."

JR: "Do you do the stretching, Ms. Ludwig, on your bed?

ME: "I believe that's a private matter what I do in my bed, and I don't know that that's even relevant in this court of law."

KELLER: "Well."

ME: "Do you see what I mean about professional manner? Is that professional?

KELLER: "Well, Ms. Ludwig, just don't do this. Ms. Mark, I'm sort of missing where you're going here. Maybe is that something wrong with the stretching on the bed?"

JR: "Your honor, the children tell father mother gets naked and sprawls her legs so that she can stretch them in the presence of the children. They're afraid of her because she is so grotesquely exposing herself on a daily basis to them."

ME: "Ms. Mark is coming up with one of her claims again. Once again, I have asked for her to behave ethically and professionally. This claim is so out..."

KELLER interrupts "Ms. Ludwig answer the question."

ME: "Of course I don't. Please."

KELLER: "All right. Let me ask you the question then and so it doesn't just seem like it comes from Ms. Mark. There's been apparently an allegation that are you naked in front of your children."

ME: "They're female, and I am female. We have one bathroom. Yeah, sometimes they do see me without clothes on."

KELLER: "All right. And well, can you expand upon the circumstances under which they may see you naked?"

ME: "Well, I might take a shower or if they're getting ready for bed. I am renting a stone house and there is a landing that I've made into a reading area. And there are two bedrooms – mine is in front and theirs is in the back. And there's a bath in the corner. So it's open. We walk between each other."

KELLER: "Well, apparently there is an allegation that you lie in the bed naked with your children in the same room."

ME: "Well I don't. No, I haven't."

KELLER: "You don't do that?"

ME: "Not, no. Not that I'm aware of."

KELLER: "And you don't do something, some stretching exercises naked?"

ME: "No, I don't."

KELLER: "The children are not in your bedroom when you're naked on the bed?"

ME: "They may come into my bedroom in the morning."

KELLER: "And you're naked on the bed?"

ME: "Generally I like to use covers. I'm not somebody who sleeps without a sheet on me. I have pajama's there right next to the bed. I don't have any men. There's nobody else. It's me and two girls. I don't see why that is even an issue or an allegation."

KELLER: "All right. Well, all right. Ms. Mark, move on."

JR: "Your Honor, I would ask that you talk to the children about this matter. If she would produce the children and you can take them in chambers."

Keller orders us to another hearing next week. He yells "We are going to recess until 1 tomorrow. Wherever I am. Find me. Bring the children." I say "The children have day camp and they need the activity. They need to get away from their parents." Keller answers "There's more apparent, immediate concerns. Mr. Stepien has arranged for some counseling. The children need counseling. Let's address those issues. I'll see you on the 1st at 9." JR says to Keller "We don't want her to create another problem of losing another counselor for the children."

On August 1st, Chet brings the girls to Keller. Keller takes them to his secret chamber with only himself and a transcriptionist. He repeatedly asks 9-year-old Beth if she sees me naked. Beth finally answers "A leg." Keller says "How do you feel about that?" Beth answers "Yucky." When Keller asks Kathy if she sees me naked, she answers "No." Back in the courtroom, Keller issues his order: "Mother must not be naked in front of the children and must not make them ride their bikes on the gravel. Mother is ordered to Dr. Rottenberg to determine if she is incapacitated."

After this hearing, I cross the street and go to the local domestic violence group, Berks Women in Crisis. I sit in the waiting room and cry that my husband is abusive and the court won't listen. A counselor takes me in her office and I tell her "I divorced my abusive husband. He told Ring he hit me but Ring ignored it, and they are giving Chet my children and they ordered me to Rottenberg to call me incapacitated." The counselor is shocked that Ring ignored the abuse. She schedules an appointment for me.

A few days later, I go to work and then drive to Reading for the counseling appointment. The Director, Mary Kay Bernefski comes out, wearing her tailored suit, hair perfectly coiffed, and tells me "I canceled your appointment. I tried to reach you, but this counselor is new and she is not properly trained. I don't want her speaking to you." I have been waiting to talk to the counselor, I cannot believe Mary Kay will not let me, so I tell Mary Kay "I divorced my abusive husband." She responds "People get divorced for many reasons." This domestic violence worker did not even validate my experience! She says to me "Let me look at the report." I say "It has not even been done yet." She answers "We cannot do anything for you. We have no lawyers. Try legal aid." So I leave and walk the two blocks to legal aid. Val West is sitting at the front desk. I tell her that DV sent me to her. Unlike Mary Kay, Val listens to me compassionately and says "We have no lawyers who will go against them. We would have to find one who is ready to retire. I don't know of any."

A week later, at the hearing under Meyers, JR hands me a notice to be in court on August 15th for a contempt hearing and to bring the children.

When two parents are sharing children, each is given a week of vacation. I have taken my week, but we are to go to court on Wednesday. That morning we are getting ready to go to court and Elizabeth is sitting on the toilet saying "I have stomach pains." I didn't realize it at the time, but she knew she was being used by JR and Daddy. It was having physical effects.

I actually call Keller's office and tell them we are going to be ten minutes late because Beth is in the bathroom, not knowing I have given the court the perfect opportunity to start the elimination trial without me. That is what they do. So the transcript, the written record of what occurred, has Chet testifying about how I show my vagina to the children. He goes on about how he is afraid of me. I am not there and I am never permitted to cross-examine Chet about his false allegation.

The children and I sit on a bench outside the courtroom because we are late and they have closed the courtroom doors, while Chet is inside weaving his fabulous tale. We are huddled together. Kathy says "They can't take us because we are on vacation." I say nothing. Suddenly, I am called by the security guard. The children have to sit outside; they are not allowed to go inside. I sit, the guard blocks the door, he won't let me go back out to check on the children.

Chet and JR take the children and leave. This becomes the last time they see me, their mother. This is the last time they see their personal possessions and their dog, Anna. They will never again see their maternal family: grandparents, aunts, uncles, cousins.

I am called to stand in front of Keller while he reads his order "We find by necessity, by her conduct, that we need to modify the order of August 1, and we hereby do until further order of Court. Chester Stepien, father, shall have primary and sole legal and physical custody of Elizabeth Stepien and Kathleen Stepien. The mother is prohibited from having any contact with the children by phone or physically until further order of Court. We will consider supervised visitation, but only after the mother petitions for it and the Court would order it."

Keller ends his order "Hopefully, it will be done without any undo emotional scarring to the children. This order is entered solely because of the conduct and actions of the mother, Doreen

Ludwig, and as a result of her conduct."

Since it's a contempt hearing, Keller orders "Mother will pay $1,000 to Ms. Mark for father's legal fees."

I look at Keller and say "Dr. Ring is unethical and apparently so are you."

Two security guards forcefully grab my arms and manhandle me out of the courtroom and into the elevator. I say to the guards "JR has a collage of the children in her office. She told Melissa's children "I didn't get pictures of the first ones so now I get a picture."

At home, I hold Anna. She is shaking; the kids must have given her a tearful, terrified goodbye. I walk around with the camera and take pictures. Beth took her Pooh doll, Baby, and a few stuffed horses. Kathy got only her blankie.

I am relieved because I didn't tell the girls that I needed to work on our vacation week, that there was no money for us to go anyplace, and, now, I will not have to ask family at the last minute to watch the girls. For the next two days I go to a retirement center and unpack a kind, single, elderly man's kitchen, unpacking and arranging spices, utensils and pots.

I tell Melissa "I'll file an appeal." I look up the rules of appellate procedure. I print and read them three times, highlighting the important parts. I have ten days to write a memo stating my intent to appeal. It is a simple memo so it gets filed the next week.

In response, I get an order in the mail that I have to file a Statement of Matters Complained of On Appeal. I write how Judge Keller did not follow the law, consider best interests of the children, and especially, how there was never any cross-examination of Ring and Chet's vagina claim. I get the Statement date stamped at Berks County.

I research how to file a judicial conduct complaint. When I

complain to authorities about Keller's improper actions, I'm told "You have to file a judicial conduct board (JCB) complaint." I research the judicial code and the complaint filing rules.

My friend Kathy and I drive to Harrisburg to file my finished complaint and the appeal paperwork. The first thing we do when we get to Harrisburg is take my judicial complaint to the JCB office. We enter a vestibule. At the far end, a secretary sits behind a glass wall. I tell her "We are here to file a complaint." She refuses to open the door. She replies "Leave it on the chair." I ask her "How do we get to 3rd street where the Superior Court is located?" She snaps "I don't know where that street is." It is only a few blocks away. When we leave, Kathy remarks "That was very strange."

We find the Superior Court filing office. When we enter, the clerk looks us over and briskly retorts "What do you want?" My voice shakes and my eyes tear as I mutter "I am here to file an appeal." The clerk grabs my paperwork and angrily stamps as I start to cry. Kathy says "They have taken her children."

The paperwork is filed. Next I must learn how to write an appeal brief, which is basically a school research paper with its own format. At first, I look for case law books at Berks County's law library located on the 10th floor of the courthouse. Keller has ordered the security guards to follow me whenever I am at the courthouse, so I cannot do research without having a tail. I discover a large law library in Harrisburg, across from the state capitol building. The librarian gives me appeal briefs, so I can see the finished product. I take photographs rather than spend money making copies. I look for case law. I find continual reference to the best interests of the children without any definition of what factors are considered, only an article citation.

The Harrisburg library does not have a copy of the legal journal cited. I am told that law schools will permit non-students to use their libraries, so one Sunday I drive an hour away to the University of Pennsylvania. I find parking and walk around. I find the law library. I ask to enter and they tell me I am not allowed. I say "I telephoned and they said I could use the library." A guard says "Not on the weekends. It is too busy." I start to cry, "I drove and I have lost my children and I can't find it anywhere." I can't stop crying. A librarian approaches, listens to my cries, and finally agrees "You can come in to find only what you need and then you are never allowed to return." I'm escorted inside. As I give the librarian my driver's license I say "This is the citation." I follow a student around the library, walking up stairs and down hallways with my head down and eyes red while the well-to-do students do their research. But I get what I need and I leave, never to return. I buy coffee to drink on the ride home. I drive the Schuykill and I take the citation home. I assemble the case law, including the definition of best interests of the children, the standard for judging custody. I add the citation to my appeal brief argument.

Melissa is still fighting with Keller and JR over her children. Melissa found out early that Ring was bogus, so she refused to see him. Instead, Keller appointed Dierdre Young to be the custody evaluator. Melissa never went to see Dierdre Young. Dierdre's training is in art therapy. The court let's an art therapist decide custody! I telephone Dierdre and ask "How do you determine custody?" She answers "I just meet with the parents and get a feeling." Even though Dierdre never met Melissa, Dierdre submits a report to Keller claiming that Melissa is "untreatably mentally ill."

Melissa works as a long-term substitute teacher in her children's school district, a job perfect for being able to take care of school-age kids. In late September, she receives an order from Keller "Father is to have primary custody. Mother must vacate the home within ten days." At the time, Eric, the father, was renting an apartment, but Keller decides Eric should move back and take care of the kids while working his second shift job.

Melissa has no place to move to and no money. Since I am now a professional mover, I work during the day and drive to Melissa's house to help pack, bringing boxes and packing supplies. Melissa has a friend who comes and helps us move her things to a storage unit. He puts her up in a motel and somehow they find a small apartment that she can move into. One afternoon Melissa and I use the storage unit van to move her things to the apartment. Melissa is permitted to see her children every other weekend, so we attempt to make things comfortable for three kids to be in a one bedroom apartment. The kids never care about the space; they just want to be with their mother.

During the week, Melissa's kids are now being watched by their father's mother. Grandma arrives at the three bedroom ranch home when they get home from school to supervise homework and cook dinner since dad works the 3 to 11 shift. The kids prefer Melissa. Grandma is a chain-smoking, miserable, old lady, a bad cook, with a history of smacking the kids when they bother her.

Melissa files an appeal one month after my appeal is filed. So now we are working together on appeals. This gives us lots to discuss and each night we talk for hours about case law, and procedure. On Saturday, we go to Harrisburg's law library together.

You get 30 days to file your brief. I file mine just before the deadline. Melissa files hers early, a week later. That night Melissa telephones "I drove to JR's office to deliver my brief. She was out in the hallway. JR looked like she was having a heart attack when I handed her my brief." I laugh "Now, she'll be required to file two reply briefs within ten days, just before

Christmas!" JR solves the problem by filing small briefs containing the exact same argument in both of our cases. Whole paragraphs are identical!

Chapter Four

Jail For Mothers

Fall, 2006

Meyers finishes the distribution of assets. Of course it is manipulated to favor Chet. Meyers claims a bank account belongs to Chet's father. The pension fund is improperly valued at $40,000, a tenth of true value, since no actuary was retained. Meyers lists a $7,188 certificate of deposit as my property, knowing that it was cashed out by Chet on December 2, 2004; the money is mine on paper only. Even when I file a separate motion for payment, Chet is permitted to steal my money. (An appeal resulted in the Superior Court claiming the cashing out was in dispute, even though the redemption certificate, signed by Chet, was provided in the exhibits.)

The manipulations result in my settlement being much lower than entitled, but due to our years of work and frugality, the final award is still sizeable. Chet is supposed to pay within thirty days, by December 3rd, 2006, over two years since the day the divorce was filed. Of course, he never pays and I have to file a Motion for payment.

In his August order, Keller ordered me to Dr. Larry Rottenberg, at Reading Hospital for an evaluation to determine if I am an incapacitated person under the law. That means, I am unable to make basic financial, health and safety determinations for myself. (This order was predetermined as Keller informs JR of his intent at the beginning of the July 26th custody hearing. It is part of the set-up. I was begging and pleading for the children, they were making outlandish accusations without any proof.)

Getting an order that a litigant is incapacitated is a legal strategy to give the lawyers control of a parties money. A guardian ad litem (GAL), usually a lawyer, would be appointed by the judge and they would receive an initial payment of $25,000 out of my divorce settlement with complete control of my finances and all the divorce settlement. On July 26, Keller made it clear that this is his ultimate goal.

Melissa, being younger than me, is more proficient at computer research. She finds out Rottenberg, who I call Dr. Rotten, is Jewish, left Europe for Canada at a young age to avoid the Holocaust. He published an article proclaiming Jews to be superior beings. Melissa finds a similar case, where Berks County court was attempting to call a divorcee incapacitated. The divorcee is Gail Savage, the ex-wife of the local auto dealer, The Savage Auto Group. I call Gail and we have lunch. We talk about who's who and the local connections among the players including the Ullmans, who were instrumental in setting her up. Gail tells me "I hired my own psychiatrist, a doctor from Pittsburgh with high level credentials. He determined that I was not incapacitated. But, in the month the court was playing this game, the Ullmans were able to spend over $30,000 of my money."

"The court put me in jail for one year. They claimed I attempted to murder my husband because I rear-ended his vehicle. I was never charged, just locked-up, in maximum security, with murderers. Ironically, the entire sheriff's department received new Jeep Cherokee's compliments of Savage Auto Group." As we eat our salads, Gail tells me "I keep my telephone listed so maybe I can help other women. One woman who contacted me is a doctor. She had to live in her office." At the end of our meal, Gail says "My children have been ruined. But you can't fight City Hall."

I do not have money to hire my own psychiatrist so I go to see Rotten, thinking I will give him the chance to be honest. Rotten's evaluation consists of contacting Ring and using his evaluation, asking a few psychological questions like "Why would you not yell fire in a movie theater?" "What is wrong with throwing stones at glass houses?" and "If you could have one wish what would it be?" Rotten spends the remainder of our visit yelling at me about my custody case. He says "Why would you argue with a respected member of our community?" I think he means Ring but he could mean Keller, they are very worried about the ethical complaint because they know it is legitimate. I answer "He may be respected in your community, but he is not in mine." Rotten really doesn't like me; my ability to stand up to them because my morals and belief in right and wrong are strong. When I explain "I got my sense of right and wrong from a strong church upbringing and from the fact that my father, grandfather and great-grandfather were Philadelphia fireman" Rotten sneers at my analogy, he doesn't understand fear and weakness did not exist in my family.

Rotten never finds out if I am able to handle my money: pay rent and utilities on time. He never finds out how I manage any medical concerns, if I make doctor visits and follow instructions. He does not visit my house to see if I am able to shop for food, prepare meals, clean and organize my home, care for my dog, nor does he question my landlord to verify that my habits are those of an incapacitated person. Melissa and I know that Rotten will deem me incapacitated.

While I'm waiting for Rotten's report, I work moving seniors, taking classes at West Chester, and working on my appeal, often driving to Harrisburg to file papers and research at the law library.

One weekend I drive alone to New Jersey to attend my nephew Chris and Jen's wedding. When I find my table, my Aunt Nancy smiles as she tells me "I'm divorcing Carl, too!" She and the kids are glowing because Carl is an alcoholic and they are all thrilled he is out of the house. No one mentions that Beth and Kathy are missing. I put on a strong façade, being pleasant, only briefly thinking that my children will never be able to be a part of their cousins wedding. I write an IOU for a gift.

I call Rotten's office and ask the secretary "Where is the report?" She answers "You will get it once Judge Keller is finished looking at it." It is supposed to be an impartial report, Keller is not supposed to have input. (Later, when I sue Rotten, he will write that he "was just doing what the Judge wanted.") When the report shows up in my mailbox in an open, unsealed, manila envelope, I don't even read it, I just look at the last page, where Rotten has written "Doreen is an incapacitated person, but this doesn't mean that she is not a good person, but it is our duty, out of our goodness, to help her."

Keller schedules a hearing for the next week. I file a motion stating "By law the court is required to give thirty days notice in order to prepare a defense and get witnesses and exhibits, so therefore the hearing is not legitimate and I will not participate." Knowing that they were going to do this anyway, I had typed, notarized, and filed a legal Power of Attorney, appointing my uncle my guardian should I ever become incapacitated, using a copy of the Power of Attorney he had for his brain-injured son. By doing this, I stopped Keller from giving away my finances to an attorney. My finances were the legal property of my uncle.

Keller appoints Rebecca Stone "in custody only." I believe

Keller wants Stone to drop the ethical complaint against Ring on my behalf. I call Stone and tell her "The first thing you are to do on my behalf is to file a suit against Ring for malpractice and violation of my due process rights." She doesn't. Stone is the daughter of another prominent local family, her father is a contemporary of Keller. Stone is mousy and afraid, when we are in Keller's courtroom, she literally shakes.

Early in January 2007, I receive an order from the Superior Court regarding my custody appeal. It says my appeal is DENIED. I am not allowed to appeal because Keller said he did not get a copy of my Statement of Matters Complained of on Appeal. Keller was supposed to write an Opinion explaining why he made his orders of August 1 and 15, and he is supposed to point to the place in the record that confirms the evidence for his order. He doesn't do this because there is no evidence for any of his orders. Instead Keller's written Opinion is that the Superior Court should deny my appeal because he did not get a copy and because my Statement was long. For proof, Keller attaches a copy, proving that he did indeed have a copy, filed and date stamped by Berks County. By law, the Superior Court is not allowed to deny appeals (due process) by using the copy rule. Even JR admits that this is a bogus claim. She acknowledges in her reply brief that the PA Supreme Court overturned denial in a previous case where a Statement was not even filed.

I have spent the fall taking classes, working, researching and writing my appeal. I met every deadline. My argument is solid. I knew the Superior Court would not permit my children to be taken based on Ring's, JRs and Chet's lies. None of the lies were proven. The law required them to consider the best interests of the children. Yet, in the mail I get a one-page document saying my appeal is denied. My blood freezes, my heart seizes, my mind spins, my pulse races. I look around the room at my kids' stuff. There must be something that I can do. I grab the yellow pages, and I call the news stations and say "I have a story." I want to drive to their offices and insist they put my story on the air. We mothers are calling news stations and papers begging them to print our stories. They won't.

I think "I must drive to the house and just talk to Chet. Surely, he will show some sense and we can talk and stop this already." So I drive out there and the house is dark. I walk to the neighbor's house. Diane answers the door. I ask her "Do you know where Chet is?" She answers "No." I tell her "I want to talk to him. He is abusive."

I leave. I drive, thinking I will go to the news station in Philadelphia. But I don't get far. I go back to the rental and curl up in bed thinking of ways to kill myself.

Keller mails me an order to show up in court or be arrested. During Christmas, Keller telephoned my Uncle, Pop, to find out how willing he was to pay a lawyer for my case, basically, if my Power of Attorney Uncle is going to cooperate with the money scam. On the hearing day, Rebecca Stone is present. Pop meets me at court. I am wearing brown corduroys, a tan cable knit sweater and Born clogs. By this time, I am aware that every action of Keller is a set-up. Keller begins by telling Rebecca "What I want you to do…" I direct my interruption to Rebecca "If you do anything I don't want I will sue you." Keller yells "Arrest her! She is in contempt! You will go to jail for ten days!"

There are always many security guards in family court, divorce court (remember: my crime is filing for divorce). Several security guards grab me and Pop takes my stuff. The guards drag me through the back doors down to the basement of the courthouse where the prisoners go. I am not fingerprinted because I am not a criminal, just a divorcee.

In the fall I had visited the FBI office in Allentown and met with Agent Markowitz who looked at my documents, including the underlined transcript. He had told me "There is something here. We will investigate." When I am left with a phone, I pull out his card because I want to call him with this latest development in the corruption scam. I have filed a claim with the ACLU and I call them and say that the court is putting me in jail because of my corrupt case.

The guards put me in handcuffs, leg irons and a waist chain connecting my legs and hands. They take me on the jail bus. They put me on a bench in the back of a closed-in box truck; girls on one side, boys on the other, separated by a tin wall.

When we get to the prison we are unloaded in the processing area. They take off the chains, which were put on so tight there are welts on my wrists. They put five of us in a cell which contains a small bench and a toilet.

They give me the jail uniform, pants and shirt. They give me the thinnest of blankets and a Bob Barker hygiene package. The game show legend owns a line of jail necessities: toothbrush, comb, soap, deodorant. They give me a pair of bobo's in a bigger size so they flop off my feet when I walk. If I was wearing sneakers, I could keep them, but I am dressed for divorce court. (Mothers, take this word of advice: wear your sneakers to divorce court when your judge is abusing his power. Fatherhood judges are jailing mothers in order to intimidate, threaten and prove who is boss.)

I am told I can shower because I won't be allowed again for three days. One of the other girls says "I'm going to shower" but I decline.

I am taken to the women's cellblock, it is evening social hour, so the girls are out exercising, walking, and watching TV. But my group is being taken to quarantine. I won't be allowed to be part of the general population until a TB test has cleared.

It is the other people who get you through, you are not alone and that makes it easier. There is a black woman who has to do one year. There is a Latina who has to stay for thirty days because her teenage girl is cutting school. Since she is the mom, she has been fined, owes several thousand dollars which she doesn't have, so she has to do jail time for the fines. "What can I do, I take her to school and when I leave she walks away. Now I will lose my job and maybe my house." There is a pretty white twenty year old who has to do ten days like me because she owes three hundred dollars for a parking ticket. She is told to pay or go to jail. She doesn't have the money to pay and hopes she will still have her job at a local commercial dessert processing plant when she gets out. These are the woman I am put in with. They tell me what will happen. We talk to each other through slots in the door.

When I am in quarantine I sit by the door in a chair. I get the top bunk. The beds are made of cold, hard metal. The mattresses are thin. There is no pillow. It is early January, the room temperature is about fifty degrees, mold grows on the wall. I wear a thin, short sleeve shirt. They refuse to give everyone a sweatshirt. The blanket is threadbare. Butter, saved for moistening dry lips, doesn't melt or soften.

My mind is racing but I think to myself "You cannot go crazy because that is why Keller put you in here. He wants you to lose your mind." The other prisoners say "Ten days. I could do that no problem."

There is some routine and that helps. I talk to the therapist. When I explain I am there because of divorce they look sympathetic, but useless. I guess they think I am lying. There is a woman that comes around with bibles. She is willing to talk. She gives me a small new testament.

There are books and I ask for something to read. The guard gives me a thick paperback, an american revolution historical romance. It keeps me busy.

There is a young latina woman in another cell who comes to her door and talks, mostly about her kids. She has a young boy and girl. She has an older son that she doesn't see because Berks County gave him entirely to the father. She has to pay $500 a month in support. She doesn't have a job but she can waitress. She said she overslept and missed a support hearing. I understand she didn't go because she didn't want to be re-abused. So now she is in jail for owing back support and her young children are in foster care. She is street tough, but once in a while she says "I have to go away now." She goes to her bed and silently cries.

The twenty-year-old cries out loud a lot. She calls her mother and asks her to pay the parking ticket but her mother tells her "You'll have to serve the time. I don't have the money either."

On my first day in jail, I share the cell with a girl who didn't respond to a subpoena to be a witness in a criminal case. During the day, she leaves on the jail bus to go before the judge. When she gets back she is soon released and I am alone until the middle of the night when someone is thrown in.

The new roomie begs me to give her my mattress while I sit in the chair and she begs for my blanket because I can only wrap the sheet around myself while I sit in the plastic chair. I curl my feet up in the chair as I listen to everyone talk.

I get my period and I ask for a pad and I am glad they supply me.

The worst part is that you can't scrub your teeth, there is no dental floss and the toothbrush is toddler size and the paste barely works. You can't wash your face because you have no soap so your face gets oily and pimples emerge while your lips crack from dryness. If you get caught saving butter to moisten your lips, you'll be sent to the "hole."

The meals always contain butter and bread. They are heavy on carbs but the meals are the best part and I eat with gusto. To drink, we are given kool aid juice. One girl says "I don't drink that juice, I put it down the toilet. It's jail tydibowl."

On my second day of incarceration, I am called to the front processing area where I am served with a protection from abuse (PFA) order filed by Chet. He claims he is in fear of me because I visited the neighbor's house. The form asks Chet to list any prior instances of abuse against him and the children. He writes "There have been no prior instances against the children." (Remember: I have been eliminated because of The Vagina Claim. I guess that abuse escaped his mind. Mothers fighting true sexual abuse of their children would never miss an opportunity to rehash the abuse and list their proof. Chet has proven again that he was lying in August when I was eliminated.)

The guards read me the PFA. When they get to the part about taking away weapons, they say "Do you have any guns?" I give them the "What are you stupid?" look. (I'm in jail. I don't think I have guns.) They laugh. The PFA hearing is scheduled for next week, while I am still in jail.

After three days of quarantine, I am allowed to go to the general population. I can shower every night and walk outside in the "yard" and make phone calls. I can order things with the money that was automatically taken from my wallet, about forty dollars. The prison will not return my money when I leave. I will have to request a return and they will only return half.

I am allowed to shower during evening free time. The open showers have clear white, light curtains. They are located in a corner of the top floor and everyone can see your shadow as you lather and rinse.

I get new books. I go to the library.

I get a new cellmate who doesn't speak much English. She tells me "My son was shot five years ago. Since then I do drugs and get put in jail." I let her use my money to purchase things. When I first entered her room I could see she has nothing, very few personal belongings. The only money she gets is welfare. (Some jailbirds have people on the outside sending them money.) She buys envelopes, instant coffee and tons of candy. When it arrives the next day, she stays up all night crunching what sounds like jaw breakers. She has a toothache the next morning.

I am told if you want contraband, you get an outside person to give money to a correction officer. That's how they smuggle you cigarettes and drugs.

We get common area time in the evening. The girls watch Cops on the small TV, comparing stories and prison info.

One night another cell has something stolen and they accuse my cellmate and search our stuff. I am convinced that Keller has set me up and I panic as I wait in the hall. But eventually the real burglar is found in another cell.

When you first enter prison they ask if you have medical needs and they say they will supply what you need. I ask for a contact case which I am not given, nor am I allowed to have cleaning and wetting solution. My contacts have to come out of my eyes so I use two leftover juice cups which I store in the bottom of my jail supplied plastic container. When we are outside, the guards go through our stuff. We are not permitted to keep things like juice cups and they throw out my specialized contacts. I come back to my room and say "Where are my cups? My contacts were in them. I need them to see." Again, I am panicked. My cellmate finds the contacts in the cups in the trash.

On Thursday I am to be transported to court for the PFA hearing. Wednesday was laundry day, so I get to wear clean clothes. I will be gone the whole day. In the morning I get chained and put in the box truck with another girl. She is also a drug addict; a pretty girl with missing front teeth, she flirts with the guards. She is pregnant and excited about having the baby, due in a few months. The guard takes off her chains every time she asks to go to the bathroom, while we wait in the holding room in the basement of the courthouse. There is another lady in there who has spent the night chained to the bench. She is wearing pointy cowboy boots. She says she was chained up because she had a fight with her boyfriend and he called the cops and she kicked the cops. I raise my eyebrows and say "With those?" She answers "Yes." I start telling her how she will get treated in jail. My pregnant friend pokes me and whispers "Shut up, don't say anything, do you want her to start freaking out?"

Two guards come to take me to Keller. One is holding something in his hand. I say "What is that?" He smirks and his eyes gleam. I realize it is a taser and he is just looking for an excuse to use it on me.

I enter Keller's courtroom the back way. I strut into the courtroom with my head held high, smiling, not even hindered by the leg chains. I coolly say "Hi" as I stroll past JR and Chet who are sitting together at their table. Keller goes through his spiel. He asks "Ms. Ludwig, do you want to contest the charges?"

I answer "No. You are going to do what you want to do so I don't need to sit here. I am tired." They take me downstairs. An hour later the guards call me and take me back to Keller who says "You have been called as a witness."

Chet claims that because I spoke to the neighbor, I threatened him. I say "The neighbor needs to be here to testify." Keller orders a two-year PFA against me. At the end of the hearing Keller says to me "You must get back to this court. Unless I get out of this prison of a courtroom and win the lottery you must get back do you understand? Do you understand?" I derisively answer "I understand."

The next morning is Friday. I'm released early. I get my belongings back except for my money. So I have no money to make a phone call or to pay for a ride home. I walk. I walk two miles and get to a shopping area. There is a convenience store. I ask a truck driver to take me into the city if he is going that way. He thinks about it and says "No." I go to a CVS drug store and ask if they have a phone book and if I can call a taxi. They let me call a taxi, an older man arrives. I tell him "I was in court for divorce and got put in jail and my car is at the courthouse parking garage." He says "It was probably put in the impound lot. I'll take you there first." But my car is not there. I tell him to park in front of the bank around the corner from the court garage and I get fifty dollars, the last of the money in my account. I pay the driver and have just enough left to rescue my car. I drive home. My friends have stocked my freezer with frozen meals. Stephanie, my friend's sister-in-law, is caring for Anna.

Pop has my money from the divorce. It is 12 o'clock so I call him and drive to his house to get my settlement check. Jeff's health aide has a husband in the army. She asks "What was jail like?" I answer "I guess a lot like being in the army."

That night, my friends, the play group moms, come over and bring food and wine. Lori says "What is it like being in jail?" I'm glib. "I'm from Philly so I could take it. You just curse a lot."

On Monday I stop at the bank before going to a lunchtime work meeting. Everyone is glad I am OK. I clean a house on Saturday. Everything is moved out and I get extra pay by being the staff who does the final house clean. I get five hours pay for cleaning floors, bathrooms and cabinets.

I've been waiting for the divorce money so I can pay off the credit cards. I spread the cards out and call each to agree on a payoff amount. I authorize bank account withdrawals. The settlement disappears quickly. I pay overdue bills: electric, water, heating oil. I pay rent.

Within days of my release, I type a letter to the Rules Committee of the PA Supreme Court. Before being sent to jail, while doing my legal research, I noticed the court planned to change their rules to make greater use of the custody evaluator (the Dr. Ring's). The deadline for commenting occurred while I was imprisoned, but I write a comment anyway. I type three pages explaining that evaluators are acting under no requirement to be ethical. I make a point to write that the court should have standards rather than make it easier to use these outside, for-profit businesspeople who have no training in the law or rules of evidence. I include an article reiterating that point. In response I receive a letter saying "We cannot represent you." I write back "I did not ask you to represent me."

What I don't know is that the court and legislature are passing a law that no one can file an ethical complaint against any mental health practitioner involved in custody in Pennsylvania. That means that the courts are working to make it easier to use these business people while simultaneously ensuring there is no ethical requirement. (At this time, I still think it is only one person, Dr. Ring, running a counseling scam.)

Chapter Five

Working to Correct, Looking for Help

January, 2007

    I file an appeal against the PFA. I devote myself to writing another brief. I write a masterpiece proving that Chet is the abusive person. I include research proving that abusive men use custody to continue their abuse. Because I was not permitted to see my children based on Chet and JR's Vagina Claim and Chet acknowledged in his PFA application that "there were no prior instances of abuse," this simple admittance proves father's fraud in the elimination of me, mother. The Vagina Claim was bogus and he admits it in his PFA application. So I point out that Chet admits there was never any abuse in the first place. Since I was never allowed to have an appeal on the elimination of my children, I use my PFA appeal to point out the fraud of the custody decision. As exhibits to my appeal brief I attach professional research proving abusive men use custody courts to continue their control. I base my argument on these two simple factors, supplemented by evidence I raised at my original trial that I was not allowed to present which proved that Chet is really the abusive party, not me. I include Dr. Atkins 12-page letter which includes many references to abusers and invalid custody evaluations. I spend my money on ink, copying, and packaging. I spread the exhibits along the sofa and window sills. I collate. I drive to Harrisburg and file my paperwork.

At the Supreme Court of Pennsylvania, I file for Permission to Appeal the denial of the original, Vagina Claim custody appeal. (In five months, the PA Supreme Court will deny my right to appeal the denial of The Vagina Claim appeal. So, during the summer of 2007, I take the train to DC and file a Writ of Certiorari at the U.S. Supreme Court focusing on the denial of due process: my right to appeal and cross-examination of Ring and Chet. The US Supreme Court clerk will return the 10 copies by mail, three times, each time holding a copy, writing me that I sent an incomplete package because I did not include a copy of the trial court Judge's (Keller's), Opinion. I return the packet, writing that the denial of my right to appeal is Keller's Opinion. I finally get so frustrated at the returned "incomplete" packet, that I telephone and tell the clerk "Call Keller's office and ask them why there is no real Judicial Opinion." After that they process my Writ, and eventually deny me a right to appeal.)

Most of the money I get paid is taken out for support so I file an appeal against the support order. When assessing the amount of support each child requires, the master uses Chet's higher income, but when the master factors percentage each parent contributes, the order is written so that Chet and I make the same amount of money: about $20,000 per year. He makes $65,000 to $80,000 as a union millwright, which is like being a mechanical carpenter. I have never made more than $17,000 as a clerical worker, I have been a stay-at-home mom for ten years, my computer skills are severely out-of-date, and I have visual limitations. I spend an entire week writing the support brief. It makes me familiar with how finances are manipulated and how easy it is to assign distorted, false incomes.

I begin another semester at West Chester University. I work, but 60% of my take-home pay is deducted for support. Sometimes, the seniors we unpack give us tips. The tips keep me in gasoline and coffee.

I still try to get help. One day I write Pennsylvania's National Organization of Women chapter and ask them if they can recommend a lawyer. The response says "Liz Richards just made a presentation to NOW about how women are being treated in court." I email Liz and when I come home late one night from visiting my sister, I have an answer telling me about welfare's fatherhood program funding custody case rigging for dads. I email Melissa "This is it! It is a racket! It is not us!"

Liz writes "For fifty dollars I will send you a packet that will explain the racket. With financial proof the court will become afraid and they will back off, the corruption will stop." Liz's packet is difficult to understand. It contains articles and case rigging proof. It tries to outline the fatherhood program. A lot of the articles are old and from other states. The problem is that the fatherhood welfare program is huge and Liz is one person. The scope of the corruption is not comprehended even by Liz, as she has worked to "out" the program, the fatherhood and its internal court network has successfully grown the program.

Because I don't understand it, I research Liz's information by searching the internet. Using key people and words, I find current, reliable, relevant research.

Meanwhile, I work, packing and unpacking seniors moving from homes into retirement centers. I see their houses. I notice that some men treat their wives gently. I notice how these couples act with love, kindness, respect. Eighty-year-old Nancy has dementia and alzheimer's. Her husband Bill is selling their home and moving them to a retirement center, in southern Chester County. Nancy worked as an elementary teacher. She accumulated collections of crystal and hummels. We pack so many boxes of crystal we run out of paper. When we unpack at the much smaller apartment, vases and statues are bunched on every surface, even on top of the refrigerator! Bill doesn't care because the crystal makes Nancy happy. She picks up an item and says "Oh, this is so pretty!" The only time Bill raises his voice is when Nancy forgets to take her pills. When it is time to leave, he wraps her up in a sweater and brings her with him to walk us to the exit. Later, when I clean their empty house, I notice a handwritten sign at the top of the steps saying "Nancy, when you get to the top go left and step into the bathroom and wash." A realtor stops by and says "How sweet is that note?" Later, I tell my family "I have met the man I want to marry and he is eighty and already married."

Another client needs an organization because his wife died a year previously and he needs someone to go through her things. The front rooms of the house contain all her clothes because that is where she lived for the last year of her sickness. This man is still grieving and cannot get rid of her presence. He tells me "I was the first black law clerk in my state. My wife was such a good woman. My sons are all doctors. I miss her so much."

When I am not working I do school and legal work and I research the fatherhood. My friend Kathy brings her children to visit or I'll drive to their house. When it's Kathy's weekend without the kids, I go with her to clean the office. Other times, Melissa comes over and we do research and law work. Other nights we'll talk on the phone and she'll say "Keller looks like Dana Carvey doing Saturday Night Live's Church Lady, the way he shrivels up his face and shakes."

Melissa's appeal is read and the Superior Court determines that Keller should have dropped the custody case because it was not resolved within six months. The higher court sends the case back to the lower court for another hearing. Immediately, JR resubmits Dierdre Young's false custody evaluation calling Melissa "untreatable mentally ill." JR and Keller quickly have an ex-parte hearing and Keller orders exactly the same thing that had just been overturned on appeal! Melissa quickly types up a Motion and I drive it to Harrisburg and file it since I have more time flexibility. The Superior Court orders Keller to desist ex parte hearings. (Ex-parte hearings are held without one or both of the parents present. Many mothers are eliminated by ex-parte orders. They have never been given the opportunity to refute the charges against them.)

Because Keller's custody order is overturned, Melissa's kids return to her primary care, so they move into the one-bedroom apartment for the summer while dad continues to live in the 3 bedroom marital home. Even though the space is small, Melissa's son and two girls are happy to be with their mom, they never complain. Melissa's a teacher, so she is free to be with the children, who are glad they aren't being watched by grandma all summer. When I visit, we get pizza, take walks to see horses at the farm, and play yard games in the backyard.

Keller schedules another custody hearing for Melissa to take place on four different days. Keller and JR begin to rig another case. After two hearings, I telephone the AOPC (Administrative Office of PA Courts) and leave a message "Why is there no due process in the Dietrick case?" At the next hearing, there is an unknown person watching. Melissa submits a copy of dad, Eric's myspace page. On it, Eric has written "I've been assured getting custody is no problem." This infuriates Keller. The case is quickly resolved with Melissa receiving primary custody and dad getting weekend visits.

I am still owed $55,000 in divorce settlement but JR and Chet have tied it up by keeping it as retirement funds rather than buy me out, paying the amount in cash which is the standard. The Union, which holds the money, refuses to give it to me and I have to go to court over this. Meanwhile, I live off what is left from the first half of the settlement. Most of the money I get paid is taken out for support. I get paid very little, about $200 to $300 a week and the court takes 60% of that; a $200 check leaves me $90; a $300 check leaves me $140.

The car needs new tires, my windshield gets hit with a rock and needs replacing, and it is time for inspection. There is no extra money, so I don't get anything done.

Every few months, I call the State Department and ask "What is happening with Ring's ethical investigation?" They have many excuses. "We have a lot of work." "Dr. Ring would not give us his records so we had to go to Commonwealth Court to get them." "We are sending the report to an expert for their review."

One day, a recusal from Keller shows up in the mail. I telephone Melissa. "Keller is not my judge anymore. Judge Lash is assigned." I take this as good news. Actually, what happened is that the Judicial Conduct Board (JCB) has refused to do anything about the unethical Keller, instead, administration told him to get off the case. The JCB sends me a letter stating "There is no reason to investigate." A JCB annual report will confirm "Over 50% of complaints are resolved by a phone call to the Judge."

Melissa and I decide that I will file for a custody hearing in front of Lash. I type an Emergency Petition stating that father does not allow the children to see any of their maternal family, their mother, or any of their possessions. I again state that Chet is abusive and the Pennsylvania custody statute requires custody to be determined by history of abuse and which parent allows the other parent to see the children (the friendly parent provision). A hearing date is scheduled. I spend the day before the hearing cleaning the rental, wiping each and every one of the girl's possessions.

When I get to court, Judge Lash claims he cannot do anything about what Keller did and he refuses to have a hearing. In effect, whatever Keller did is AOK; Ring will never be held accountable for his unethical report; a custody determination based on the truth will never occur. I immediately get in my car and drive to Philadelphia to the Administrative Office of Pennsylvania Courts and I knock on their locked office door. I ask the staff opening the door "Why is there no due process? Why are you not investigating?" She answers "The Attorney General and FBI should investigate. We only do training." Then she calls the security guard to escort me out of the building. On my drive home, I stop in Conshohocken and find the offices of the Philadelphia Inquirer. I leave a message that I would like a reporter to contact me about a story.

I am still unaware of the fullness of the fatherhood program goal to give custody to dads and to eliminate mothers and make mothers pay dads support. It will take me years to realize the full scope of the program and the political cover-up of fatherhood custody case rigging for abusive men.

I still try to get help. I get lists of groups that are supposed to help abused women. I call. The Pennsylvania Coalition Against Domestic Violence tells me "Pennsylvania courts are very corrupt." They offer only that, no help. I call and ask if they know of any lawyers who can help. They know none, in the entire State! I call Lancaster County and Philadelphia domestic violence groups. They know of no lawyers. I call national domestic violence groups, Battered Women's Justice Project (BWJP) and the National Coalition Against Domestic Violence (NCADV). They know of no lawyers. Since she claims to be a national coalition, I leave a message for the NCADV Director, Rita Smith, asking for the name of someone in Pennsylvania who is working on the battered woman's custody problem. She knows no one.

I'm told to ask for legal representation from a victims assistance group. A woman returns my call while I'm at a home working with Mark to clear out items left after the move. When I explain I am looking for legal representation because my abusive husband was given my kids, she yells at me "They give children to men who have been in jail for years!" I hang up shaking, almost in tears. Mark tells me "Take this extra stuff, this mirror in the window frame painted with hot air balloons, cookbooks, bookcase, pots and pans."

I call the Governor. I ask for a meeting with a member of his staff. I ask them to expedite the ethical complaint. They refuse. Eventually they make it so my phone number is not accepted. Again, I don't realize the scope of the racket and the range of the players.

On weekends her children are with Eric, Melissa comes to my rental and does her laundry using my basement washer and dryer, saving money and a trip to the Laundromat. She plays on the computer while I do things around the house. I'm upstairs cleaning and I start to look at my kids belongings. I pull their socks and underwear out of the drawers. I take them downstairs and give them to Melissa saying "Take these for your girls. It's been a year and Beth and Kathy wouldn't fit them anymore." I get sad and angry. I cry. Melissa leaves, taking the socks and underwear.

I decide to sue all the players for violation of my due process rights. I go to the Harrisburg law library and look up the Rules of Federal Court. I read how to file a federal suit. As I read the rules,

I panic. I say to myself "Calm down, you know what a Motion is." "You know what a Pleading is." I read the rules and they make sense the first time.

I go home and look on-line for more rules and forms and I write my claim. I list JR, Keller, Ring, Rotten, Meyers, Ullman, even the local District Attorney for refusing to investigate. I type up the Petition succinctly listing the steps taken by all players to deny my rights to a fair trial. I send each of them notification that they are being sued.

They lawyer up. They all get lawyers and respond. Ring takes over thirty days to respond, waiting until the deadline has expired. He claims he is late because he was away and didn't open his mail. Of course, I mailed the suit by certified mail to Ring's business. The district attorney claims "prosecutorial discretion." Unlike your local police who prosecute street criminals, district attorney's and attorney generals, who typically go after white collar crime, are under no obligation to investigate and prosecute crime. JR claims lawyers are permitted to lie in Pennsylvania because it is representing her client. Ring and Ullman claim they are judges and entitled to immunity from prosecution. Rotten states he was just doing what the judge wanted. In the end, the third circuit will allow each of the players to get off with these claims.

When the spring college semester ends, I apply for acceptance into West Chester University's Women's Studies program, hoping this will give me a chance to focus on writing. I am accepted. I apply for a federal grant and receive an amount which will cover half the cost of tuition. I keep trying to get the marital funds owed to me but the court and union refuse to pay me. I am not permitted to take a hardship withdrawal to pay for tuition. What I now know is that the fatherhood program works to financially disable mothers so they have no means for legal representation.

I get my transcript from Philadelphia Community College. But the time for me to pay West Chester's fall tuition expires. I am not willing to take out a bank loan. I would have to pay for living expenses if I went to school for several years. I cannot earn enough to pay my rent, utilities, food and car maintenance. I still believe that the money is owed to me and it is only a matter of time until it is paid. I file a federal suit against the Union, thinking this will force them to pay.

In September I sell my paid-for car for $4,000 so that I can pay the rent until appeals are complete. I'm still believing the court will rule in accordance with the law (ha, ha).

I cannot go to school and I cannot work. I call work to tell my employer "I cannot work anymore. I had to sell my car." They answer "We don't know how you could work anyway with all the money they are taking out."

I walk into town and take a bus which runs once in the morning and once in the afternoon, to Reading where I apply for food stamps. When I receive an emergency payment, a friend sends her brother to take me shopping.

During the winter, Melissa found a blog called the Pennsylvania Progressive. John Morgan, the blog editor and chief writer, writes about Berks County corruption. Melissa tells John about the corruption in family court. John emails me "Do you know about Drinking Liberally (DL)? Liberals get together at a local restaurant and drink, eat and talk politics." I am so thrilled! I would never go out alone and get a drink. So Melissa and I attend one February night. DL meets every two weeks. I become a regular. I learn more about the local political machine, what I call "The family."

Some of the other DL regulars are male. Because I've spent twenty years in an abusive relationship, I'm still learning how to interact with men. Dave Miller is head of the local group supporting John Edwards for President. The first time we talk, Dave shows me a picture of his dog, Brandy. During the spring and summer, Dave and I talk and email but I remain distant. I am not interested in pursuing a relationship. In one email, I explain my court case to Dave ending by writing "This is not going away."

One night at DL I show my federal suit against Berks County to Chuck Brown. Chuck reads it and says "I can tell you are a good writer. Will you submit a piece for an on-line paper I'm producing called CommonSense2?" I email my personal abuse story. John Morgan puts my federal lawsuit on his PAProgressive blog.

In September, when I sell my car, Dave comes to my home to take me to the county democratic dinner. Another weekend, he takes me to a political fundraising event at a committee women's farmhouse. Dave drives me and another John Edwards supporter, Jeannie, to Philadelphia for the Presidential debate. We stand outside Drexel University and watch a taping of the Chris Matthews Show. We hold signs up high as the candidates enter the building.

In November, I tell Melissa "I need the money I loaned you, $1,000." Melissa responds "I can't pay" even though she just received over $4,000 in a tax refund. I need the money for rent so I tell Melissa "I will take you to court if you don't pay." Melissa mails me a check and we don't speak after that.

Dave is an easy person. He doesn't push or put pressure on me. He is quiet but talks. Slowly, a relationship builds. We spend weekends together either at my place or his. I'm more comfortable in my place since it is filled with my children's possessions. There is no cable, but Dave tapes Monk episodes and he fixes the TV so I get more local channels with better reception.

We take our dogs, Anna and Brandy, for long walks at French Creek State Park. We walk off-road trails. At first, Anna stays by my side but after a few walks, she is out in front only occasionally looking back to make sure we are still there. Anna likes to run in front of Brandy, Dave's mixed terrier rescue dog. Brandy is older and mellower than Anna. Sometimes she looks like she is exhausted by my hyper Anna. The two dogs have a secret language to get treats from Dave's knapsack with Brandy barking and Anna standing guard. On one walk we get lost and are out for hours. The dogs are tired and thirsty; the trail becomes dark. I begin to worry, but we make it back to the car just before dusk.

I can tell Dave is falling in love. I don't want a relationship, my friends say I hate men, but I get attached and Dave becomes a part of my life.

By Christmas the money from selling my car runs out. The Superior Court won't force the trial court to give me my divorce settlement. I have to wait for the suit against the Union for payment of the second half of the divorce settlement. In the settlement a $7,188 certificate of deposit is listed as my money, but Chet actually redeemed it. I submitted a receipt proving that he took money that is listed as mine, but Keller and the appeals court won't make him give me my money. I call the police because technically it is stolen money. Claiming it is "a family court issue," the police and district attorney won't prosecute theft.

Dave says "I will take money from my retirement account and give you a loan." I write an IOU and get it notarized. I pay January rent.

I want to go to the Battered Mothers Custody Conference which is held in Albany, New York the week after New Year 2008. I find out about the conference from a yahoo group. Group members are women who left abusers and now are being professionally abused by the courts and mental health people, court business affiliates. These women know all about the fatherhood and its origins. Many of the women have children who are being sexually abused and the courts and their associates refuse to help the children or stop the abuse.

I use Dave's money to get to, and pay for, the conference. I take the bus into Reading and then take a bus to Kutztown where another mom, Karen, picks me up and drives to Albany. I pay for the hotel room since she is driving.

Karen is angry because Berks County eliminated her from her two son's lives years ago. The sons have aged out; they are over eighteen. Karen is free to make contact and is slowly developing a relationship. Karen is sad and resentful for the loss of those years.

At the conference, I conduct a workshop on representing yourself so the conference fee is waived. I hand out my resume, hoping that one of the advocate groups in attendance will hire me so that I can work on this issue. I have no means of providing for myself in the future and I am willing to move to another state.

I meet other moms who I communicate with online. One mom has a 15-year-old son who has been raped by his father but she is deemed to be the danger because she is called alienating. California courts decided she has made the son hate his father, not that the son hates the father because he is getting screwed by him. The courts and father have sent the son to a Christian lock-up facility. Mom gets infrequent visits and she tells me "When I see him, his eyes can't focus. He is drugged out of his mind."

Another mom has a nine-year-old daughter who is being raped and filmed by her father. The court has also called this mom a danger for trying to stop the abuse. Both of these women are gentle, kind, caring, and soft. I say "You seem like the perfect mothers, I would love to have you as my mom."

During a presentation, Wendy Murphy talks about child sex abuse, explaining in detail the rips and tears inside an abused child's sexual parts.

When I get home I am sick and depressed.

A week later, my landlords knock at the door. Elsie says "Sign this paper that you will leave the house within fifteen days." I have paid the rent but they don't like Brandy, Dave's dog, and they don't like me having a man I'm not married to stay overnight. I respond "I will not sign." After that, I don't pay the rent. I wouldn't have been able to pay much longer anyway.

In February, my sister Debbie asks me to babysit her dogs while her family vacations at Disney World. My brother-in-law picks me up and I spend a week at her house typing the brief for my federal lawsuit against Keller, Ring, JR, Rotten, et al, for denial of my right to due process. One day I drive back to my place and work on my legal argument. It snows heavily as I drive back to my sister's. Driving uphill, the car spins out of control and smacks the guardrail. I spend borrowed money on copying and mailing of the brief and $500 for the deductible to repair the front of my niece's car.

I've been eating off food stamps and what Dave brings over on the weekends. The welfare clerk tells me "Welfare doesn't provide job training and it certainly does not pay for college." I receive a letter saying I am no longer eligible for food stamps because I am a single person.

In March, the landlord files an eviction notice. I can't go to the hearing because I don't drive. The eviction notice gives me thirty days to get out. The landlord comes by and asks "When will you be moving?" I say "I have thirty days."

Since our first winter, I receive government heating assistance (LIHEAP). The old house has no insulation and has holes in the walls. I keep the thermostat at sixty degrees and use lots of blankets and ceramic heaters given to me by a lady I moved.

On EBay I sell things given to me by people I moved. I use Craigs List to sell my retro porch gliders and Bosch washer and dryer which Pop insisted I take when I moved out of the marital home.

I post an ad on Craigs List that I will analyze cases and that is how I meet Nancy. We agree that she will pay me $200 to look at her case. One night Nancy arrives at my rental with her legal documents. Nancy weighs about 300 lbs. She wears a wig of blond hair piled up in a haphazard arrangement. Nancy is heavily drugged with pain killers which she claims she takes for back and leg pains. She walks with a cane. I look at the documents and listen to her case, a long, detailed, back and forth, encompassing years, which never settled financials because Nancy wants him to come back. That neglect gave him plenty of time to hide and drain assets. Nancy has been living in their house where she wants to stay. After many years, Nancy has been told to vacate the home; it is her ex-husband's property. Nancy appealed the decision because her only income is disability and she shares the house with her daughter and granddaughter. I look at the paperwork and quickly notice that the lawyer who wrote the appeal merely took Nancy's money. Nancy's appeal brief would never pass legal muster since it does not follow the Rules of Appellate Procedure. Nancy's lawyer did not even include a transcript of the hearing being appealed.

Nancy pays me. It's late and I need to work in the morning, a friend pays me to help her clean houses. Drugged out Nancy can't get herself back in her car to drive an hour home so she sleeps on the couch. In the morning I leave while Nancy sleeps. She wakes up in the afternoon when I return home. Since this is the time of day when Nancy gets going, she wants to go out to eat. I just got her money so I have to pay for our dinner. Finally Nancy leaves. I use the money to buy a new contact lens.

I have to be out of the house by the end of May. I have to pack. Beth and Kathy's belongings are exactly as they were the day they were taken; I have been waiting for them to come back. Leaving forces me to confront the fact that Beth and Kathy are not coming back; our lives will not resume at the place when they disappeared. Almost two years have passed. That time will not be reversed.

Dave brings boxes from his electronics company and I pack. I have a lot of stuff. I think I could ask my family to move in with them, but don't want to do this as I have nothing to offer. Dave wants me to move in with him, but I feel this would be admitting defeat, a finality I am not ready for. I don't want to be living with a man when my children return.

I have been looking for a job that offers housing. One guy is in prison serving a DUI. He gets work release to his house where he fixes computers. He advertises for someone to live in his house and drive him back and forth to jail. Dave drives me to tour the house and get more details about the job. I leave completely depressed. I can't do it.

I still want to correct the fraud, the problem. Jim has been commenting on the battered mothers yahoo group. He's a psychologist from Pennsylvania. Pennsylvania took his license away because he reported the sex abuse of a client's powerful father. Now Jim is living in West Virginia. He tells me he has contacts who are going to do something. He says he has nothing but a place to stay and I say "I have the stuff for the inside of a house." So a night before I have to be out of the rental, I decide to drive to West Virginia and stay with Jim, thinking that we will work together and the crime will finally get fixed. Dave comes over and helps me pack stuff into a moving truck. I give furniture to my family and friends. We fill up the truck. I take a load to my niece's basement for storage. I tell my sister and niece that I am going to go and work against this. I think Jim has made headway towards resolution.

Anna and I spend the night in Virginia and the next day I drive the Shenandoah Valley. Jim lives an hour from the nearest town. The roads are steep and twisty. Jim meets me at the Dairy Queen. After we eat ice cream, I drive the truck to his place, a ramshackle building barely hanging onto the steep hill it's built on. The truck is slanted at 45 degrees. I pull the emergency brake and hope it holds. I pull a mattress into the house and sleep alone in a back room.

The next morning I clean because the place is filthy. I am disgusted. The walls are thin wood. The building smells like rot. In the afternoon, the neighbors, two teenage girls and a twenty-two-year old man help me unload. They like my stuff. I have a modern purple sofa and many pocketbooks. I give pocketbooks to the girls.

When Jim gets home from his counseling job, he is surprised by all that was done. He exclaims "You have a vacuum cleaner." For dinner, Jim drives to a Chinese restaurant, showing me the depressed local community. Jim tells me "There is a conference in DC and they want me to testify." These are the things he told me to get me down there in the first place. He led me to believe he was getting results and on the way to solving the problem. But the more I listen, the more I see that he is getting no results for all his efforts.

The next day I need to return the truck. I drive an hour to the nearest big town. Jim says he will pick me up after work. I drop off the truck and walk across the street and buy groceries. Jim meets me and we go to another restaurant to eat.

The next day I continue to unpack and set up the kitchen. A technician comes to install cable. The place is so rickety that the cable guy has to put the wires through an open window which now can't be closed. When Jim gets home I cook dinner. Jim wants to set up a stereo. He slices his finger when he uses a knife to strip wires. Blood pores from his finger. I run to the neighbor and ask "Where is the hospital and how do I get there?" I spend hours in the emergency waiting room while Jim gets his finger stitched. At one point, Jim tries to get comfort from me and I turn him away. He is gross.

Dave calls and says "How is it?" I answer "It is horrible." I need this to be a path to correcting my problem, to outing it, to getting my kids and my life back. But how is this horrible place with this horrible man going to be anything positive?

The next day is Saturday and Jim doesn't work. He gets a letter in the mail and is angry. "They are denying to investigate the fraud in my case." I stay in my room while he talks on the phone. When he is finished he tells me "I was talking to someone and told them that you are staying here. They got mad, said I am crazy and now they won't talk to me." He continues "I don't know if this was a good idea. I'm afraid of losing my job. I don't want to lose it because you're here." He can't have a license in Pennsylvania; West Virginia is the only job he can get. Believe me, there aren't many people who would work in this West Virginia pit.

I answer "Then I'll leave." Jim replies "You will?" I say "Yes, just take me to a bus station." In my head I am making my own plans to go to Washington and revisit my Senator, Arlen Spector.

On Sunday Jim drives an hour away to the bus station. On the drive he says "I want to buy your sofa." I say "OK $300." He says "I can't afford that, how about $75." Then he goes to the ATM and gets me the money. Meanwhile, I have left all my stuff except a few clothes, my contacts and supplies, a toothbrush and court documents.

I tell the cashier at the bus station not to tell Jim where I bought a ticket to.

There is a switchover at McDonalds. I have to wait a few hours for the new bus to arrive. I sit and talk to a drifter. We have a philosophical discussion about freedom and standing up for what you believe in.

Early Monday morning, I arrive in DC and I walk to Senator Spector's office where I ask for his staff, Reagan Blewitt. Two months earlier, me and another mom (New Jersey family in Chapter 10 "The Players and Their Methods"), had visited with proof of case rigging. I ask Reagan "What are you going to do about the case rigging corruption?" Reagan answers "Nothing." I walk around town. I arrive at the Hoover building and ask to speak with an agent. I am told to leave.

The next morning I go to the emergency room and tell them I want to kill myself, I haven't done anything but I think about it. This is called suicide ideation.

The hospital lets me stay. They put me in the psychiatric unit and I sleep. For several days they feed me. I talk with the other patients, many are homeless. A counselor looks at the PFA transcript and says "Any Judge who says this about winning the lottery is sick, but you have to think about the people in China who lost their kids in the recent earthquake, thousands were killed." Another staff says "Corruption exists and it will exist five years from now."

I call Dave and tell him where I am and why. He wants me to come back and stay with him and this time I agree. Dave rents an in-law suite attached to Harry and Barb's house. It is on the top of Mount Penn which overlooks the City of Reading. There are a lot of trees, a nice park with a lake, three minutes away. Shopping is close.

The next week we get a truck and drive back to West Virginia to get my things. We arrive on the hill just before dark. Dave gives the neighbors $20 each to help us load. Jim wants to keep the sofa but we take it. He wants his $75 dollars back and I say "No. You took advantage of me and I could report you."

When we get back to Pennsylvania we put the sofa in the middle of Dave's living room and we get rid of his sagging sofa. We put my new mattress in the bedroom. I clean the kitchen and put my dishes, cups, and pots in the cabinets.

Chapter Six

Rebuilding

Summer, 2008

While hospitalized, I promise I will get treatment for my depression. They show me a list and make me pick someone saying "You need to trust; not wanting to go to counseling in Reading is paranoid." I agree to go to Reading Hospital's counseling center. At our first session, the counselor says "You need to have goals. Let's make a five year plan." Textbook treatment; not suited to individual circumstances, or the cause of my depression, just a billable hour.

I go to the welfare office and reapply because now I have a disability. They give me food stamps and cash assistance of $200 a month while I wait for my social security disability application to process. I know my disability is my eyesight but the psychiatrist signed paperwork that I am too depressed to work.

Because we need the money, I take Dave's car while he works, and look for a job. I get hired to work in the deli of a new supermarket. They tell me "We do not hire full-time. We pay $7.65 per hour; you get thirty cents more for working in the deli."

After two and a half years of waiting for the ethical complaint to process, a Rule to Show Cause shows up in my mail. There are seven ethical charges against Dr. Ring. The legal paperwork starts with the facts of the case, a beginning summary. It says Chet and I were sent to Ring for a custody evaluation and, at that time, I had primary physical custody.

The first charge is that Ring did not follow the recognized standards for the evaluation and finished report. The first charge states that Ring's report contains several inconsistencies, including, but not limited to, the following:

> a. On page 24 of the report, Ring recommends a change in primary physical custody to the father based in part on the mother's yelling to the point where it frightens the children, however, on page 20 of the report, Ring reports that when asked if her mother's yelling scares her, Elizabeth responded "no."
>
> b. On page 22 of the report, Ring based in part his conclusion that the mother had an unstable history by stating that "she essentially entered her relationship with Chet as an escape from her family of origin," and yet on page 3 of the report, Ring reports that Doreen was living on her own in an apartment at the time she began her relationship with Chet.

The first charge is that Ring "improperly focused primarily" on my alleged *[by Chet]* mental illness rather than parenting ability and the psychological and developmental needs of the child and the resulting fit. It charges that Ring has no data, evidence, examples, or information to support his claims that my *[made-up]* mental illness adversely effects the children; that I cannot parent because I am mentally ill; that I cannot maintain an appropriate home environment while going to school and working; for recommending changing custody to father; and, fails to explain why changing custody to father is best for the children and why father is a better parent.

The first charge is that Ring failed to get any proof or confirmation from other sources for believing Chet's statements that mother kept a dirty home. It charges that Ring failed to review school or medical records, talk to teachers, and did not visit the parents homes in order to confirm any information.

The first charge ends: Ring's "conclusions and recommendations are unsupported by the data and information contained in his report and reflect a lack of objectivity and impartiality in his assessment" and, based on the first charge, Ring "displayed gross incompetence, negligence or misconduct in carrying on the practice of psychology."

The second count charges Ring with committing immoral or non-professional conduct. The third charge is that Ring deviated from APA guidelines for child custody evaluations in divorce proceedings by failing to focus on parenting capacity, the psychological and developmental needs of the child and the resulting fit. Charge four is that Ring failed to use multiple methods of data gathering. Charge five is that Ring drew conclusions not adequately supported by the data. Count six charges Ring with failing to make recommendations based upon what is in the best psychological interests of the child. Count seven charges Ring with failing to maintain an objective impartial stance.

To me, this is proof that the entire custody change was a fraud. I file for another custody hearing, this time in front of Judge Lash. I subpoena Ring. I go to Legal Aid and file a request for them to represent me. The lawyer tells me she cannot take the case because she will "get burn-out." When Dave and I show up at court for the hearing, Ring is sitting in the pew. I say to Dave "This is Dr. Ring." Lash refuses to have a hearing claiming "Nothing has changed." I appeal. In contrast to Keller, Lash writes a real opinion stating that there are no new matters and

"Mother is just trying to re-litigate old issues." In their opinion, the Superior Court will blame me by writing:

> "We reject Mother's contention that she has never had a full and fair opportunity to litigate the issues surrounding Dr. Ring's evaluation since he has never been subject to cross-examination. **The trial court's ruling on March 27, 2006, which did not require Dr. Ring to testify, was a direct result of Mother filing a complaint against him** with the Pennsylvania Attorney General's Office *[in fact, the ethical complaint is filed with the State Department Bureau of Licenses]*. **Mother's action has consequences to which she is bound**. As such, we conclude Mother's claims are without merit." The Superior Court of Pennsylvania, 815 MDA 2009

The court has determined that custody evaluators can submit completely false and unethical reports and parents have no right to contest these false reports! It was Ullman and Keller's responsibility to review the report for adherence to standards and truth. But, because the entire fiasco was conducted solely to provide false evidence to justify giving father custody, Ring's bogus, false report was endorsed. Ring is protected by the court because he is a fatherhood practitioner.

I have an appointment with Reading Hospital's psychiatrist so he can continue my antidepressant prescription. He wants to talk about what happened and I say "I am sane because I haven't done anything to any of them, including Pam Ullman, and JR gave me her home address; an insane person would try to kill them for stealing their children." Of course, this psychiatrist is cut from the same mold as Dr. Rotten, they are colleagues. He responds "I am going to immediately institutionalize you. You have just made a threat." I reply "I am not going to do anything to anyone. I don't even know how to use a gun. I have a court hearing this afternoon and I need to be there." The counselor comes down and says "I don't think she's a threat, but what do I know." Dave comes in and says "She is no threat. She has no car. I am with her at all times." But Rotten's colleague answers "I'll have someone else assess you first." He tells his staff to escort me to the emergency room; again, I am treated like a criminal. While Dave and I wait for someone to talk to me to determine if I am a threat, a nurse tells us "No one is coming. They are just going to do it (302 me)." While we are sitting there alone, Dave convinces me to walk out.

I think security will chase us down while we are walking to the car but no one approaches as we fast-walk across the lawn towards the car. We buy lunch at McDonalds and race off to court. After the hearing on Chet not paying my medical insurance, as required by the divorce decree, Dave and I decide I will have to commit myself. I want to go anywhere but Reading, because of their pattern of corruption and collusion and fraud. So we decide we will go to Lancaster Hospital. While we are driving, the State Police call Dave. I hear Dave say "No. I will not tell you where she is. I am taking her to the hospital now." The trooper answers "Fine, then our job is done."

When we arrive at the hospital, I get a call from the staff who is trying to 302 me. I tell her "I didn't do anything." She answers "You are crazy." I counter "You have never met or talked to me."

Dave and I buy dinner in the hospital cafeteria. After we eat, I admit myself, telling the staff "Reading was trying to 302 me but I came to Lancaster because Reading is part of my corrupt court case. I only want impartial treatment." The next day I meet with Lancaster's doctors and tell them about my corrupt custody case; what Ring and Rotten and Keller have done. I give them a copy of

Ring's ethical charges.

I have entered another industry. I have coverage from Medicaid, so the hospital is happy to keep me since everything is paid for. They force me to take a psychotropic drug, Risperdol. It becomes evident that they have called Reading and they will back them up rather than believe what I've told them. I tell a male nurse "I don't want to take that drug." The nurse answers "If you behave and take the drug, you will get out sooner." I answer "I will take it under one condition: that you call Dr. Atkins and talk to her about me." Dr. Atkins practices in Lancaster. He answers "OK."

During the day I stay in the community room so I'll sleep soundly at night. If I nap, or lay in bed during the day, I risk being awake at night. While hospital staff huddles around the nurse's station, the patients stay in the community room, telling stories of attempted suicide, depression, and assault. Some patients are severely mentally ill. One older man in particular is completely out of touch, but harmless, and me and another girl entertain ourselves by talking with him. He tells me how he used to drive a bookmobile and enjoyed the children. I write a story about the bookmobile driver. He enjoys it immensely.

After several days of being on Risperdol, I can't feel my feet touching the ground. My pupils become so dilated that this patient screams at me one morning "Get away from me with those eyes!" But when I'm given my ten-second meeting with the psychiatrist I'm told the drug is not working and that they want to keep me longer and increase the dose. I tell him "I can't feel my feet." He replies "You'll get used to it." I say "I have a life I need to get back to, including a job." The hospital workers could care less, they only like positive answers, saying "Surely, your employer will hold your job."

Finally, after five days, the social worker calls Dr. Atkins. She tells me "You are not good at representing yourself." Apparently, instead of them not listening, it is my fault for not talking properly. Dave tells me later that he called and spoke to the social worker and said "What have you done to her? You took someone healthy and now you have her so drugged up she cannot function." Instead of keeping me locked up, they decide to release me. A young male social worker tells me "We cannot let you leave until you pick a counselor to visit." I answer "Who do you have who is ethical?" He answers "Phil Haven is founded by Mennonites."

As we drive home from the hospital, Dave talks and I say "I can't even focus on what you are saying because of that drug." He stops at a diner for food saying "Food will help get the drug out of your system." I answer "Yeah, they hardly even fed you there. The food was lousy and they gave you small amounts."

Before I left the hospital, I asked the doctor to sign the welfare form stating that I was disabled, so welfare continues, and I work at the supermarket deli about 15 hours a week.

I write a Human Rights Petition to the Inter-American Commission on Human Rights. Several women who had been abused and had been eliminated used an international lawyer to file a petition through a group called Stop Family Violence. I use their petition and the rules I find on-line and I list all the violations while focusing on the fact that I cannot get a fair trial because of the fatherhood program. I sign and date the Petition on Elizabeth's 12th birthday, October 23, 2008.

I use a wiki page to keep documents posted on-line. This way, I have backup and I do not have to pay for a web page. I name the link "childabusecondonedbyfamilycourt." I write an outline proving welfare is funding custody and support litigation. I fax the outline to every member of the federal house ways and means committee when the fatherhood programs come up for funding reauthorization.

I write another support appeal; I still have to pay $700/month. I figure out that by using kids as a write-off, Chet pays .0007% federal taxes. I take my mathematical deduction outside where Dave is sitting reading the paper and say "He paid $7 in federal taxes. It is .0007% of his income." We both laugh.

JR files a motion "Alimony should stop because Doreen is living off her paramour." I was awarded $375 per month for four years. Not one penny has ever been paid. Dave drives me to the hearing and sits in the audience (the pews) while I sit at the lawyer table. Whenever I speak, a short, stocky female security guard bends towards my face and yells "Shut up!" I want to ask her "Do you want to shoot me?"

Chet sits in the witness stand claiming "I should not pay alimony because Doreen is always with..." rising from his chair, Chet points to Dave "THAT MAN THERE!" I turn around and smile and wave at Dave who has an enormous grin on his face. He is proud the other fighting couples filling up the pews know we are sleeping together. Lash doesn't take away the alimony, but Chet never pays it, and the court never makes him.

Welfare writes to me that I have income because I am working. I explain that any money I make is going to support. So, Judge Lash gets rid of the order that I pay $700 a month, but requires me to pay Chet $5 a month for arrears.

One day I have the car and I decide to write my children because the PFA has expired. My friend Kathy has always told me her daughter will give them a note. I go to Target and purchase folders and Hannah Montana activity books. I write my letter. I assemble two packages: one for Beth and one for Kathy. I drive to Kathy's house and ask her "Will Carly give the envelopes to my girls during school?" We talk for a while and Kathy keeps staring at the packets. She says "I don't know. I am scared. I don't want to get in trouble." I take the packets and leave saying "I understand."

As I drive down Chet's road, I call my old phone number, the message machine picks up and I say "Beth and Kathy, it is your mother. I couldn't talk to you before or your Dad would put me in jail, but I am going to leave something for you outside the door." I pull into the driveway, get out of the car, place the package inside the back door, get back in the car and drive away. The next day I get a call from the Robeson police demanding to know where I live. I refuse to tell them. The officer yells at me "You harassed Chet, Elizabeth and Kathleen. The youngest girl couldn't stop crying and Elizabeth is scared." I say "Really, you are blaming me?" He answers "I remember, we came to your house for a domestic disturbance and you were masturbating with the shower head." I say "Dave, can you believe this police officer is making up stuff?" The next day I call his superior officer and say "Your officer made up a story and you better not change the file." He answers "We do not change our files."

Because I am scared, I again call the PA Coalition Against Domestic Violence and ask "Why are you not helping abused women in custody and why can't you get media stories about how abused women are treated? You have media contacts." Nicole Lingenfelter answers "That's a good idea. I'll think about it."

I visit Berks County Children and Youth to file a report of abuse against Chet. I give them the ethical charges against Ring. The shocked staff says "Not Dr. Ring." I say "Yes, he is unethical." But they never do any investigating and they will not even acknowledge that Chet's actions are abusive. I also call the state hotline and report his abuse, but they never investigate.

I receive another PFA due to the package drop-off. Dave and I attend a hearing in front of Lash. He issues a PFA and I appeal. Lash's written Opinion concludes that, in fact, after looking at the evidence, I am not abusive. But the Superior Court decides that I am psychologically and emotionally abusive to my children and they uphold the three year PFA. In reality, Chet is the one perpetrating this abuse on the children, but the court will never admit it.

One summer morning while Dave is home and I'm driving the car, I am pulled over for passing a slow truck. The police seem to be taking a long time to write a ticket. The officer comes to the window and says "There is a bench warrant for your arrest and we are taking you in. The car will go to the impound lot." I am handcuffed, driven to the Limerick police station and put in a cell. From there, I am driven to Robeson Township, taken before the magistrate and charged with harassing Chet and trespassing. The constables drive me to Berks County jail and we sit on a bench. A security guard named Cowboy Bob comes up and says "Ms. Ludwig I just saw you in Lash's court. You were the only one concerned about the children." I'm put in the holding cell with five other women. One says "What are you in here for? Prostitution?" I feel complimented and answer "I got a nasty divorce and my ex filed harassment because I gave my children a note."

I fill out a prison form, writing "diagnosed with depression." Instead of being put in the women's unit, I get taken to the medical unit which has single occupancy cells. Prisoners are entitled to make one phone call. Dave does not know where I am. Each time I asked to make my call during the day I was told "Later." When the security guards take me to my cell after dinner I say "I did not get to make my call. I need to make my call." A big guard says "It is too late, you are not getting a call, you'll call in the morning." He pushes me up against the wall, shoving my arm up my back. I whisper "Go ahead, you know you want it."

After lunch the next day, I finally call Dave. He already knows they arrested me. "Harry drove me to get the car and I am calling the bail bondsman. You should get out today." It is midnight when they finally let me go. Dave and I laugh at how there is so much nighttime activity at the courthouse. We say "It's a happening place."

I am given a public defender for a hearing at the magistrate. When we arrive the PD tells me that Elizabeth is going to testify and the magistrate will decide if there is cause for another hearing. I say "My daughter has not seen me for three years. I do not think this is the right time and place for her to first see me again. Do you?" He doesn't answer. I waive my right to have this hearing. At the next hearing, I have a different defender.

The new public defense attorney tells me "They want you to go to see Dr. Rotten so he can assess your mental state." I say "I'm not going to him. He is unethical. If I am going to see him, he needs to provide me with the protocol he plans to use to assess me. I am seeing a doctor at Phil Haven, he can testify." The defender answers "Your doctor is not approved by Berks County, you have to see a doctor on their list." I meet with that doctor for less than one hour at the public defender's office. I tell him "I want a trial. I did not commit a crime." I am not permitted a trial, instead, at the hearing the Judge drops the charges claiming "I have a report here saying she didn't know what she was doing." Then the Judge yells at me "Keep seeing your doctor."

While Dave and I are sitting outside waiting for the hearing to begin, Chet is there, looking angry. I am sick to my stomach. My pulse is racing. I have finally had enough of this court. I am done. I will wait for another agency to acknowledge the corruption. I resolve to write a book in order to have the story told.

One Saturday in May of 2009, on our way to visit his mother,

Dave and I stop to retrieve my mail which is sent to a Post Office Box. I open the envelope from the Pennsylvania State Department as we are driving and read a Withdrawal of the Rule to Show Cause against Ring. Bridget Guilfoyle, Prosecuting Attorney for the PA State Department, has determined that since Ring completed 16 hours of training from the APA, and because he volunteers for the Red Cross, Ring is no longer a danger to the general public so all charges will be dropped. I start to shake and cry. I yell at Dave, "They have stolen my children! He gets to lie and now they are just going to let him get away with it!" Dave says "I guess we are not going to my mothers." He turns the car towards home. After several minutes of silence, I say "No, we'll go." On Monday, I call Bridget and ask her "Why were the charges dropped?" She yells at me "I'm not going to get into this with you."

Both Federal and State legislators, House Representatives and Senators, have Judiciary Committees. They oversee and recommend laws applicable to the Judicial Branch. I have contacted federal legislators many times, especially Arlen Spector who is a member of the Judiciary Committee and past Chairman. Spector, a lawyer and one-time Philadelphia District Attorney, was a member of the Senate's fatherhood task force which could explain his unwillingness to acknowledge the illegal nature of fatherhood custody funding. This time, I decide to contact my State Judiciary Chairman, Senator Stewart Greenleaf. His staff, Greg Warner, tells me "We are in the process of rewriting state custody laws and you can attend a working group meeting in Harrisburg."

The legal changes being proposed make it easier for MHPs to be appointed to decide custody and for lawyers to be appointed for children. The new law requires parents pay for any court appointee or be jailed. The new law continues to protect MHPs from ethical complaints, forbidding parents from filing complaints during the process of litigation. I write a lengthy response, starting strong and ending by including credible research, proof and solutions.

> "I contacted Mr. Warner because I have documented a lack of due process in child custody, especially in cases involving abuse. Custody decisions are made not by Judges, but by Psychologists who call themselves evaluators. The custody evaluator does NOT adhere to law or Rules of Evidence. They do not investigate or verify false allegations. They often rely solely on hypothetical tests and do not question collateral witnesses such as the children's school, doctors, family, friends, or police reports. They have no training or hands-on experience in abuse and control. They have a profit motive and they are giving custody to abusers to continue cases and award themselves perpetual counseling fees which tend to be higher than the market average.
>
> THERE IS NO REMEDY FOR AN UNETHICAL, PERJURIOUS CUSTODY EVALUATION THAT DOES NOT PROTECT VICTIMS OF ABUSE!!!! See Dr. Ring's report stating "abuse was mutual."
>
> The Pennsylvania Supreme Court DENIES appeals, against the PA Constitution, in order to permit custody to be determined solely on the basis of the custody evaluation, even when it is proven to be written for one parent only. Likewise, Court Administration DENIES that custody evaluators are submitting fictitious reports. The Rules Committee refuses to hold evaluators to Standards."

I send a copy of my packet to all members of the state Senate

Judiciary Committee and House Judiciary Committee, and I send a copy to the PA Coalition Against Domestic Violence (PCADV). Dave takes a vacation day and drives to Harrisburg so we can attend the meeting. We sit at a table stacked with fathers rights group members. Two PCADV staff are seated at the far end of the long table. Their only concern is that Pennsylvania not mandate shared custody. I introduce myself and they refuse to speak with me. Dave later remarks "They are no help. They just want status quo."

Greg Warner's staff sends an email to working group members inviting us to join a follow-up phone meeting including an attached copy of Pennsylvania's Changing the Culture of Custody plan. I notice the plan admits that cases that have numerous court appointees, have the lengthiest litigation, yet the entire plan is a blueprint for assigning court appointees. On the day of the phone meeting, I call in late. Mike McCormick of ACFC, a pedophile-centered father's rights organization, is speaking about how important it is for states to have laws that protect MHPs and punish parents with contempt charges. He brags "Right now, I'm sitting in a federal legislator's office. My group has Richard Warshak as a board member." I quickly respond "Warshak has written a book telling fathers how to rig custody cases. Why is he speaking? He is not a constituent of Pennsylvania." Greg Warner answers "We consider lots of opinions." Later, Warner tells me that the plan is being put into effect. No Pennsylvania legislator ever contacts me about my widely distributed concerns.

I am approved to receive social security disability because of my Kerataconus. Because I stayed home caring for Beth and Kathy, not getting paid for work, I am not eligible to receive SSD. I can only get SSI, $698/month. I have to prove that I have no assets. When I am asked if I own any annuities, I explain the divorce, that there is money owed to me which is being held in retirement funds. I have to prove that I spent the original divorce payment. The social security staff becomes belligerent and refuses to process my approval. After a year of telephoning, I get assigned a new caseworker, who takes another year to process my paperwork. Eventually, I am given SSI, medicaid and food stamps. I tell Dave "What makes me the angriest, is that they did not let me get a degree so I could make enough money to take care of myself."

The recession hits and Dave's company downsizes, eventually closing. Dave gets a job an hour's drive south. Dave looks for a new rental and finds one in Elverson, the same town I used to live in, where Chet and the girls live now. I don't want to move, especially near Chet, who likes to get me arrested, but the place winds up being too nice, there are three bedrooms and a washer and dryer. We move to northern Chester County, out of Berks County. Dave and I settle into a nice life. Dave expresses his love by paying attention, anticipating my needs and emotions, starting my coffee every morning, even though he doesn't drink it, and supporting all of my efforts. I have a love that lets me thrive!

I continue to stay connected to battered mothers groups, the California Protective Parents Association (CPPA) run by Connie Valentine. I attend several marches in front of the White House. In the summer of 2012, CPPA hosts a workshop and march. I ask Connie if I can do a presentation on welfare's fatherhood funding of custody litigation. I tell her I can do it in 15 minutes, so I race through my two-page outline. Other speakers include Rita Smith, of National Coalition Against Domestic Violence. She stands in front of the group and says "The problem is bad judges. We just need to get rid of the bad judges." Rita is always saying her group is going to help someone someday in the future. Rita's new hire is training the mothers how to lobby. She says "You need face time. You need to tweet. You need to give political contributions. You need to build coalitions." I respond "You, DV groups, already have the coalitions. You already have access to media and politicians. You need to stand up for us. You need to step up to the plate." They get mad at me for saying something, but many of the mothers are glad because they, too, have been sold-out by DV advocates. In the end, the mothers determine that addressing fatherhood should be one of five priorities for combating scandalous custody cases.

I attend the 2013 Battered Mothers Custody Conference, held in Washington, DC. I had mentioned that I felt the conference should take place in DC, not Albany, so that mothers can visit legislators and legislative staff can be invited to attend. Joan Meier, a professor at George Washington University Law School and head of DVLeap (Domestic Violence Legal Empowerment Action Project) conducts a workshop about new legislative happenings. She is enthusiastic because the Office of Violence Against Women (OVW) has new grant money and DV groups will be able to apply for grants to hire attorney's to represent battered women in custody litigation. Joan wants the mothers to lobby legislators to pass a resolution, what I call the "whereas" document. The document lists three pages of DV statistics, including how abusers behave in custody litigation, and concludes that congress should suggest that states have standards for evaluators and others working in family court. It would not be a law, merely a resolution, a recommendation for states to act on. Joan says that it is difficult to get legislators to listen and do something because the federal government does not fund family court. I say "Yes, they do, through the fatherhood program. I have proof." Joan responds "We can't say anything about fatherhood. Fatherhood is apple pie." At the end of the presentation, Connie approaches me and says "We can bring that up when we get our investigations." I anxiously reply "She has her research and I have mine which is legitimate, too." The next day, I give Joan my proof. I never hear from her, or any of her DV compatriots.

Since we live in my old neighborhood, we get the local newspaper. In May, 2014, Dave says "Elizabeth is in the paper." He shows me a section of Twin Valley high school graduates. There is a picture of Beth, who looks like me and other members of my family. I look through the pictures noting the children I remember from the years when I was homeroom mom.

Several days later, I am driving past The Greenery, the local flower shop, and I think "I should send flowers." I know I am impulsive, so I resolve to think about it. A week later, Dave mentions that I should send a card. I tell him "I am thinking of sending flowers with a note. I think the flowers will get in, not be intercepted by Chet." Dave says "This time, if you are arrested and they have a hearing, Elizabeth needs to testify. I know you were protecting them before, but they are older now." I answer Dave "The problem is, I have a nice life now. What if they contact me and, especially, Kathy, wants to leave, I am not sure I can help. I have no money for a lawyer. I may have to tell them that I can do nothing."

Several days later, I tell my niece my flower plans asking if I can use her telephone number as a contact in my note. When I show her my sample letter, she tells me to simplify it further, stating "They may not be ready to contact you yet. This just gets them to start thinking about it." The flowers get sent. Dave and I wait for the police to show up. When we take the dog to the park for walks, we drive by Chet's cabin and Dave sees flowers sitting on a bench on the porch. "Well, we know they got them. Why would he put them outside?" I guess "The local police won't arrest me so he'll take them to court on Monday and file for another PFA claiming the flowers prove I am threatening them. I don't think they will give it to him this time. The kids are older. It's almost over. He doesn't have JR working for him anymore."

This time I'm not arrested or taken to court for a PFA hearing.

PART TWO

The Research

Chapter 7

ABUSE

The emphasis on ending domestic violence been has defined simply as hitting. It used to be okay for a husband to beat his wife since marriage was seen as a form of ownership. But the women's movement shed light on males who beat women, and said it was wrong. The mood was that women should leave these men; that it is not safe to stay, since a violent man is capable of causing severe harm, even death. Safety, which started as part of the women's movement, evolved into a monopoly of Domestic Violence (DV) groups who receive large government grants which they use to offer shelters, counseling and protective order legal help. DV groups have huge administrative costs and little of the funding goes towards direct services. DV groups have evolved into political entities that use their status to dominate the definition of abuse. DV groups keep the focus on women who are beat and murdered because physical violence is more sensational and easily classified.

In order to give women and children the protection they deserve, and the right to fully leave abusive males, we must stop allowing political, government-funded, DV groups to monopolize the topic of abuse with their limited definition and problem-solving. We need to stop allowing violence to be the sole indicator of male mistreatment. We need to define the wider picture of abuse and we need to reconfirm women's right to leave abusive men completely, even if that woman has had children with her abuser.

DEFINING ABUSE

Abuse is a bigger category than domestic violence. Abuse is more than hitting. It is about treatment: one person's thinking, behavior, mannerisms and actions towards another. Our society accepts one person having power over another: employer/employee, teacher/student, parent/**ch**ild, husband/wife. All relationships have the ability to be abusive, the person with power uses it inappropriately. While I believe our society needs to address abuse in all our structural systems, this chapter and book focus on male to female abuse and what happens when the female tries to leave an abusive male.

This chapter relies on other people to explain abuse. In order to get across my point that abuse is more than physical violence, I have listed words that can be substituted for abuse, taken from my first authority, Webster's Thesaurus. To understand abuse, fill in this sentence: "An abuser purposely ___(insert thesaurus description)___ another."

> *Abuse: (to treat badly) insult, injure, hurt, harm, damage, impair, aggrieve, offend, misuse, disparage, berate, maltreat, mistreat, wrong, persecute, molest, victimize, oppress, ruin, mar, spoil, vulgarize, reproach, rail at, outrage, do wrong by or to, mishandle, pervert, profane, prostitute, desecrate, pollute, harass, manhandle, do an injustice to, overstrain, overwork, overtax, overdrive, overburden, violate, defile, impose upon, deprive, taint, debase, corrupt, squander, waste, dissipate, exhaust; do one's worst, do one an injustice, knock about*

Whew! There are many ways for one person to abuse another! Using this long list of interchangeable words, we learn that the abusive male has multiple behaviors to choose from. While everyone mistreats the one they love sometimes, the highly abusive male goes well beyond occasional mistreatment. The mistreatment is intentional; it is designed to maintain his control and dominant position in the personal relationship.

Abuse as Coercive Control

Abuse is much more than physical violence! Evan Stark, a social worker helping abused women since the 70's, decries defining women's experience of abuse through the standard of physical violence. In his book, *"Coercive Control: How Men Entrap Women in their Personal Lives,"* Stark points out that rating abuse by violent incident belittles the oppression directed at women by men. Violence permits abuse to be classified by incidence and harm. He beats her severely, but she is not hospitalized and suffers no permanent wounds. Three months later, he gives her a black eye. The DV community focuses solely on the two incidents, they rate the first as more severe, but not that bad, and they make the wrong assumption that the male has committed no abuse in the intervening three months. In fact, abuse has been prevalent.

Stark has coined a better term, "Coercive Control," to define the abuse that occurs in those non-violent three months. Because Stark spent years talking and actually listening to women, even sheltering them in his home, he learned that violence is not considered to be the worst part of life with an abuser. It is the means men use to maintain power and control over women that causes the real, permanent harm. Harm is ongoing and cumulative. Stark recognizes that males perform self-interested behaviors in order to maintain their privilege and dominate women. These behaviors are intentional. They can be broken into two tactics: behaviors meant to hurt and intimidate, and behaviors meant to isolate and control.

> *"Viewing woman abuse through the prism of the incident-specific and injury-based definition of violence has concealed its major components, dynamics, and effects, including the fact that it is neither "domestic" nor primarily about "violence." Failure to appreciate the multidimensionality of oppression in personal life has been disastrous for abuse victims. Because of its singular emphasis on physical violence, the prevailing model minimizes both the extent of women's entrapment by male partners in personal life and its consequences.*
>
> *Coercive control entails a malevolent course of conduct that subordinates women to an alien will by violating their physical integrity (domestic violence), denying them respect and autonomy (intimidation), depriving them of social connectedness (isolation), and appropriating or denying them access to the resources required for personhood and citizenship (control).*
>
> *The micromanagement of how women perform as women lies at the heart of coercive control and is emblematic of how coercive control violates their equal rights to autonomy, personhood, dignity, and liberty. Compliance with "rules" that extend to the trivia of daily life makes abusive men appear omnipotent and women like nothing."*

This type of abuse that women experience stems from males belief that they are superior to women and that they have the right to control her thinking and actions. The steps that males take to ensure that they are able to dictate every area of the personal relationship becomes the abuse. Women may not realize that this man wants her to be a mere extension of him; to exist to serve him, make him feel good. The abuser does not respect women as individuals. Since women <u>do</u> think and act for themselves, the male must design a range of covert, subtle, manipulations aimed at reducing the women's confidence, self-esteem and will.

    Many women are caregivers. They are happy to act to make others content. They will make a favorite dish, adding less salt if he has high blood pressure, buy flannel sheets if they know he likes to be warm at night, they may not complain when he watches football because they know he enjoys it. But the abusive male feels this attention is his due. He will insist on just the right amount of salt in his food and if it is wrong, he may scream that "you don't know how to cook," throw the food in the trash, or insist that an entirely new meal be prepared. Some men will insist that the sheets be 500 count, ironed, white-only, and if they are not, he will throw a fit, maybe rip the sheets from the bed. He may demand complete silence during the football game, yelling at his wife if he is interrupted. His over-the-top reactions are designed to ensure that the woman gets it right next time. His negative reaction to the most trivial actions creates enough fear and insecurity to cause her to change and question her behavior.

    Women want to please the male because that is what you do when you love someone. The abusive male uses that normal desire to gain control. He may mention that he likes women to wear dresses, so she wears more dresses. Slowly, she may find that he gets angry when she wears pants. It may be as simple as uttering a harrumph, or raising his eyebrows, or commenting "Those pants make your backside look large." Soon she finds that she only wears dresses even though she likes wearing pants. The abuser has subtly dictated her choice of clothes.

The abusive male will find reasons for disliking her family so that she talks with, and visits them, less. He will criticize and make fun of her friends so that she will not invite them over. He will have problems going places: the ride is too long; he doesn't go to restaurants because he doesn't like to wait. This ensures the woman is his and his alone, it ensures that she stays close, that others do not influence her, and she has no one to talk to or compare her experience with.

One woman involved in an abusive divorce told me that her husband would take the toilet paper and food that she purchased and then pretend that she never brought it home. She would keep the receipt so she could prove the purchase to herself. This abuse is called "crazy making," attempting to make the women think she is nuts. Another woman told me that against her will, her husband would make her go out and pick up men to bring back and have sex with in front of him. This is a form of sexual abuse that does not respect a women's right to control her own sexual experience.

Women have been conditioned to accept the subservient role: to put themselves second. His opinions are more important, his likes and preferences take precedence. It becomes part of the female psyche and that allows an entrance for the highly abusive male. I have attended two weddings where the marriage sermon included a speech telling the women to be subservient to her husband; one Catholic and the other Jehovah's Witness. The Catholic priest stated that in a marriage someone must give up themselves and that had to be the woman. The Jehovah's Witness preached to the bride that she must obey her husband as he was in charge, the leader. Coercive control is an ordained way for men to keep woman in line!

When researching the ideology behind religious condoning of abusive behaviors, I found a website which posted sermons offered for Pastor's use. One sermon was entitled "How to Lead Lovingly." The writer gave this example of leading lovingly "If your wife chooses the wrong peanut butter you should not be angry but lovingly accept her mistake." Since when is there a wrong peanut butter? People may have different preferences, crunchy, smooth, Jif, Skippy, but there is really no wrong choice of peanut butter and if the male thinks there is, and that the women purchased the wrong kind, and he needs a sermon to learn to control his anger, it is almost certain he is a highly abusive male. Some women don't want a relationship where the purchase of peanut butter is considered a wrong decision nor do they want to live with someone who thinks he gets to choose the peanut butter even when she goes to the store.

I was watching an episode of Archie Bunker and realized that Archie is an abuser. He continually demeans Edith, he makes disparaging comments and faces, he treats her as if she exists merely to cook and clean. He yells when dinner is not on the table at 5 o'clock. In that episode, Archie is mad because dinner is not on the table. Edith had spent the day with her new friends, neighbors Frank and Eileen. Frank, a gourmet cook, brought dinner. Archie made his usual fuss. Edith told him "You find something wrong with all my friends and you chase them away." All In the Family made the 70's commonplace abusive husband lovable and comedic, funny. Edith acts overly jovial, dimwitted and unaffected by Archie's continual verbal lashing. The writers orchestrate events so that Archie looks foolish and occasionally, sympathetic. However, in reality, most women who live with men who think they are above everyone else, become diminished and beaten down by his behavior. Many abused wives present a false front of gaiety. In real life, Archie would increase his tactics and could become violent when Edith asserts herself.

The abusive male is dehumanizing the woman and treating her as an object which he has the right to control by whatever means it takes. Because the abusive male thinks so much of himself, without any empathy for his subject, he falls into the narcissist, sociopath, psychopathic continuum. Arrogant self-love can easily lead to justification of mistreatment of others. That internal justification can easily lead to sociopathic and psychopathic behaviors, as the abuser increases his tactics without any empathy for his prey.

Abuse as Narcissist, Sociopath, Psychopath

In contrast to Evan Stark's clinically kind treatment of the abusive male, Dr. Sam Vaknin in his book *"Malignant Self Love - Narcissism Revisited,"* http://www.narcissistic-abuse.com/ takes a no-love-spared assessment of the abusive male's behavior. Stark identifies threats as part of the intimidation class of male coercive control; Vaknin lays the behavior out when he lists attributes.

> *"Abusers are insatiable and vindictive. They always feel deprived and unfairly treated. Some of them are paranoid and sadistic. If they fail to manipulate their common children into abandoning the other parent, they begin treat the kids as enemies. They are not above threatening the children, abducting them, abusing them (sexually, physically, or psychologically), or even outright harming them - in order to get back at the erstwhile partner or in order to make her do something."*

Stark identifies four classifications for coercive control: physical violence, intimidation, isolation, and control. Vaknin identifies the not-necessarily-violent yet all-encompassing form as

Ambient Abuse. Because Vaknin has done such a good job of explaining the psychology of the abuser, and because this form of abuse is prevalent in abusive custody cases, rather than paraphrase, I have reprinted an extended excerpt from web postings retrieved in 2007 and again in February, 2014.

> "Ambient abuse is the stealth, subtle, underground currents of maltreatment that sometimes go unnoticed even by the victims themselves, until it is too late. Ambient abuse penetrates and permeates everything – but is difficult to pinpoint and identify. It is ambiguous, atmospheric, diffuse. Hence its insidious and pernicious effects. It is by far the most dangerous kind of abuse there is.
>
> Ambient abuse is the outcome of fear – fear of violence, fear of the unknown, fear of the unpredictable, the capricious, and the arbitrary. Ambient abuse is perpetrated by dropping subtle hints, by disorienting, by constant – and unnecessary – lying, by persistent doubting and demeaning, and by inspiring an air of unmitigated gloom and doom ("gaslighting").
>
> Ambient abuse, therefore, is the fostering, propagation, and enhancement of an atmosphere of fear, intimidation, instability, unpredictability and irritation. There are no acts of traceable explicit abuse, nor any manipulative settings of control. Yet, the irksome feeling remains, a disagreeable foreboding, a premonition, a bad omen.
>
> In the long term, such an environment erodes the victim's sense of self-worth and self-esteem. Self-confidence is shaken badly. Often, the victim adopts a paranoid or schizoid stance and thus renders themself

exposed even more to criticism and judgment. The roles are thus reversed: the victim is considered mentally deranged and the abuser – the suffering soul.

There are five categories of ambient abuse and they are often combined in the conduct of a single abuser:

I. Inducing Disorientation

The abuser causes the victim to lose faith in her ability to manage and to cope with the world and its demands. She no longer trusts her senses, her skills, her strengths, her friends, her family, and the predictability and benevolence of her environment.

The abuser subverts the target's focus by disagreeing with her way of perceiving the world, her judgment, the facts of her existence, by criticizing her incessantly – and by offering plausible but specious alternatives. By constantly lying, he blurs the line between reality and nightmare.

By recurrently disapproving of her choices and actions – the abuser shreds the victim's self-confidence and shatters her self-esteem. By reacting disproportionately to the slightest "mistake" – he intimidates her to the point of paralysis.

II. Incapacitating

The abuser gradually and surreptitiously takes over functions and chores previously adequately and skilfully performed by the victim. The prey finds itself isolated from the outer world, a hostage to the goodwill – or, more often, ill-will – of her captor. She is crippled by his encroachment and by the inexorable dissolution of her boundaries and ends up totally dependent on her tormentor's whims and desires, plans and stratagems.

Moreover, the abuser engineers impossible, dangerous, unpredictable, unprecedented, or highly specific situations in which he is sorely needed. The abuser makes sure that his knowledge, his skills, his connections, or his traits are the only ones applicable and the most useful in the situations that he, himself, wrought. The abuser generates his own indispensability.

III. Shared Psychosis (folie a deux)

The abuser creates a fantasy world, inhabited by the victim and himself, and besieged by imaginary enemies. He allocates to the abused the role of defending this invented and unreal Universe. She must swear to secrecy, stand by her abuser no matter what, lie, fight, pretend, obfuscate and do whatever else it takes to preserve this oasis of inanity.

Her membership in the abuser's "kingdom" is cast as a privilege and a prize. But it is not to be taken for granted. She has to work hard to earn her continued affiliation. She is constantly being tested and evaluated. Inevitably, this interminable stress reduces the victim's resistance and her ability to "see straight".

IV. Abuse of Information

From the first moments of an encounter with another person, the abuser is on the prowl. He collects information. The more he knows about his potential victim – the better able he is to coerce, manipulate, charm, extort or convert it "to the cause". The abuser does not hesitate to misuse the information he gleans, regardless of its intimate nature or the circumstances in which he obtained it. This is a powerful tool in his armory.

V. *Control by Proxy*

If all else fails, the abuser recruits friends, colleagues, mates, family members, the authorities, institutions, neighbours, the media, teachers – in short, third parties – to do his bidding. He uses them to cajole, coerce, threaten, stalk, offer, retreat, tempt, convince, harass, communicate and otherwise manipulate his target. He controls these unaware instruments exactly as he plans to control his ultimate prey. He employs the same mechanisms and devices. And he dumps his props unceremoniously when the job is done.

Another form of control by proxy is to engineer situations in which abuse is inflicted upon another person. Such carefully crafted scenarios of embarrassment and humiliation provoke social sanctions (condemnation, opprobrium, or even physical punishment) against the victim. Society, or a social group become the instruments of the abuser.

Abusers often use other people to do their dirty work for them. These - sometimes unwitting - accomplices belong to three groups:

I. The abuser's social milieu

Some offenders - mainly in patriarchal and misogynist societies – co-opt other family members, friends, and colleagues into aiding and abetting their abusive conduct. In extreme cases, the victim is held "hostage" - isolated and with little or no access to funds *or transportation. Often, the couple's children are used as bargaining chips or leverage. <u>Ambient abuse</u> by the abuser's clan, kin, kith, and village or neighborhood is rampant.*

II. <u>The victim's social milieu</u>

Even the victim's relatives, friends, and colleagues are amenable to the considerable charm, persuasiveness, and manipulativeness of the abuser and to his impressive thespian (acting) skills. The abuser offers a plausible rendition of the events and interprets them to his favor. Others rarely have a chance to witness an abusive exchange first hand and at close quarters. In contrast, the victims are often on the verge of a nervous breakdown: harassed, unkempt, irritable, impatient, abrasive, and hysterical.

Confronted with this contrast between a polished, self-controlled, and suave abuser and his harried casualties – it is easy to reach the conclusion that the real victim is the abuser, or that both parties abuse each other equally. The prey's acts of self-defense, assertiveness, or insistence on her rights are interpreted as aggression, or a mental health problem.

III. <u>The System</u>

The abuser perverts the system - therapists, marriage counselors, mediators, court-appointed guardians, police officers, and judges. He uses them to <u>pathologize the victim</u> and to separate her from her sources of emotional sustenance - notably, from her children.

Forms of Abuse by Proxy

- *Socially isolating and excluding the victim by discrediting her through a campaign of malicious rumors.*
- *Harassing the victim by using others to stalk her or by charging her with offenses she did not commit.*
- *Provoking the victim into aggressive or even antisocial conduct by having others threaten her or her loved ones.*
- *Colluding with others to render the victim dependent on the abuser.*
- *But, by far, her children are the abuser's greatest source of leverage over his abused spouse or mate."*

The research contained in Evan Stark's and Sam Vaknin's books expands the domestic violence definition of abuse. Both men take the reader into the inner world of abuser and prey. Anyone who claims to, or wants to, understand abuse, the motivations of the abuser, and the experience of the prey should purchase and read "Coercive Control" and "Malignant Self-Love" in their entirety.

ABUSE BY PROXY

Abuse by Proxy, which Vaknin has expanded upon, is the form of abuse used very successfully by the fatherhood in family court. Welfare fatherhood programs give full approval to males to use custody and litigation to continue to control and terrorize their female and child victims. While the welfare program is geared to help men, court players are not beyond helping the narcissistic female to use litigation to abuse (get at) the male. However, the abusive male is more prevalent since he often has wealth and business and political connections, and as Vaknin confirms, the majority of narcissists are male.

Lundy Bancroft, is a third researcher whose work is integral to enlightening the industry and public about the psychology and behavior of abusers and prey. Bancroft has worked in battering male treatment programs and as a custody evaluator. I rely on quotes taken from Bancroft's articles which have subsequently been published in the book *"The Batterer as Parent: Addressing the Impact of Domestic Violence on Family Dynamics,"* another necessary resource for those requiring education on the topic of abuse in custody court.

Bancroft profiles the abuser in his 1998 article, *"Understanding the Batterer in Custody and Visitation Disputes."* Again, the profile is not very flattering and the abuse goes well beyond hitting.

> "The batterer is controlling; he insists on having the last word in arguments and decision-making, he may control how the family's money is spent, and he may make rules for the victim about her movements and personal contacts, such as forbidding her to use the telephone or to see certain friends.
>
> He is manipulative; he misleads people inside and outside of the family about his abusiveness, he twists arguments around to make other people feel at fault, and he turns into a sweet, sensitive person for extended periods of time when he feels that it is in his best interest to do so. His public image usually contrasts sharply with the private reality.
>
> He is entitled; he considers himself to have special rights and privileges not applicable to other family

members. He believes that his needs should be at the center of the family's agenda, and that everyone should focus on keeping him happy. He typically believes that it is his sole prerogative to determine when and how sexual relations will take place, and denies his partner the right to refuse (or to initiate) sex. He usually believes that housework and childcare should be done for him, and that any contributions he makes to those efforts should earn him special appreciation and deference. He is highly demanding.

He is disrespectful; he considers his partner less competent, sensitive, and intelligent than he is, often treating her as though she were an inanimate object. The unifying principle is his attitude of ownership. The batterer believes that once you are in a committed relationship with him, you belong to him. This possessiveness in batterers is the reason why killings of battered women so commonly happen when victims are attempting to leave the relationship; a batterer does not believe that his partner has the right to end a relationship until he is ready to end it.

Each batterer has his own mix of controlling and entitlement. Some monitor every move their partners make like a prison guard, but at the same time are somewhat lower in entitlement, contributing more to housework and childcare than other batterers (though still less than non-batterers). Other batterers don't control their partners freedom as severely, but become irate or violent when they are not fully catered to, or when victims remind them of responsibilities that they are shirking. The levels of manipulativeness and overt disrespect also vary, so that each batterer has a particular style.

> *Most abusers do not express these beliefs explicitly; they are more likely to deny having them, or even to claim to have opposite convictions that are humane and egalitarian. An experienced batterers' counselor may have to spend several hours with the abuser before the underlying attitudes begin to show. These attitudes are generally evident to victims, however, who often feel frustrated at the batterer's ability to present a markedly different face to the outside world. This dual aspect to his personality also helps to keep the victim confused about what he is really like, and can contribute to her blaming herself for his abusive behaviors."*

ABUSE IN FAMILY COURT

These three experts have actual hands-on experience working with battered women, men who batter, and narcissists. From their experience these three men have explained that abuse is much more than hitting. Stark, Vaknin and Bancroft understand the underlying dynamics of an abusive relationship. They do not feel that men have an inherent right to dominate women. They know that feeling superior leads to abuse in a wide range of forms. In contrast, the welfare fatherhood custody program (called access/visitation) is built on the conviction that fathers are superior to mothers. The design of the welfare program has led to a large industry that supports male superiority by diminishing abuse, blaming the victim, and giving parity to abuser and prey by branding it "high conflict."

Every State includes abuse as a determining factor in child custody statutes. The fatherhood custody program was invented to go around these laws by instituting a federal administrative mandate. Instead of relying on the legal process, determining fact by the rules of evidence and adhering to law, state statutes, fatherhood access/visitation programs mandate the use of court service providers to give fathers custody. Protection from abuse is omitted from the fatherhood custody mandate.

Since its inception, this mandate has led to increasing amounts of children being sentenced to spend their youth with abusive fathers without the protection, comfort and often physical presence of their mother. The DV community is well aware of this problem, yet for the most part, they have bowed to the fatherhood custody mandate. The DV community has not organized legislative awareness campaigns, they have not used their influence to generate a media spotlight, nor have they organized qualified legal opponents to represent battered mothers. When battered mothers stuck in abusive litigation call for help, they are routinely shunned; the government-supported DV community tells them "We have no money to help." The only vocal response to the problem from the DV community is to call for identification of abuse, while still permitting the emphasis to be on violence.

Lundy Bancroft, Sam Vaknin and Evan Stark have written about abuse and how it plays out in custody (that welfare program again). The most egregious outcome has been the number of incest cases ignored by family court. In fact, an entire industry has been built on providing false evidence in order to permit dads sex abuse and punish mothers for taking a stand against it. Research and court's ignoring incest have combined to create a small group of professionals calling for inclusion of domestic violence in child custody decisions. In order to placate those calling for awareness of abuse, fatherhood promoters and trade association members have developed their own system of classifying violence which relies heavily on the writings of Janet Johnston and others who receive their funding from fundamental conservative groups and government fatherhood grants.

MINIMIZING ABUSE BY CLASSIFICATION

If you control the information, you control the dialogue and outcome. To that end, the court trade association AFCC (see Chapter 8, War on Women) relies on Janet Johnston's model which breaks abuse into five categories. In 2007, AFCC worked with the National Council of Juvenile and Family Court Judges (NCJFCJ), a judicial association, and held the "The Wingspread Conference on Domestic Violence and Family Courts." The intent of the conference was to bend family court DV categorizing towards the Johnston model. To prepare for the conference, AFCC asked participants to read the 2005 article "Differentiating Types of Domestic Violence: Implications for Child Custody," by Nancy VerSteegh. I found a free copy at http://open.wmitchell.edu/facsch/217.

VerSteegh relies heavily on the work of sociologist Michael P. Johnson who also types domestic violence calling it Intimate Terrorism, Situational Couple Violence, and Violent Resistance which is only mentioned as a part of Situational Couple Violence. AFCC convened this conference to forward their propaganda that there are two types of domestic violence and only one type is true abuse: Intimate Terrorism. The others, Violent Resistance and Situational Couple Violence, fall into the High Conflict category where the woman is blamed equally for any violent episode, or for if she uses physical means to protect herself or the children. There is no category for fathers who sexually, physically or emotionally abuse their children. Nor is there any mention of father's abuse of children in the 55-page typology or the resulting 22-page conference report.

Renaming domestic violence is extremely advantageous to AFCC trade association members who profit off abusers who use the court to continue their control, manipulation, threats, intimidation, abuse by proxy, etc. Classifying cases of abuse as being merely high conflict permits trade association members to appoint themselves to be custody evaluators, guardian ad litems (lawyers for the children), parent educators, mediators, supervised visit monitors, and parent coordinators. Recognizing that the male is abusive would require the court to offer protection to women and children. Protection is bad for business, so the court is heavily motivated to classify abuse as situational couple violence or high conflict.

Below, I have listed Johnston's type taken from her Typology of Batterers, the AFCC Wingspread conference classification, my comments, and Lundy Bancroft's comments excerpted from his 1998 article *"Understanding the Batterer in Custody and Visitation Disputes, Janet Johnston's Typology of Batterers and the AFCC Risk Assessment: The Quest for Simple Solutions."*

TYPE A

Johnston: Ongoing or Episodic Male Battering; what Johnson calls Intimate Terrorists

AFCC Wingspread: *Violence used by a perpetrator in the exercise of coercive control over the victim.* "Sometimes referred to as "classic battering," this type of violence occurs when an abuser (usually male) uses force as one tactic in a larger escalating pattern aimed at intimidating and controlling the victim. Physical violence and sexual abuse are often accompanied by threats, psychological and emotional abuse, isolation of the victim, manipulation of children, and exercise of economic control."

Doreen says: Courts and their service providers rarely classify a case as true violence. Women must have large amounts of physical harm documented with a large police record. Even when a police record exists, a mother can be blamed for staying and putting the children at risk. The industry uses supervised visits to quickly "cure" the violent father, making him eligible to be alone with the children where he is free to abuse them. The wealthier the father, the quicker he will be deemed acceptable.

Bancroft comments: *Type A is considered the real batterer; he is very frequently and severely violent, and he uses violence to control his partner. The "A" type of batterer is considered the only real batterer; he is described as having a victim who is severely traumatized, who is passive and withdrawn, and who rarely starts arguments or challenges the batterer.*

TYPE B

Johnston: Female-Initiated Violence; Violent Resistance under Situational Couple Violence; High Conflict

AFCC Wingspread: Also calls it *Violent Resistance or self-defense.* "This type of violence occurs when a victim (typically female) uses violence to protect herself against a perpetrator who is using force as a part of a larger pattern of coercive control." Note: The connection to self-defense is noted in the conference report, yet the VerSteegh article does not recognize male abuse as the problem, but prefers to classify self-defense as Situational Couple Violence.

Doreen says: Courts and their service providers are singularly calling these cases High Conflict. There is never any recognition that a mother has stood up for herself, used physical means to stem father's attack of her or the children. Women are classified as creating conflict because they have resisted the abuser. The majority of women who wind up in family court have shown enough self-esteem and strength to make the first move towards leaving. Leaving is not a sudden decision in most cases and only taken after a long time of attempting to change the abuser, usually by fighting and resisting. A woman is usually very angry and emotionally exhausted. This makes it very easy for courts and service providers to belittle the abuse by calling it high conflict, giving parity to abuser and prey.

<u>Bancroft comments</u>: *Type B is violence that is initiated by the victim; she gets hurt because she is smaller, but her behavior is the problem. Type B, where the victim initiates the violence, needs to also be treated with care. The question of which person strikes first is of limited value in assessing domestic violence; the more relevant questions are which party is in fear, which party is being systematically torn down or controlled, and which party is suffering the long-term psychological damage. Careful evaluation sometimes reveals a picture quite different from the initial impression.*

TYPE C

<u>Johnston</u>: Male Controlled Interactive Violence; Situational Couples Violence; High Conflict

<u>AFCC Wingspread</u>: *Violence driven by conflict.* "This type of violence takes place when an unresolved disagreement spirals into a violent incident, but the violence is not part of a larger pattern of coercive control. It may be initiated by either the male or female partner. However, female victims are more likely to suffer negative consequences, including injury, than are men."

<u>Doreen says</u>: Courts and service providers hate women who aren't completely subservient to men, who stick up for themselves and their children. The overwhelming majority of custody cases are being classified as situational couples violence, or high conflict, blaming the women for the abuse because she deserves it!

<u>Bancroft comments</u>: *Type C is violence caused by "mutual verbal provocations," and again the woman is the victim only because she is physically smaller; she is considered equally abusive.*

A woman who is stronger, angrier, or generally more unpleasant to interact with, would be likely under Johnston's approach to be seen as mutually abusive and provocative, the "C" type of relationship; she would thus be considered largely responsible for the man's violence. In reality, most abused women, even those who are terrified, do not give up all forms of fighting back, and continue attempting to protect their rights and the rights of their children. The more that the victim refuses to submit to the abuser's control, the more likely he is to escalate his violence. Under Johnston's typology, the more courageously a woman attempts to defend herself and her children, the less responsibility the abuser has for his actions. Using this approach serves the batterer's interests well, but endangers the children. The result of this approach is that some of the most dangerous abusers, those who are the most determined to dominate at all costs, are ironically declared to be the lowest risk to their children. Studies of trauma survivors also demonstrate that symptoms will vary greatly from person to person. Some battered women may become passive and withdrawn, but others are more likely to show hostility, disjointed thinking, or extreme mistrust, precisely as a response to the severity of the abuse they have endured; the second group is the most likely to be labeled "provocative." Women in this group run the greatest risk of having their abuser win custody or extended unsupervised visitation, which he can then use to continue terrorizing her and the children.

Abusers almost always characterize their relationships as mutually abusive, if they acknowledge any behavior problems of their own at all. Under close investigation, however, most domestic abusers, even those who use relatively low levels of physical violence, are revealed to involve extensive patterns of verbal degradation, psychological abuse, and other types of cruelty on the abuser's part, and to involve a marked imbalance of power. There is no substitute for careful evaluation to see if this is the case.

The concept of "violence resulting from mutual verbal provocations" is in itself a disturbing one. What kind of arguing is a woman permitted to do before she is defined as provoking violence? A woman who is being abused is likely to have multiple sources of resentment: the unrelieved burden of childcare, the insults and name-calling, the degrading sexual comments, the affairs, the neglect, the violence. If she periodically becomes enraged and confronts her abuser about these things angrily, is she provoking violence? Is there any way in which she can forcefully defend her own interests, or her children's, without being labeled provocative? This characterization can only serve the interests of the abuser. In fact, it appears to be an adopting of the batterer's view, endorsing his way of characterizing his victim as holding responsibility for his actions. Johnston even goes so far as to say that if a woman "tried to leave or refused to communicate with him," the abuser's violent response should be considered part of a mutual provocation.

In sum, the danger that a domestic abuser represents to his children can only be assessed by examining him (as common sense would dictate), not by examining his victim.

TYPE D

Johnston: Separation and Postdivorce Violence

AFCC Wingspread: *Separation-instigated violence* "With this type of violence, the first violent incident occurs at the time of separation as a response to the trauma of separation on the part of an individual with no history of coercive controlling behavior."

Doreen says: It seems safe to say that courts and service providers think it is OK to hit a woman who is leaving. There is no recognizing that the male becomes violent when he is not getting his way. It is a well-known fact that violence escalates and danger to prey increases dramatically when they try to leave.

Bancroft comments: *The "stress of separation" category, (type "D") is also a risky one. As discussed above, separation may occur as the result of an escalating pattern of abusiveness, with the physical attack being the last straw. Such an escalation would be likely to continue post-separation, with important implications for the children. The formation of this type also raises an important clinical question; is Johnston suggesting that there is no significant difference between men who use violence in response to the stress of separation and those who do not? In fact, most men do not use violence towards intimate partners, even during an acrimonious divorce; those who do so are likely to have the other characteristics typical of batterers.*

TYPE E

Johnston: Psychotic and Paranoid Reactions; not mentioned in VerSteegh article

AFCC Wingspread: *Violence stemming from severe mental illness.* "Some perpetrators of domestic violence evidence psychosis and paranoia, and their violence is driven by severe mental illness."

Doreen says: Courts and service providers are terming the mothers "mentally ill" and then determining that fathers have a cause for hitting them. Like high conflict classifications, force is justified because she needs to be put in her place.

Bancroft comments: *In cases where a batterer does have a mental illness (Type E), the disorder cannot be assumed to be the cause of his battering. Most mentally ill batterers also have the typical attitudes and behaviors of batterers, and therefore addressing the mental health problem alone will not necessarily reduce the domestic violence. Johnston appears unaware that a person can simultaneously have a mental health problem and a battering problem, neither of which is reducible to the other.*

OMITTING ABUSE OF CHILDREN

In his assessment of the AFCC/Johnston typology, Lundy Bancroft **does** recognize that fathers abuse children. The courts only purpose is to determine custody. Welfare fatherhood programs require courts to give fathers as much custody as they want without any consideration to what is best for the child: the welfare program assumes that a father is the only thing a child needs. In his article Bancroft makes some excellent points in addressing the trouble with ignoring the children when pigeon-holing abuse.

> "A few other problems are high priorities to mention. First, this approach is based on the assumption that the risk to children from visitation comes primarily from exposure to new acts of physical violence. As serious as this risk is, it is not in fact the greatest one; the far greater danger is of physical, sexual, and psychological abuse by the batterer during the visits. Children from domestic violence are particularly vulnerable psychologically because they are already scarred by the violence they have been exposed to. Johnston's typology does nothing to identify those batterers who are most likely to abuse their children post-separation, does not examine what kind of atmosphere assists children to recover from the trauma of divorce and domestic violence, and does not discuss any other indicators of a batterer's risk to children other than his level of physical violence.
>
> Second, this typology does nothing to help assess the risk that an abuser will batter in his next relationship. Although abusers blame their violence on their current victim and on the specific relationship dynamics, both research studies and clinical experience make clear that the problem lies within the abuser. Abusers have a high

rate, regardless of their level of physical violence, of battering in their next long-term relationship. Children of batterers are therefore at risk of exposure to domestic violence in their father's new relationship.

Johnston sometimes accepts abusers' explanations of their actions at face value. She writes, for example, about men who she says slap their partners "in a misguided effort to quell her 'hysteria'". Batterers are known for their violent punishment of partners who attempt to express anger, which Johnston is apparently unaware of. She is actually describing a batter who is highly intolerant of his victim's efforts to have a voice, which has far-reaching implications for both her and her children.

Johnston appears to have no awareness of the overlap between battering and incest perpetration. In one of her articles (Johnston, July 1993) a striking passage describes the relationship between girls younger than seven or eight years old and their batterer fathers: In general, there were poor boundaries between these men and their daughters, especially among the substance-abusing men, with mutual seductiveness and provocation of his aggression. These fathers needed validation of their masculinity and attractiveness; they pulled for this affirmation from their little daughters." Johnston shows no sign of recognizing this as incest, although it reads like a description from a training course on sexual abuse. It is also important to note that she is holding these girls equally responsible for the dynamics of their relationships with their fathers, which certainly raises questions about her judgment in assigning responsibility for abuse in adult relationships.

Children of batterers are at particular risk for sexual abuse (Herman 1991; McCloskey et.al.; Paveza; Sirles; Truesdell et. al.). The profile of an incest perpetrator is similar in many respects to that of a batterer. The incest perpetrator typically has a good public image, making it hard for people know him to believe him capable of sexual abuse. He is self-centered and believes that the child is responsible to meet his needs. He is controlling and often harshly disciplinarian as a parent, while at other times giving the children - particularly the incest victim - special attention and privileges. He often prepares the child for months or years in a "grooming" process, akin to the charming and attentive behavior used by batterers early in relationships. He usually will have no diagnosable mental health condition. He will tend to confuse love and abuse; just as a batterer may say, "I hit her because of how much I love her," the incest perpetrator believes that his times of sexually abusing the child have actually been moments of special intimacy. Incest perpetrators define themselves as having been provoked, just as batterers do; for example, he may say that a four-year old child "came on to" him. He often sees the child as a personal possession, feeling that "no one has any right to tell me what I can do with my child." This list of similarities continues, making the high statistical overlap between battering and child sexual abuse unsurprising. (See Groth; Herman 1981; Herman 1988; Leberg)"

Minimizing abuse against the mother, blaming mother for the abuse, leads to physical, emotional and sexual abuse against the children.

PROFITING FROM ABUSE

AFCC, which consists of court employees and those who profit from protracted litigation, has a clear motivation for ignoring abuse and renaming it high conflict. Simply put: money. The second part of the AFCC Wingspread conference report and VerSteegh's article asks the question: *What court services are appropriate for each type of domestic violence?*

Trade association members see themselves as being in charge of parenting for divorcing parents. The Wingspread report states *"In addition to deciding cases that are presented to them, court systems are increasingly involved in managing cases. What is sometimes referred to as "differential case management" involves early screening of cases, assessment of family needs, creation of a service plan including referral to services and appropriate court processes, development of a parenting plan, and potential post-decree monitoring. Thus, the role of the court has expanded beyond decision making to encompass potential ongoing involvement with some families."* The court welcomes men who use the system to further their abuse!

The only services being offered to parents are custody evaluation, guardian ad litems, parent education, mediation, supervised visits, and co-parenting coordination. These services are not "offered," they are ordered by a judge or lawyer acting as a judge (usually called Masters or Hearing Officers). The services are not free. A parent faces penalties of jailing and/or monetary fines for refusal to participate (called contempt), often supported by state laws. Service providers charge exorbitant, above-market prices, routinely charging 100's of dollars per hour. VerSteegh recommends that in cases of situational couples violence (high conflict), a *"parenting coordinator should be appointed to continue the educational process, monitor conflict levels, and assist in mediating day-to-day decision making."* At several hundred dollars an hour, parents will pay a lot of money for this day-to-day decision maker!

VerSteegh admits that these mediators, custody evaluators, parenting coordinators, etc. have no training in domestic violence and rarely even screen for it! The abuser thrives in this environment! What occurs is that abused women are abused by court employees and court service providers. The evaluator, mediator, parenting coordinator, and judge, demean, threaten, intimidate and control. They use their power over the mother. Financial abuse is prevalent. Women are not permitted to recover because they are stuck in the court system until the children turn 18, the money runs out, father dies or is given full custody or mother walks away, which is the most common outcome of these abusive custody cases!

PROTECTION AND RECOVERY INSTEAD OF PROFIT

Instead of being required to pay business people who will only re-abuse, mothers would benefit from services that help them recover and become emotionally and financially stable. The Office of Violence Against Women has funded a report which outlines the services abused women **do** need. The report, titled "Domestic Violence Practice in Louisiana" was written in 2005 by Mark Moreau of Southeast Louisiana Legal Services. Louisiana legislature passed the Post-Separation Family Violence Relief Act (La. R.S. 9:361-369) because when a woman leaves her abuser the abuse often escalates and child custody and visitation, family court, becomes the new forum. Moreau outlines how legal aid lawyers can help victims. By doing so he lists the services that would help women recover.

- A protective order can make abusers less threatening. Abusers are not always rabidly violent, they are often weak and therefore, afraid of being jailed, so an order can make abusers "back off". An order can remove the abuser from the home, giving the women the time and space necessary to recover, and the confidence to make her own decisions about her family's future.

- A quick divorce will provide the victim with financial protection. Many abusers control the family finances and women must live for years, without any financial resources. Moreau states that some abusers no longer view their spouses as property after a divorce is obtained; certainly, a quick divorce would help send the message that the prey is allowed to leave.

- Moreau recognizes that many abusers use custody litigation to continue their harassment and there is a high probability that he will abuse his children. "The proper resolution of child custody and visitation is essential for the protection of women and children. Many abusers also physically, sexually of emotionally abuse their children."

- A newly freed abused woman may need spouse and/or child support. Abusers may not pay support to force the mother to return. The traumatic effects of abuse may make employment difficult. A controlling male often completely controls the financial assets of a relationship.

- Quick resolution of division of property: car, home, savings, pensions, is essential to keeping a job and securing economic independence.

- Women need help with housing. Women may become homeless from fleeing. It can cost thousands of dollars to rent or relocate. An abuser's conduct can cause eviction. Eviction can cause the loss of rent subsidies. Abusers may not pay mortgages or rent. Women may need to relocate closer to family for support. Leaving a home that holds memories of abuse may be the best prescription for recovery for mothers and children.

- Women who are employed at the time of leaving need help keeping that job. Requirements to be in court or at a court service provider result in work absence, loss of income and job loss. Job protection is essential to economic independence from the abuser.

- While financial independence should be the goal, women fleeing abuse may need public benefits.

- Abused women may need tax assistance and reduction of consumer debt.

Moreau has listed areas where lawyers and the court as a legal entity, can help women fleeing abuse. This includes a wide area of expertise. For that reason, government financed help for women should come from the legal aid community, not from the domestic violence community. Moms may not be getting assistance because government reports admit fatherhood programs direct men to legal aid for custody assistance. Perhaps it is too difficult for legal aid to represent both sides of the custody equation. Sadly, the domestic violence community offers only help getting protective orders; they are not equipped to offer the wide range of services necessary for mothers with children to actually terminate a relationship with an abuser. Termination of an abusive relationship requires protection from protracted litigation and court services. Currently, the "services" being ordered by family court are merely another abusive method meant to keep mothers and children subservient to fathers.

The DV community has never protected women from the abuse of court service providers. The DV community does not keep a list of lawyers who would offer abused women and children protection from court service providers. Nor do they offer any pro bono (free) legal help. DV administration is often in bed with local court service providers. It is my opinion that domestic violence groups who get paid under the Violence Against Women Act through the Department of Justice's Office of Violence Against Women, are not qualified to legally represent abused women in custody litigation with an abusive male. Rather than encourage women's autonomy, recovery which only happens by truly getting away from the abuser and becoming self-sufficient, the DV network has been forcing fatherhood: telling women that they must allow the abuser access to the children, that no matter how abusive, the father is best for the kids. They believe only the most documented violent men should be required limited access through supervised visits and he can slowly be given unsupervised time with the child. DV staff have stated to me that, even if he beats his wife it doesn't mean he will abuse the children. Alarmingly, they support handing over child rearing decision making to a parenting coordinator. We need to be clear: a parenting coordinator only perpetuates abuse, keeping women and children in a relationship with their abuser!

BUILDING THE PROFIT NETWORK

By reading Pennsylvania's plan "Changing the Culture of

Custody in Pennsylvania," I found out that the court's and the trade association's plan to address the question of abuse during litigation is to employ someone at the court who will determine if a relationship is abusive, classify the abuse. The employee will do this in the first month of any court filing. It is logical to assume that there will be a heavy caseload and women will have severely limited time to make their case that they are indeed abused. The male abusers will also get equal time to make their case that they have been wronged. Many women leaving abusers are in the throes of Post-Traumatic Stress Disorder, they are struggling with accepting the severity of the abuse, they are in no condition to immediately relay the many levels of control, intimidation, harassment, fear, direct violence or fear of violence, and are in no condition to convey their experience to an outsider. This problem would be compounded if the outsider is male, as abused women can become fearful, nervous and anxious around males since her experience with males is abusive. Abused women are not conditioned to relate to males as equals or as sympathetic listeners.

The DV community wants these jobs so they are willing to go along with the court and business practitioners (court service providers) in order to get those jobs. Pennsylvania has 57 court jurisdictions. If one staff is hired in smaller districts, and big cities hire several employees, at least 70 jobs would be created seemingly for experienced DV workers. Classification provides a nice employment opportunity when funding is being cut in other areas. The court employee will be pressured to limit their "true" abuse classification. What I have found is that the level of domestic violence and the protection offered by the court and its service providers, including anyone appointed to make a DV classification, will be determined solely based on the size of any bank accounts, even when those accounts are controlled exclusively by him!

Two DV people who attended the AFCC conference are Loretta Frederick, Battered Women's Justice Project (BWJP) and Nadine Neufville, U. S. Dept. of Justice Office on Violence Against Women (OVW). That resulted in BWJP, working with AFCC, being given an OVW grant to create a tool for creating a Parenting Plan (custody order) for cases where there is domestic violence. The large grant resulted in a long, complex process of relationship analytical questions, called "Domestic Violence Interview Guide." BWJP uses another of its subsidiaries to sell this form ostensibly to courts for determining the type of domestic violence classification. The parent interview consists of seven topic areas; each topic covers multiple subjects. As someone who has lived an abusive relationship, I can attest that it would take several hours to conduct an interview of this nature, that the material involved would be highly sensitive, traumatic and emotionally draining. The interview offers no accommodation for protecting the mental health of the subject; for the possibility of exacerbating Post Traumatic Stress Disorder symptoms. Abuse as a subject matter should be explored with a sympathetic, qualified counselor, not in an "evaluator" setting. Abusee's who have just left often do not have a clear understanding of the abuse and how it played out in the relationship. It takes time and space to recover and confront the dynamics of an abusive relationship, and to heal to the point that an objective discussion of events can occur. Supplying the correct answers would be dependent on intellect, personal understanding, and verbal, communication skills.

Once it is determined that the abuse is not just violent, but meant to coercively control (Type A), BWJP has created an analysis which uses the colors of red and green purportedly to represent severity. It uses the shading system to look at how the abuse affects children. This assessment again is heavily centered on episodic, violent abuse. It does not measure the effect of insidious, ambient abuse, the type that is constant and pervasive. It does not measure the sophistication needed by the child to decipher the complexities of an abusive relationship, nor does it acknowledge that abuse would be the norm in that household. This analysis will be used to determine what level of custody the abuser receives and the services the court will assign. The recommendation being: assignment of a co-parenting coordinator for all but the most violently extreme cases.

Proposing the use of this type of assessment, reminds me of Bricklin's parenting perception subjective tests covered in Chapter 9 "Players and Their Methods." This level of scrutiny is currently supposed to be part of a custody evaluation. BWJP forms have not been peer reviewed or scientifically validated. The tests do not assess the caregiving duties each parent performs. Abusers rarely assume responsibility for mundane child care tasks. The BWJP tests do not assess how each parent treats, and relates to, the children. Abusers rarely put the child's needs first. The assessment was clearly created by a non-lawyer; someone with no understanding of the legal process. Results merely create off-the-record hearsay, already an enormous problem in family court. Actually, an evaluator would need a physical, factually confirmable, record in order for the outcome to adhere to the rules of evidence. The entire evaluation would have to be recorded so that any conclusion could be challenged under due process rules. Apparently, I am not the only one to conclude the uselessness of BWJPs assessment; the court service providers in the test market (Henry County, OH) were hesitant to use it. Court service providers are interested in quick and easy profit. A competent review would be too time-consuming, the entire evaluator problem stems from the refusal to devote the necessary time required to properly assess abuse characteristics. This grant money was spent on a non-solution to the problem.

Other scales for testing for abuse exist. The government should not pay grants to reinvent the wheel; to decide how to give abusive men "parenting time" which is just another word for custody made to sound like it doesn't involve litigation. What needs to be done is to actually use what is already available. Research already proves that abusive men use custody and litigation to continue their abuse. Research already proves that men who mistreat their wives have a much higher probability of abusing their children.

BWJP's solution was presented to mothers at the tenth annual Battered Mothers Custody Conference in a workshop called "Help Us Help You." Claiming that these forms were going to protect mothers and children, who, as BWJP and OVW know, are being severely abused by fathers, courts, and court business practitioners, the mothers were told that they should go through the interview portion with their lawyers (I'll conclude because they knew the service providers were not going to use it). I pointed out that lawyers charge several hundred dollars an hour and I was not one to share this type of intimate, personal information, especially with someone acting in a business relationship with me. I also mentioned that Child Abuse Solutions, Inc. (http://childabusesolutions.com/) had developed very good checklists. BWJP staff responded "There are several methods out there."

While denying federal funding of fatherhood courts to mothers during the conference, BWJP was simultaneously working with the Office of Violence Against Women to get their DV parenting plan assessment mandated and funded by the Child Support Act, as part of President Obama's 2012-15 budget. However, Congress refused to force DV assessment when signing The Sense of the Congress (Pub.L. 113-183) which continues to tie custody to support orders, instead, makes assessment of abuse merely voluntary.

AFCC and BWJP are collecting government funds to develop guides for cases with domestic violence so that judges will rule appropriately since there is a huge problem with the current status of judicial handling of abuse custody cases. Yet, judges already have access to guidelines. They are called Benchbooks, because they give guidance for ruling from the bench. Almost every State has developed a DV Benchbook which relies on legal practice and state law to aid family law judges when they come in contact with women and children fleeing abuse. The majority of these benchbooks have been available to judges for over a decade, yet these high quality legal directives are rarely put into practice. Additionally, the National Council of Juvenile and Family Court Judges (NCJFCJ) developed "Navigating Custody & Visitation Evaluations in Cases with Domestic Violence: A Judge's Guide" (revised in 2006) for DV cases and now markets "Specialized Family Violence Information Packets" which are excellent resources if only they were used.

The problem is: welfare has mandated father's custody. Classifying abuse, ignoring probability to abuse children, and ruling only the most violent of men unsuitable for custody, while permitting all other forms of abuser to be granted liberal custody, results in abusers using litigation and court service providers to further threaten, intimidate and control their victims. If the abuser wants complete control of the children or wants to punish the mother for leaving, he has help. Court players will eventually create a record by fraud and misuse of process that will turn mother into the abuser and give the <u>real</u> abuser, father, complete power.

CONCLUSION

Who gets to say if a relationship is abusive? Shouldn't it be the person leaving? No one can know what someone else is experiencing without patiently listening for hours. Coming to terms with abuse is a long process, even a woman who has decided to leave may not realize all the levels of abuse since she has been accepting and dealing with it on some level in order to stay and protect herself and her children. Most women do not decide to leave suddenly. She has most likely tried to change the relationship first. Like Bancroft confirms, her attempts to challenge, or change, his actions, result in increased conflict. That leaves the abuser with ammunition to use against his prey. Court and business people are more than willing to call the relationship "high conflict" instead of acknowledging that one person is leading the conflict and the other is attempting to stand up for themselves in a non-passive manner.

It is easy to blame the woman for getting into an abusive relationship. She should have been able to tell. It is her need to please, or her religious beliefs, that got her into an abusive relationship. She deserves to be treated badly because she doesn't feel good about herself. But those attitudes do not take into account the insidious, devious nature of concealed abuse. Our society likes to blame the victim, it is easier than changing the structural systems that help perpetuate coercive control/ambient abuse/battering. Not all women are victims. They do not cower and blindly obey. Many make choices of when to fight, disobey or exert their right to do what they want even knowing resistance will result in more abuse as he increases his methods to control, intimidate, isolate and instill fear. Women in these abusive personal relationships often work very hard. It takes courage to survive coercive control, let alone challenge or resist abuse.

In my abusive marriage, the coercive control increased after the birth of the children. Children bring a new dynamic into the relationship. They are additional people that the abuser must control. As Stark confirms, he wants to micromanage woman's functioning in everyday tasks; children add a new level of need. However, many women's bonds to the children are so strong that they are willing to fight in areas that just were not that important before. When I got pregnant I was determined to go to a birth center mostly because I did not want to have an episiotomy. I had read a book called Nursing Your Baby and I was determined to do the best for the child. My will was so strong that my abuser instinctively knew that his efforts to control me would not be successful. So he could be grumpy and negative, but I would ignore him, and since he wanted the children too, he was not going to take the abuse to the physically violent level.

But there were many moments when he would revert to his ambient abuse tactics. He had what he wanted: a wife who cooked, cleaned, stayed home caring for the children so he never had to, the house was in his name only, bank accounts were under his name only, he wasn't asked to do chores or child care. His sole household responsibility was mowing the grass. One time I said to him "If I ask you to sit with the children while I run the vacuum, you act like it is something special, but when I stay with them and you cut the grass, it is nothing." He would sometimes say "Other women do the grass cutting." His one job and he wanted me to do that too, but when I said I would cut the grass and got on the riding mower, he did not like that either because he sees himself as the master mechanic and he does not want me ruining his machine.

Am I supposed to recount this to a court employee? A lawyer? A Psychologist? How much will I be billed? $100's per hour? These stories occurred for years, even decades. How much recanting will a lawyer, court employee, psychologist sit through without becoming tired, annoyed, blaming me for staying? It sounds silly even to me. Isn't it our cultural nature to determine I asked for it? There is obviously something wrong with me for putting up with it for so long. There must be something sinister motivating me to leave now. Most likely, I want to be free so I can party, have multiple sexual partners, and live off his money.

The court and its service providers are not set-up to comprehend the complex dynamics of these relationships. No amount of training will compensate for a true lack of proficiency especially when the motivation is to perpetuate the profit business model. Women leaving abuse need well-paying jobs which may require education and training, affordable quality child care including after-school, holidays, and summer programs, safe housing and neighborhoods, and high quality education for children. Women and children do not need court-ordered high priced decision-makers who merely siphon family resources.

As Evan Stark concludes, helping the survivor regain control of her life is the over-riding goal of the entire therapeutic process, restoring her capacity for free and independent decision-making, social connection and self-direction, to restore the hopes and dreams that have been foreclosed by coercive control. **"To treat the harms we must advocate that women be given full status as persons. Ending coercive control and establishing sexual equality are inseparable."** Gender specific fatherhood funding of custody fails to protect mothers and children who have said "NO" to abuse!

Chapter 8

War on Women

Welfare fatherhood programs are a war on women and children! Children have lost their mothers; they are motherless because of welfare's fatherhood program. Children are forced to live with incest and other forms of abuse because of welfare's fatherhood program. Mothers are not allowed to be good mothers because they refuse to permit father's abuse.

Women's groups like NOW and media commentators cry that the war on women is against a woman's right to choose to have an abortion when the real war is against women's right to live free from abusive control of men. Not just the right to terminate a pregnancy, the war on women is against a women's right to make her own decisions, to control the outcome of her life and that of any children she has birthed. The war on women is singly a movement to maintain male control which is inherently abusive to women. You cannot control someone against their will without resorting to abusive tactics. This chapter covers the male groups that worked to institute government welfare programs that would favor fathers, forging a welfare funded war on women in their role of being mothers.

I have chosen to highlight four special interest groups: a right-wing religious ideology group; a fatherhood group; a male-centric custody & support network; and a court membership trade association. I explain each groups' area of specialization, how each colluded to institute welfare policies that fund mother and child abuse through fatherhood programs, and, how they work to this day within the family court system. The first three groups instituted the program and the last group, AFCC, enacts it.

FROM IDEOLOGY TO WELFARE PROGRAM

Institute for American Values

I chose the Institute for American Values (IAV) as my example of a right wing, religious group's involvement in the development of mother-abusing fatherhood welfare programs because its founding director, David Blankenhorn, was instrumental in writing and passing welfare fatherhood legislation.

The Institute for American Values represents the right-wing religious backlash against the women's movement. Not everyone is happy that women gained more individual liberty. Being able to get good jobs and support themselves meant women developed less tolerance for abuse within the home. Before World War II, women had to put up with an alcoholic husband. If he refused to work or came home and expected to be waited on, created an atmosphere of fear for his wife and kids, if he slept with other women, a woman was expected to stay in the marriage until death.

When WWII took men out of the workforce to military service, women were encouraged to staff the factories making military goods. Women wanted to be Rosie the Riveter and many needed to provide for children and parents. But after the war, when the men came back, women found they liked getting paid cash for their labor, and the families liked the increased income which purchased suburban houses, cars and appliances. Thus began the trend towards greater numbers of females in the workforce, many being wives and mothers.

When reliable, easy-to-use birth control became available in the form of the pill, women did not have to be constantly pregnant. Wives and mothers became free to pursue other interests like getting a higher education, leading to better paying jobs. Women no longer had to get a husband to provide food, housing and other basic needs. Having more freedom, having accomplishments outside the home, having their own money, gave women confidence and self-respect.

Conservatives like the status quo. They do not like change. The women's movement is threatening to their idea of the natural order. Religious conservatives believe the bible ordains males as husbands and fathers, as natural leaders, with god-ordained rights to rule over wives and children. A favorite quote comes from Ephesians 5:22 "Wives, submit to your husbands as to the Lord." Paul repeated this hierarchy of God-husband-wife, used by conservatives to justify male domination.

Since few people want to be dominated, as women gained more strength in society, resistance to male domination became greater. Men who could not adapt, who refused to treat wives as equals, found themselves the recipients of divorce actions. While there are many causes of divorce, negative male behaviors are the greatest cause of female initiated divorce. Without acknowledging the negative male behaviors that contribute to their being dumped, conservatives created dogma against women's freedom, name-calling women looking for simple human rights: feminists, man-haters, femi-nazi's.

A 1995 report issued by the Institute for American Values (IAV) blames divorce and single motherhood for all society's problems. Right wing, religious conservatives' answer was to use government, social service, and education to force marriage and fatherhood. The report outlines the true agenda of fatherhood and marriage promotion programs which have nothing to do with supporting women's right to live free from male negative behaviors. In fact, this report makes this preposterous claim: *"As Senator Daniel Patrick Moynihan has noted, poverty has historically derived from unemployment and low wages; today (1995) it derives from family structure."*

The belief that marriage is the problem, not poverty, formed the building blocks of welfare programs. The first welfare program that is set-up to be against women is called Marriage Promotion. I do not know how many Americans realize that welfare funds such a thing as promoting marriage, and surely, most Americans don't realize that the intent behind marriage promotion is to keep women subservient to the male. Marriage promotion welfare programs designed by right-wing religious conservatives belittle women's reasons for leaving marriage. The IAV report states *"Marriage has come to be regarded as the problem and not the solution. Marriage, so we are told, **is** restrictive, confining, oppressive, and unliberating. The solution, many of us have come to believe, is the unencumbered life, the life without binding commitments, the life of new beginnings—a life that can often be achieved through divorce."* Leaving a marriage because of abuse is written off as being frivolous and self-indulgent.

In the IAV report conservatives lament the loss of the status quo: *"Divorces that involve children used to be in the category of the shameful, even the unthinkable. One measure of the acceptance of divorce involving children, the proportion of persons who disagree with the statement "when there are children in the family, parents should stay together even if they don't get along' has jumped from 51 % in 1962 to a remarkable 82% as of 1985."* Even as society in general realized the negative effects of abusive marriage on children, these conservatives held firm to their idea of the male-headed household.

The IAV report laments *"the trend toward a divorce culture"* claiming academic research and scholarly discourse on family issues conducted since 1965 (the start of the women's movement), contain a strong anti-marriage bias and that textbooks *"openly propagandize against any privileged cultural status for marriage and quite often even against marriage itself."* Welfare marriage promotion programs are designed to give that missing cultural privilege back to marriage.

Why would welfare be interested in creating a cultural privilege for marriage? Because, as the wordy diatribe of the report states: *"The genius of marriage is that, through it, the society normally holds the biological parents responsible for each other and for their offspring. By identifying children with their parents, and by penalizing people who do not have stable relationships, the social system powerfully motivates individuals to settle into a sexual union and take care of the ensuing offspring."* This thinking resorts back to the God-husband-wife philosophy. God takes care of man, man takes care of wife, and wife takes care of children. Divorce upsets the natural order. Welfare was rewritten to ordain marriage instead of assisting poor, single mothers, demonized as lazy free-loaders!

As the IAV report laments single motherhood, we are informed of the conservative belief that women are no longer looking after these men.

> *"The explosion of nevermarried motherhood in our society means that fathers are increasingly viewed as superfluous, unnecessary, and irrelevant. Remarkably, unwed parenthood has now reached virtual parity with*

divorce as a generator of fatherless homes in the United States.

This growing belief that fathers are superfluous should be a major social concern for our society. First, fathers are vitally important to the task of childrearing. Certainly, we have never met the child who did not say that she or he wanted to be raised by both a father and a mother. And children know whereof they speak. The importance of fathers to childrearing is strongly supported by social science research.

Second, it is extremely important to the larger society that men remain involved in family life. For men, married fatherhood is a civilizing force of no mean proportions. Conversely, having a large number of men disconnected from the patterns and satisfactions of family life—and thus much more prone to unhappiness, deviance, and crime—has always, and properly, been one of society's worst fears. In too many of our nation's communities today, this fear is becoming a reality."

Crime and poverty is blamed on women, not on the male himself. He is absolved of any responsibility for his own negative behavior. Also not acknowledged is the truth that children of abusive and alcoholic fathers would prefer to live alone with a non-abusive, non-alcoholic mother, and they would be better for it.

The IAV report gives clues to how welfare programs will be designed. This 1995 report lists recommendations for every segment of society that have the ability to influence discourse and policy including legislators, media, educators, social workers, health practitioners, community advocates, religious leaders, employers. The devious intent to endorse patriarchy is hidden in the report's recommendations. Family law and judicial recommendations hint at what will become the structural foundation of welfare fatherhood programs.

> *"Family court judges often seem more interested in promoting "divorce counseling" than in promoting marriage counseling. Policymakers in government, impersuaded that anything can or even should be done to reverse the basic trend, settle for half measures aimed at damage control. Instead of Fatherhood, child support. Instead of marriage, divorce reform."*

The only reason for an individual to come in contact with a family court judge is for a divorce. Judges would have no business ordering marriage counseling to people filing for divorce as that decision is made by the wife and/or husband. One could argue that the right to decide to divorce is a liberty guaranteed by the US Constitution. These conservatives are against no-fault divorce and they would like to go back to the days when divorces were denied. Lastly, this quote is important because it admits the intent of the conservatives designing welfare programs was to negate child support, equating increased fatherhood to increased custody. The dollar amount of support, and the parent receiving support, is determined by custody. Claiming child support is a damage control half measure, and by admonishing judges to award fatherhood instead, the IAV report endorses the custody-for-father mandate that became an integral part of Fatherhood Initiatives, Access/Visitation program run out of child support offices.

Another IAV recommendation to judges and lawmakers that confirms the child support custody-for-father mandate states: *"fundamentally reassess the current state-federal child support enforcement program, seeking whenever possible to foster not simply more child support but also more marriage and more fatherhood. Expecting child support payments in the absence of committed fatherhood is an elusive and probably ultimately futile goal.*" This recommendation is how fathers were able to get an entire welfare system to fund them getting custody and create a family court culture that prefers to give fathers custody over mothers!

In the same year, 1995, IAV founder David Blankenhorn authored a book entitled "Fatherless America: Confronting Our Most Urgent Social Problem." In the introduction to his book, Blankenhorn claims that *"men are not ideally suited to responsible fatherhood. Men are inclined to sexual promiscuity and paternal waywardness. Males are increasingly unwilling to invest energy and resources to the care of their offspring. Cultures must devise and enforce the fathers role for men coaxing and guiding them into fatherhood through legal and extralegal pressures. Only an authoritative cultural story of fatherhood can fuse biological and social paternity into coherent male identity."* This view of males should be insulting to monogamous, decent fathers. But, Blankenhorn uses his belief in the inherent unruliness of males to justify government forced fatherhood; awarding custody to fathers regardless of his caretaking history, pattern of abuse against mother and/or children, criminal background, or judicial application to custody law and best interest standards! Ironically, Blankenhorn states males are inherently unfit to parent and then advocates for legally forcing fathers to parent.

I have outlined David Blankenhorn and his group of right-wing, religious ideologues beliefs behind the formation of welfare fatherhood programs. Conservatives have many groups that they use to promote their control of women thinking. You will hear code words "fatherhood" and "family values" emanating from speeches during C-PAC events, in literature disseminated through the Heritage Foundation and Family Research Council, and by candidates working to be endorsed by the mysterious Council for National Policy (CNP). The beauty of these conservatives is how they work together to achieve often hidden agendas. They are good at creating new organizations to promulgate a specific portion of their overall objective: control of women.

National Fatherhood Institute (NFI)

Under the vein of focusing on promoting the importance of fatherhood, David Blankenhorn joined with Wade Horn and created the National Fatherhood Institute (NFI). In keeping with Institute for American Values recommendations, NFI would be a lobbying and networking group for the formation of welfare programs favoring fathers over mothers. NFI would justify these programs through a media campaign geared towards extolling the virtues of fatherhood; how necessary fathers are to children. The Annie E. Casey Foundation has written a comprehensive history of the fatherhood movement (or field); how it developed from conservative ideology to social policy. Like Blankenhorn, NFI is credited with being a major factor to prioritize fatherhood over motherhood and other social poverty-fighting initiatives. *"NFI works directly with policymakers and with communities. NFI organizes conferences, bipartisan congressional task forces, and community fatherhood forums; provides resource materials to organizations seeking to establish support programs for fathers; and conducts research on fatherhood."* "Making Fathers Count: Assessing the Progress of Responsible Fatherhood Efforts" Annie E. Casey Foundation 2002
http://www.aecf.org/KnowledgeCenter/Publications.aspx?pubguid={5931A803-4E1C-421B-844C-65644D6968E6}

Government and privately funded research was created which would obliterate any negative behaviors of fathers. Men no longer drank. Even abusive men were deemed to be good for the children by reports and studies paid for by charitable foundations such as The Annie E. Casey Foundation. In July 1994, The National Center On Fathers and Families (NCOFF) was established at the University of Pennsylvania with core funding from the Annie E. Casey Foundation. Ralph Smith is the founding director. He quickly became a staff of the Casey Foundation, helping divert funds intended for child welfare towards fatherhood promotion. To this day, NCOFF does not include the study of abusive, alcoholic, promiscuous or other negative behaviors of males as part of their fatherhood research. Research highlights only the positive impact of fathers.

Fatherhood foundations, right-wing groups and the Bush Administration were very successful at creating "research" that supports their objectives. The Casey Foundation endowment, which was created to benefit children's welfare, was used to hold conferences and fund reports which would publish research concluding that fathers were necessary for children. Lip service would be paid to "healthy marriages and responsible fatherhood." Fatherhood promoters would claim to be for healthy marriage while ignoring abuse and other negative father behaviors, refusing women's right to protect themselves and their children from abusive men.

Wade Horn testified before Congress in 1999. *"Federal legislation must clearly promote married fatherhood as the ideal."* NFI strongly supports marriage as the most reliable way to promote responsible fatherhood. Casey's historical report "Making Father's Count" confirms, *"NFI's prominence in the fatherhood movement has ensured that the marriage debate remains at the center of fatherhood policy discussions."*

The NFI became so integral to welfare that Wade Horn was appointed by George W. Bush to be the Assistant Secretary for the Association for Families and Children, (ACF), commonly known as welfare. Wade Horn had no experience in administering government funds. Wade Horn had no financial training whatsoever. His training is in psychology. He was a conservative columnist for a newspaper out of Lancaster, Pennsylvania. While he was completely unqualified to command a welfare program, he was perfect to enact the welfare fatherhood agenda in the conservative war against women.

Through his welfare position which he held from 2001-2007, Wade Horn was able to direct welfare money back to NFI in yearly allotments of $500,000 for NFI to then redistribute to local fatherhood groups of its own choosing. NFI was given a six-year contract paying over $2 million a year for a total of $12.5million. During this time, the portion of Temporary Aid to Needy Families (TANF), state welfare block grants, going to fatherhood and marriage promotion programs was increased and encouraged. No longer were food stamps, housing, education, daycare programs that benefited mostly single mothers and children, funding priorities. Rather, money shifted quietly to fatherhood programs run out of prisons and family courts.

Horn resigned his welfare position after disclosure of his kick-backs to NFI and his wife, Claudia Horn. In keeping with the government tradition of the revolving door, Horn now works for Deloitte Consulting where he assists state governments in setting up social service welfare programs. I believe he is encouraging states to divert TANF, MOE, OCSE funds to fatherhood and marriage programs.

The focus on fatherhood has not reduced poverty. Poverty rates have increased since 1998 up to 16%, 20% for children, in 2012. Nor has the focus on marriage and fatherhood decreased federal funding. Dollar amounts of TANF grants have stayed steady. Pennsylvania has received TANF grants in the amount of $719,499,305 since 2006. The premise that Marriage Promotion and Fatherhood Initiative programs would benefit families by making them more financially secure has not panned out.

In contrast to conservative rhetoric, welfare marriage and fatherhood programs were not really designed to alleviate poverty, but, instead were designed to keep women and children in submissive-to-men roles. Analyzing the special interest groups behind the development of fatherhood programs shows the true objective of punishing and controlling women who leave.

BUILDING THE MOVEMENT TO LOWER DAD'S SUPPORT BY INCREASING CUSTODY

Children's Rights Council (CRC)

In addition to conservative ideologues, in order to understand who is invested in welfare programs that favor fathers over mothers, we need only to look at the men who administer, and are members of, the Children's Rights Council (CRC). I found an archived newsletter from the years 1989-92. Three years of this newsletter more than adequately displays the special interests behind the creation of welfare fatherhood programs.

CRC is an umbrella group for Fathers Rights groups. As women left abusive men, they filed for support. Government has an interest in men paying support so that children would not live in poverty. Fathers did not like paying support to women and children they could no longer control. So the men networked and created Fathers Rights groups with names like Daddy Justice, Father4Father, Fathers for Equal Justice. Together, these fathers would cry that support payments were too high and that they were expected to pay without seeing their children. These men coined the term "access" which would become a fatherhood program unto itself. Access is custody! Courts realized that women are usually better fit to care for the children, that they were usually the primary caregiver during the marriage, so in divorce women would receive the greater portion of custody, with men being awarded visitation, usually every other weekend and, sometimes, a few hours during the week.

While the children benefitted from having a stable home, the fathers created a story that they had to give support without having access/visitation. In reality, these middle and higher income men realized that custody and support are intrinsically tied, in direct proportion to each other. The men knew that increasing custody lowered support. The amazing thing is that these men were able to get the government to ignore the motivation of lower support payments when it funded welfare's fatherhood access/visitation program. CRC is the father's rights umbrella group that worked to implement the government program that would favor courts awarding custody to fathers over mothers, lowering father's support obligation, even requiring mother's to pay father's support.

CRC was originally called the National Council for Children's Rights. They built on the conservative wish to reduce divorce, claiming that they want to "reduce divorce by strengthening divorce and custody reform, substituting conciliation and mediation for adversarial approach, assuring a child's access to both parents, and providing equitable child support." As is common in fatherhood programming, these goals contain a lot of double speak and hidden agenda. First, it is impossible to reduce divorce by litigation. An unstated goal of fatherhood is to force the mother back to the abusive father by threatening to take away the children. Abusive men commonly threaten a women that if she leaves they will take the children. Welfare marriage promotion and fatherhood programs help dad achieve this goal by favoring him getting custody over the mother. Many women stay with abusers because they do not want to leave the children with the abuser; they tolerate the abuse in order to protect the children.

CRCs second claim of being for conciliation instead of adversary is a boon to abusive men. Courts use conciliation hearings to threaten battered women and coerce them to give the male abuser his way or else the women losses "access" (custody) of her children. Women are threatened that they will lose custody all together if they do not "submit" to fathers. Courts like to appoint businesspeople, lawyers and mental health practitioners (MHPs) to be the conciliators who charge exorbitant fees for their services. These business people are trained in fatherhood, not abuse, and they are highly motivated by abuse because it keeps business continual. Conciliation makes no acknowledgement that abuse and other negative behaviors like alcoholism, drug addiction and criminal behavior are not good for children, so, in some cases, equal access, or custody is not in the best interests of the child. Conciliation and mediation hearings and conferences are all kept off-the-record. That means, any abuse perpetrated during these events, any threats, or any true conciliation made by the mother, is covered up. CRC and welfare fatherhood programs have been the major impetus to family courts denying due process by substituting conciliation for fair trials based exclusively on evidence, facts and law.

Finally, CRC claims to be for equal access and equitable child support, admitting that they are fundamentally concerned with support payments, since members realize that increased overnight custody decreases support. While a father can be with his children during the day, waking hours, he must have overnight visits in order to receive reduced support. Rather than find ways to have quality time with their children and return them to a stable home in the evenings, these men are concerned with getting court-ordered overnight access/visitation.

To reiterate: claiming to be for the healthy development of children of divorced and separated parents, CRC lists four goals for which I have written their true intent:

1. <u>divorce and custody reform</u> - in actuality, lobbying for forced joint custody and fathers receiving primary custody.
2. <u>conciliation and mediation</u> - in actuality, sessions which permit the abuser to continue his abuse and maintain his control of his subjects: women and children, all off-the-record, outside of court, with no due process protections.
3. <u>access to both parents</u> - in actuality CRC is only concerned with fathers receiving custody, either primary or joint, meaning children have to move between two homes, switching every other day or week, rather than have one primary residence with mother and a father who is actively, positively, involved in their lives.
4. <u>equitable child support</u> - in actuality, reduced support for father, and even, orders for mother to pay father support.

CRC claims to be supported by concerned parents, but it is completely a male-centric organization with the sole goal of ensuring that males prevail in support and custody litigation. A study of three years of CRC's newsletter for the years in which welfare's fatherhood access/visitation program was formed, 1989-1992, proves that CRC was integral to developing a welfare program that helped abusive fathers dominate in family court.

Since the legal standard was "in the best interests of the child" there was no need for divorce and custody reform. Each and every case was different and it was the judges responsibility to determine what was best for the child, based on law and evidence. CRC would use the guise of claiming to be concerned for children to get laws and a welfare program that would give men custody. CRC members would form alliances with conservatives and NFI to claim that the only thing in the best interests of the child was a father! What the welfare fatherhood access/visitation program has achieved for CRC and its members is changing the legal standard to "the best interests of the father" merely by latching on to those who believe that the male should always be head of the household, the sole authority figure, the leader, in control of women and children.

The newsletter makes it clear that CRC members were awarded the original government grants to develop access/visitation programs. Government funded supervised visit centers were owned and operated by members of CRC and not by experts in violence and abuse. This has led to mothers who do not conciliate, often because they want to protect the children, being ordered to supervised visits. When fathers have severe records of physical violence, courts will order supervised visits and over short periods of time, the violent father will be deemed "safe" by the center which is staffed by fatherhood advocates.

When these access/visitation programs were first proposed, women's groups like NOW, went to the congressional hearings and testified that in cases of abuse the father was not in the best interests of the children, and, could even pose a severe threat to women and children. NOW testified that the backers of fatherhood program legislation, Blankenhorn and David Levy (CRC), were "Angry Dads" and pro-abuse, meaning they believed it was a male's right to control women and children. However, any protection for cases of abuse was taken out in committee! House Ways and Means committee staff, Ron Haskins, a CRC Board member, was permitted to obliterate protection for women!

The absence of concern for subjects of abuse is one notable element of the 3 year, 235-pages of CRC newsletters. In the newsletter pages, CRC riles against Joe Biden for sponsoring the Violence Against Women Act. The newsletter supports the idea that women are making-up charges of abuse in order to get custody. These women-hating men propose that all charges of abuse are false. Congress was in the process of passing a resolution which stated that abuse is detrimental to children and should be a factor in custody determinations. Passage would not be law, but merely a statement for States to consider when implementing their own custody laws. But the men who wrote and received the newsletter were furious that Congress should act to protect children from an abusive parent!

Automatic payroll deduction of support payments was another action of Congress proposed during the years the newsletter covers. Once again the men who wrote and read the newsletter were furious. In the past, they could just withhold payment. Payment could be used as a means of financial control, keeping the mother beholden to father. Automatic payroll deductions would negate this powerful tool of the abusive male.

The CRC newsletter lets us see how men were able to manipulate research to support their claim that fathers are tantamount to the best interests formula. One researcher, Judith Wallerstein, originally supported the idea of joint custody. However, as she studied families, she came to the conclusion that shared custody was not always best for the children, and that, in some cases, children were better off with no contact with the abuser. This turn-around due to real research infuriated CRC and its members! For the men, the newsletter lists the right research on pages 51-53, concluding that "it is unacceptable for researchers, for example, Wallerstein, who feel their research is an appropriate basis on which to formulate custody law." Only research that supports giving fathers joint custody is permitted and the men are taught which studies to cite when lobbying. CRC lambasts Frank Furstenberg, another researcher who concluded that fathers were not that important to childhood outcomes.

Battered women were gaining protection in family court. States were passing custody laws that required consideration of abusive behavior and viewed it as a negative. Laws were passed that forbid family law judges from ordering counseling for victims of abuse. Conciliation/mediation becomes very important to the fatherhood agenda of ignoring abuse and claiming that abuse allegations are false. On page 93, the newsletter confirms that the conservative group, ALEC, American Legislative Exchange Council wrote the child access/visitation dispute mediation act, and, working with CRC, sent sample legislation to each state requesting that they institute forced mediation, taking these cases out of the courtroom and into back offices of unqualified, unelected, court-appointed, for-profit businesspersons.

The most abhorrent example of how CRC men ignored abuse, created excuses, and blamed the victim for the abuse is the theory of Parental Alienation Syndrome (PAS) which is covered in greater detail in Chapter 10, The Players and Their Methods, under subheadings Bricklin and PAS. On page 150 of the newsletter we find that Richard Gardner, the creator of this bogus excuse for fathers sexual abuse of children is a presenter at the CRC conference. CRC is a heavy advertiser of his book, The Parental Alienation Syndrome.

Also on page 150 of the newsletter, we find that Jessica Pearson, who founded the Center for Policy Research (CPR), was vital to CRC and its members. CPR generated reports which would help grow the fatherhood custody mandate. I have read many of these reports and they focus solely on telling courts, court administrators and states how to increase father's custody and reduce his support. CPR reports are not financial audits. CPR advises courts to institute legal help for fathers to obtain custody; confirm that fatherhood access money is sent directly to support court; advise courts to implement contempt (fines and jail) against mothers for not allowing father more custody; advise states to supplement their court fatherhood programs with TANF funds; and even, tell states how to collude to increase fathers custody. Recently, Jessica Pearson co-directs the Fatherhood Research and Practice Network (FRPN), another organization developed to get paid to analyze and promote fatherhood programs. Jessica Pearson frequently writes for the AFCC trade association newsletter, Family Court Review.

On page 206 we find that judges are heavily involved with CRC. Judge Kaplan, of Pittsburgh, PA, sat on the Judges panel. Judge Kaplan is invested in several visitation centers in the Pittsburgh area. He was the President of the trade group AFCC (the Association of Family and Conciliation Courts) for the years of 1988-89. He served on the Judicial Advisory Committee of the Office of Child Support Enforcement of the U.S. Dept. of Health and Human Services helping to set-up the custody for fathers program. He advises Pennsylvania legislators on custody and support law. He is a member of Changing the Culture of Custody Committee of the Commission for Justice Initiatives in Pennsylvania, which is a fatherhood plan for giving judicial decision-making authority to mental health practitioners.

Page 224 confirms that a $300,000 grant went to the Father's Rights activist, Dick Woods to implement pro-father programs within the state of Iowa. Many of the initial fatherhood grants went to father's rights groups. In fact, the newsletter encourages them to get this money!

On page 201, we find that killing is not even a reason to admit that some men are just dangerous and violent. In fact, Lott, having shot two lawyers and two judges, is merely a cause for calling for more mediation. CRC believes that having mediation would have resulted in Lott's getting more custody and then he would not have shot anyone!

CRC brags that more judges and lawyers are becoming members. What develops is a friendship with a trade association that will help grow CRC philosophy. In addition to building the government welfare program that would benefit abusive males, CRC would have help from the inside. Members could team up with a trade group which would infiltrate court processes and build on the ideas of conciliation instead of protection from abuse, and increases in father's custody to lower support costs.

PROFITING FROM THE SYSTEM

Association of Family and Conciliation Courts (AFCC)

The Association of Family and Conciliation Courts (AFCC) is the trade association of the forced conciliation/mediation model. As the business of divorce increased, and more parents of underage children divorced, a slew of profiteers developed around the marketplace of family court. The profiteers included lawyers and a wide range of mental health practitioners (MHPs) with vested interests in prolonged litigation. AFCC was created to enhance the opportunity for personal wealth of these government piranhas. AFCC advocates for the handing over of the judges job of legally determining custody based on evidence, fact and law, to the private sector: MHPs. Abdication of judicial duties means judges could pawn off their responsibility to their friends and fellow trade association members. AFCC, with members in every field, could increase business by claiming to be for conciliation.

AFCC members are judges, court administrators, lawyers, mental health practitioners who work as court appointees and affiliates. It is a severe conflict of interest for judges and court administrators to be members along with those who appear before them in a testimonial capacity. Yet, AFCC actually brags on its website that its greatest asset is that its members are able to work collaboratively purportedly to reduce conflict. Unfortunately for abused women, AFCC does not acknowledge that conflict is often fueled by abuse. AFCC and its cohorts, like CRC and its members, prefer to call abuse "high conflict." Rather than identify the male's desire to control as the abuse that it is, AFCC and its members give equal responsibility to the abuser and the prey. AFCC takes the abuse-doesn't-happen claim and implements it at the everyday, courtroom level.

Membership in AFCC is kept hidden. Litigants are not told that judges and court administrators are running "conciliation" courts. AFCC subscribes to the equal parenting model. This permits its members to get positions as parenting coordinators (sometimes called mediators, parent educators, and counselors for purposes of welfare payment). AFCC has grown this unbelievable position, mostly staffed by mental health practitioners such as psychologists, where the court appoints a business person to make parental decisions! Mother and father have to pay for these services which can be charged at hundreds of dollars an hour! Key to this appointment is an abusive relationship being ignored. So when a mother leaves an abusive father, she gets ordered to conciliate, and, because abusers by nature can't conciliate, mother gets ordered to obey a third party parent and pay for the service of being told how to raise her children. Parenting Coordinators (PC) make decisions as trivial as where, when and how a child can get a haircut!

Another court business person appointee advanced by AFCC and its members is the Custody Evaluator (CE). This position has been created by the psychology industry. Psychologists are claiming they are qualified to determine who is a better parent! Instead of having a trial in front of a judge, mothers are ordered to the custody evaluator who will be permitted to decide which parent gets custody, when and how much. These appointees charge exorbitant fees, ranging from several thousand dollars to tens of thousands. Many CEs spend very little time with the children or the parents. The evaluation usually occurs within the MHPs office and not in real world settings like home and school. CEs rely on untested, made-up and inappropriately applied mental health tests to determine who will be awarded custody and how much. They have no training in the law or rules of evidence, the legal basis for ferreting out truth from allegations. They are not trained in domestic violence and especially do not understand the dynamics of coercive control and ambient abuse. Many of the custody evaluators are looking to get jobs as parent coordinators so they award custody to the worse parent in order to continue to "treat" the family.

AFCC members are trained in the fatherhood model of abuse denial because early AFCC members were CRC members. Meyer Elkin was instrumental in founding both CRC and AFCC. Only recently is lip service given to "domestic violence." (See Chapter 10, Abuse.) The effects of abuse on women and children are minimized. The need for protection from abuse and the abuser is ignored. Certainly, prey are not permitted to get away from their abuser. Conciliation courts are in the business of forcing abuser and prey into an unrelenting interaction. Conciliation courts are fatherhood courts!

AFCC and its members use gender neutral terms like "intimate partner violence" and "situational couples violence" preferring to portray the idea that women are as abusive as men, when, in actuality, abuse being control, women's traditional societal role makes them less likely to feel entitled to control as men. Additionally, a higher percentage of narcissists, sociopaths, and psychopaths are male.

Conciliation is not really conciliation. No one appointed by the court is attempting to defuse anger or identify the cause of any anger. It stands to reason that the parent being left would be angry and vengeful. The anger is never treated. The left parent is never counseled to recover and accept that they are being left and that the best thing they could do for themselves and the children is to determine what behaviors of theirs contributed to the breakup.

Often, parents are not even present at court conciliation hearings, which are held merely between judges, lawyers and MHPs. Many conciliation hearings occur at support court; instead of judge's ruling, lawyers called Masters or Hearing Officers preside. Like judges, these court paid lawyers use their positions to order parents to MHPs. They act as another layer of litigation for which parents pay lawyers for representation at mid-level hearings, precursors to judicial hearings or trials. Fees add up quickly, especially because courts schedule several family's for hearings in limited time blocks (morning and afternoon), which results in numerous continuations, meaning you have to come back another day, issues are not resolved quickly. You must pay your lawyer for the time they spend waiting for your turn. If you are lucky, you will be called first.

AFCC members look for specific dynamics that indicate high potential for prolonged litigation and thereby, incredible profits. The highest valued dynamic is an angry, controlling male with high income and assets. The highly abusive male will always contest custody because he needs to remain in control. He will spend profusely on litigation, often, much more than he would ever pay in support. He will be given "wins" in order to keep him signing the check to the lawyer and MHP.

AFCC judicial and court administration member's work to set-up systems within the court that are beneficial to prolonging litigation. AFCC members get themselves appointed to state commissions and taskforces to develop protocols and court rules that will benefit other members such as MHPs and lawyers; all designed to keep the litigation flowing.

Anne Stevenson has worked in Connecticut to research AFCC's influence over the court structure. Anne calls AFCC members "family court industry insiders who are profitability motivated." The goal of MHPs is to get court-ordered therapy, or mediation. To do this, someone needs to be deemed "sick" or made sick through the process of extended litigation. The MHP is looking for billable hours. The MHP is basically in the business of selling-back parenting time. The more you get treated, the more you get parenting time.

Anne discovered that AFCC did not have a corporate license to operate in Connecticut, so it was not paying state taxes. Yet, AFCC was working with Jessica Pearson to get itself appointed as a vendor for designing court operations like case flow management and domestic violence screening procedures.

Anne also discovered that although the MHPs were coming into court and diagnosing children with PAS, when the same MHP submitted health care bills, they used different diagnostic codes like depression, or oppositional defiant because PAS is not a diagnostic code – it is merely a legal maneuver! This is very important: MHPs are going to court and writing reports which they submit as evidence, and testifying that a child has Parental Alienation Syndrome (PAS) and needs to be treated, and then that same MHP changes the diagnosis in order to be paid. They bill with a code for another diagnosis because there is no code for PAS – it is not a diagnosis! It is important to note that many court-appointed MHPs bill at every angle: they have court contract retainers, they bill parents, and they bill health care providers.

AFCC is the group whose members enact the welfare fatherhood access/visitation program. AFCC members are receiving welfare: TANF, MOE, OCSE, and direct grants. In order to increase business, they purposely do not resolve cases. They flag financially well-off abusive men for high conflict mediation services. They use terms like conciliation to supplant their objective of extended litigation and court-ordered mental health services. They work with state legislators and court administrators to get themselves appointed to positions to develop processes that will benefit their objective of extended litigation and court-ordered mental health services. Any parent who stands up to these divorce profiteers will incur the full wrath of a judicial system that has no adherence to any ethical rules or oversight!

AFCC fosters its agenda during yearly conferences and through its newsletter, Family Court Review. A recent sampling of articles included the promotion of fatherhood programs. One article written by Jessica Pearson tells members how to increase custody business within support offices by requiring all parents filing for support orders to obtain a custody order. Another article written by VerSteegh and Davis promotes the importance of classifying abuse, a voluntary assessment recommended by Congress. Chapter 7, Abuse, contains an analysis of this model of classifying abuse as endorsed by author VerSteegh and Davis of BWJP.

The last fatherhood article contained in the April 2015 edition of Family Court Review promotes opportunities for fatherhood program evaluators. This article, "Responsible Fatherhood Programs in the Parents and Children Together (PACT) Evaluation," promotes the opportunity for evaluating fatherhood programs. The article is written by three members of Mathematica, which conducted the only comprehensive analysis of fatherhood programs. The article acknowledges that fatherhood programs had very poor program review. The article acknowledges that the programs are for fathers only. The article acknowledges that fatherhood programs give custody legal assistance and support forgiveness of up to $1,625. The program analysis merely talks to fathers; it does not interview mothers. Fatherhood programs have very low participation rates. In fact, relationship workshops had the lowest rate, only 2-15% went to half of the sessions. The most in-demand program feature is custody assistance. The fathers, many of them felons, claim "She makes it really hard to be a Dad." Mathematica admits they did not talk to the mothers. They admit that many of the men come from dysfunctional families themselves and that they have minimal education; employment opportunities are low-wage, part-time and difficult to find with felony convictions. Yet, they continue to endorse fatherhood as a poverty solution.

AFCC members know where the money comes from. They are fully knowledgeable that TANF, State MOE matching funds, and OCSE money can be siphoned off to court processes and service providers under the fatherhood program. They lobby for the movement of this money and they help legislators and administrators enact fatherhood goals. The plans they help draw up for enactment of court processes rely on the use of government money.

While using welfare funds for the goal of increasing father's custody, AFCC members know that they must keep their agenda under the radar. If all fathers were receiving custody, the public would begin to notice. That is why the preference is to play a game of custody with most cases being awarded an almost equal arrangement, shared custody, with the appointment of mediators and counselors for decision-making, treatment and fostering of continued litigation. Fathers are getting much more custody than they would under the Best Interests of the Child system where abusive behavior is a predominant determinant of parental fitness. Women with a lot of money and connections can do well in custody determinations. But abusers are the most successful since they are very comfortable in the manipulative system that is family court.

Chapter 9

Best Interests of Father

Welfare's fatherhood programs have been very successful at changing family law's legal standard from the best interests of the child to the best interests of father. Of course, no one in the legal community is telling anyone about the new precedent. Welfare programs have successfully reprogrammed the legal and legislative community to believe that <u>all</u> fathers are in the best interests of the child and the only thing that matters to a child is having a father. Judges are trained to put fatherhood above safety, security and stability. If a father files for custody, he will almost certainly receive as much as he wants no matter what his character. Alcoholics, drug addicts, abusers, criminals are preferable parents to mothers!

<u>WHAT ARE WELFARE FATHERHOOD PROGRAMS AND HOW ARE THEY FUNDED?</u>

<u>Fatherhood programs are built on the premise that single motherhood is the root of society's ills.</u>
From a Congressional Research Service (CRS) report titled "Fatherhood Initiatives: Connecting Fathers to Their Children" written by Carmen Solomon-Fears, dated October 22, 2013, we

learn:

> "Research indicates that children raised in single parent families are more likely than children raised in two parent families (with both biological parents) to do poorly in school, have emotional and behavioral problems, become teenage parents, and have high poverty-level incomes. In hopes of improving the long-term outlook for children in single-parent families, federal, state, and local governments, along with public and private organizations are supporting programs and activities that promote the financial and personal responsibility of noncustodial fathers to their children and increase the participation of fathers in the lives of their children. These programs have come to be known as Responsible Fatherhood programs."

Fatherhood programs are supposed to be an answer to poverty and poverty outcomes. Growing up in extreme poverty creates problems for children. They live in dirty, dangerous, depressed neighborhoods. In the inner cities, these neighborhoods have high crime rates, buildings are abandoned, falling apart, unsafe and blighted. Streets are dirty and trash strewn. Green space, parks and trees, are non-existent. The air and water are polluted. These neighborhoods have long histories of offering very poor education and minimal jobs. Drug use is prevalent. Opportunity for self-improvement is non-existent. The simple task of getting around, to work, school, can be a dangerous daily obstacle. None of these factors contribute to crime rates, behavior problems, emotional problems, generational early childbirth and persistent, family poverty. Fatherlessness is the problem and having a father is deemed to be the cure!

Fatherhood programs have four prototypes.

Custody is an important ingredient in each prototype with a lot of program agenda overlap and inclusion of marriage promotion goals. By operating these programs for over twenty years, the fatherhood movement has successfully created a court culture that believes fathers are more desirable as parents and that fathers are the only factor to consider when assessing the best interests of the child. Conversely, men are taught that they should fight for custody because they are the most important factor for their children's proper development. Fatherhood programs give men free legal assistance to reduce support owed and increase custody. They teach men that the best way to reduce support is to increase custody. They teach dads that they can receive the majority of custody, and then become eligible for housing subsidies, food stamps, and even support payments from mom. Mothers who have been the child's full-time caregiver are suddenly demonized when dad decides to pursue custody. Court service providers, called mediators, parenting educators, and co-parenting coordinators, are paid to force mothers to conciliate, essentially: give in to dads' demands. Mothers are not permitted to think father's actions are bad for the children. If mother does not agree to give dad authority, court appointees help dad claim mom is the abuser and she should have her custody severely reduced, monitored (supervised visits) and even, eliminated.

Fatherhood programs measure his parenting skills and knowledge not by actual observation, but by questions, sometimes only by telephone interviews, asked at the beginning and end of the program. Long-term results are not reviewed; fathers are not assessed a year or longer after completion of a program. Whether a father indeed proves to be the best parent, is not quantified. Access/visitation fathers, who are wealthier, do not have to attend fatherhood classes, instead, court appointees are assigned to automatically assume father is the best parent, or, at minimum, equal to mom, even a stay-at-home mother, who single-handedly managed all child care duties before entering family court.

Prototype One – Fragile Families

While offered to higher income, white males, this program category primarily targets low income, unmarried, minority males. The family is deemed "fragile" because they are unmarried, young and low-income. Single mothers who apply for welfare benefits are required to disclose paternity and file for support payments. Mothers who disclose paternity will become involved in support and custody litigation with the identified father. Because of his lack of income potential, support arrears accumulate. Fragile family prototype programs help the father pay support through several methods, including by filing a court action for increased custody. Two program subsets exist.

The largest subset applies to men already paying support. Men are recruited from the support office or directed to a program by a judge because they have support debt accrued, what is called "arrears." Welfare program reports refer to this population as Title IV-D which is the child support population. Most of these low-income fathers do not retain lawyers. They are offered custody services directly by support office personnel and/or by the fatherhood program. Many courts offer simplified forms to get litigation started.

From the HHS report "Catalog of Research: Programs for Low-Income Fathers," written by Mathematica Policy Research, December 2011, we learn many of these programs offer a deferment, charge-off, and modification of support for participation. The majority of programs reviewed by Mathematica admit they provide legal services for support and custody, since increasing custody is a guaranteed way to decrease support obligation. A few programs try to solve the problem of father's failure to pay support by referral to state run job placement services. In a review of 76 programs, only one offered training and education (HVAC for instance) which would result in fathers obtaining a higher income. When programs concluded the majority of fathers remained unemployed or employed in minimum wage level jobs. Illiteracy, drug abuse and unwillingness to work are mentioned as barriers to successful job placement. Fathers receive cash stipends, gift cards, bus tokens, dinner, tickets to sporting events and other incentives to participate.

Samples of this model of program include:

- "Partners for Fragile Families," operated in 13 cities: Baltimore, MD (2 sites); Boston, MA (2); Denver, CO; Indianapolis, IN; Los Angeles (3); Minneapolis, MN; New York City, NY; Wisconsin; and, West Chester; PA. Programs provide fatherhood curriculum, in this case developed by the National Partnership for Community Leadership (NPCL). Each father was given a case manager who would provide assistance with resolving visitation issues and obtaining legal representation.
- The "Devoted Dads" Project in Tacoma, WA, contracted with a private attorney to conduct monthly evening workshops on custody, visitation and child support. Individual assistance on custody, referrals to legal aid and mediation, was given by the contract attorney and the paralegal staff. Staff helped clients apply for suspensions of child support obligations while enrolled in the program.
- "Strengthening Families Through Stronger Fathers Initiative (SFSFI)," authorized by New York State Legislator in 2006; included GED preparation, financial management skills, mental health and substance abuse counseling, legal assistance, and housing assistance. Most programs also

provided assistance in arranging visitation for participants to have contact with their children. Most of the sites offered incentives to promote retention, including cash for work-related supports; stipends; and transportation, legal, and child support assistance.

- "Texas Fragile Families Initiative (TFF)," Project Bootstrap, offered at four of the eleven sites, gave men a $1,325 support credit. Other services used include: help with visitation and custody orders (23/33%); legal assistance (18%); housing (18%); primary and secondary education (15/27%); money management/budgeting (27%); child care (13%); health services (13%); housing assistance (16%); anger management (13%); substance abuse treatment/counseling (7%); mental health treatment/counseling (6%); child abuse (4%); partner abuse (3%).
- The" Young Unwed Fathers Pilot Project" aimed to help young fathers, ages 16 to 25, achieve self-sufficiency and fulfill their parental responsibilities. It was offered at six sites across the country: Cleveland, Ohio; Racine, Wisconsin; Fresno, California; St. Petersburg, Florida; Annapolis, Maryland; and Philadelphia, Pennsylvania. Participants received counseling and other ongoing support regarding family law provided through workshops led by staff or volunteer lawyers. This program review included an analysis of cost per participant: Wisconsin: $4,130; California: $4,896; and, Ohio: $5,040.
- "Colorado Parenting Time/Visitation Project" assigned staff, called a Child Access Specialist (CAS) to provide custody services, including mediation, to fathers who wanted more custody. Fathers received contact

information for parenting classes, mediation services, and forms and instructions for litigation along with a courthouse help desk to prepare and file for custody and support modification. Fifty-three percent of the low-level treatment group reported using mediation to increase custody.
- The "Maryland Responsible Fatherhood Project (RFP)" assisted with employment, child support, custody and parenting. Court fees were waived for fathers filing for custody and support modification. Dads were given McDonalds gift certificates, bus tokens and money for participating.

The second subset of fragile families aims to connect with fathers early, during moms prenatal visits or head start programs. Mothers are encouraged to identify and bring father to doctor visits and children's school. Fathers are recruited to participate and given gifts like books, baby clothes and retail gift cards. They are taught how to nurture, rock and soothe the baby, how to read to a child, and how to play. Examples are The Nurturing Father's Program with sites in Florida, Washington, Ohio, Virginia and New York, and The New Mexico Young Fathers Project.

In addition to receiving services, men are required to attend fatherhood sessions. There are usually 8 to 12 one-hour sessions on a variety of topics such as the importance of fathers; being a man, discipline, parenting, and spirituality. The men are asked questions before and after the sessions to measure learning, as if proper behavior comes from having the right answers and can be "taught" in one-hour sessions. These classes are like sunday school for dads! In addition to spirituality, NFI's program, "24/7 Dad" teaches "generally research shows that men who are married live fuller, happier lives than men who are unmarried."

Fatherhood promoters like NFI and NPCL receive payment for their program materials; they are the majority benefactor of these programs.

Prototype Two - Incarcerated Fathers

This prototype has become a common prison offering since the prison population consists of large numbers of fathers of young children. Even though many prisoners are illiterate and never graduated high school, federal funding for education of prisoners was eliminated during the 1990's and replaced with fatherhood programming. Instead of being taught reading and job skills, fathers are given reduced sentences for attending fatherhood classes. Upon release they are eligible for reintegration services, another term for custody. Public defenders and parole offices may include fatherhood custody units.

Promoting custody for criminal fathers has fostered the shift towards a family court culture of preference for fathers. If a criminal dad receives custody, surely a working, non-felonious father deserves it!

Mathematica's Catalog of Research: Programs for Low Income fathers assesses prison fatherhood programs. Examples include:

- "Missouri's Strengthening Families and Fatherhood: Children of Fathers in the Criminal Justice System Project" (known as Fathers for Life) identified incarcerated dads whose children attended head start, offered a fatherhood curriculum such as 24/7 Dad, and case management which included mediation to increase access/visitation and employment services.
- "InsideOut Dad," a fatherhood curriculum designed by the National Fatherhood Initiative (NFI), to improve dads

parenting skills and increase their contact with their child, includes a session on spirituality which, given NFI's evangelical leanings, could be interpreted as an opportunity for religious conversion. Programs operated in New Jersey, Maryland, and Ohio. Long Distance Dads (LDD) is the Pennsylvania adaptation of this program.
- "The Family Reintegration Project," TX, offered inmates and parolees help with child support, family reintegration (another term for custody), and employment.
- "Father Reintegration Project" operated in Illinois, offered fathers on work release help reducing support orders, and custody services.
- "Fathers in the Criminal Justice System" operated in Massachusetts, helped dads reduce their support, admitting that the amount owed did not increase upon release.

Prototype Three: Marriage Promotion/Fatherhood

Why marriage promotion? According to Wade Horn *"encouraging married two-parent families is the surest way to ensure that fathers are engaged in raising children."* Fatherhood programs are permitted to have a marriage promotion component, yet marriage promotion has a separate funding source, even though these programs work in conjunction.

From Annie Casey Foundation's "Making Father's Count" historical report, we learn that according to (David) Blankenhorn, one possible public policy strategy (to encourage marriage), is an early intervention plan for new parents. If the early data from the Fragile Families and Child Wellbeing Study proves correct—that for many parenting couples, fathers are present at birth, the parents are romantically involved, and at least one partner really wants to get married—he asks: *"What if these families could be connected to supports in the community—like churches or other organizations—that could help them realize their goal of getting married? Currently no one is helping them do that or encouraging them that it's the right thing to do or referring them to services."*

Low-income girls are having sex with low-income boys and getting pregnant. Some girls foolishly think he will marry them; that they can use the child to get the man. The boys are not interested in marriage, getting a good job, providing. Boys have boyish behavior traits. They do drugs and think crime is an answer to money problems. They eventually wind up in jail.

Marriage Promotion works heavily with the prison fatherhood population through public defenders and probation offices. It is estimated that half of the men in prison are fathers. They are offered early release if they get married and complete fatherhood training. Get out of jail early is a great incentive for these men to marry! While they are incarcerated, they take classes on child development, getting along with mothers, etc. They may be able to serve time at a special facility, like a halfway house, where conditions are preferable to county jails and state prisons. Moms can be ordered to take the children on prison visits.

For mothers who do not want to marry the criminal father, dads are taught and helped to immediately file a custody action upon release no matter what their level of violence, drug abuse or criminal activity. These ex-cons are now being called "returning citizens" in order to soften the stigma and create an impression of good moral character. The returning fathers can easily win custody even when mother has been the long-time primary parent.

The fatherhood movement has made criminal fathers more important for a child than an upstanding, law abiding mother!

Prototype Four – Access/Visitation

The largest prototype, access/visitation is solely designed to give fathers custody. Simply put: Access/visitation is a program to take children from their mothers and give them to dads using litigation and judicially ordered court service providers.

Access/visitation runs out of court administration in conjunction with the support office (sometimes called Domestic Relations). Because of its hidden agenda, like abusers, it is subtle and insidious by nature. Legal and mental health practitioners (MHPs) are paid to become involved in litigation for the benefit of fathers. Upper-income fathers profit the most from this program as it is designed to proportionally reduce support obligation by increasing custody (visitation). Wealthier fathers get to these services through lawyers who arrange for the court to mandate fatherhood court service providers for evaluations, mediation, counseling, to deny abuse and pathologize mother. Fatherhood court service providers operate under contracts with administration and domestic relations court not disclosed to mothers, who attend these sessions unaware of the fatherhood custody mandate. Using these practitioners, dads, lawyers, MHPs, judges and court administrators are easily rigging custody cases. Welfare subsidized service providers force mothers and children to live under the continual coercive control of fathers; mothers who resist will be eliminated; children are made motherless.

The CRS report "Fatherhood Initiatives: Connecting Fathers to Their Children" written by Carmen Solomon-Fears, dated October 22, 2013, confirms the Child Access and Visitation program funded the following activities in fiscal year 2008:

- <u>Mediation</u> – this could be a lawyer or MHP appointed by the court to be the family decision-maker; could be called a co-parenting coordinator or educator. Mathematica's report states "mediation may help parents reconsider separating" an example of one way fatherhood programs work with marriage promotion programs.

- Counselling – an MHP, usually psychologist or social worker, appointed by court again to act as family decision-maker or to "treat" claims of abuse by mother and children (for instance: PAS). A counselor could also act as a co-parenting coordinator/educator.
- Parental education – some courts order specific programs like "Children in the Middle" a film developed by the trade association, AFCC; MHPs acting as co-parenting decision-maker also bill under this "education" line item.
- Development of parenting plans – these are custody orders, when each parent gets the child, usually enacted by legal professionals, but could be officiated by MHPs. The DV community is currently attempting to get paid as experts and classifiers under the parenting plan banner.
- Visitation enforcement – enacted by legal professionals, lawyers, judges and court administrators in court actions. Contempt proceedings that could result in fines, jailing and elimination of mother.
- Monitored visitation, neutral drop-off and pickup, supervised visitation – claimed to be a protection against violent fathers. For instance, when a court recognizes that a mother has been severely beaten by father, neutral drop-off, like a local police station, would be assigned. If the court recognizes a history of father's beating of the child, a monitored or supervised visit is ordered, father is quickly cured and deemed safe for unsupervised visits. In actuality, mothers are the ones being ordered to supervised visits because they have resisted fathers

abuse, the court labels PAS or another made-up danger to the child (see Chapter 3: The Vagina Claim), and the only way she can see her children is supervised visits which she is ordered to pay for.
- <u>Development of guidelines for visitation and custody</u> – these are custody orders enacted by legal professionals, could be in conjunction with MHPs, similar to parenting plans, just another name. Could fund administrative commissions or employees tasked with developing court protocol such as Pennsylvania's Changing the Culture of Custody plan.

The congressional report tells us some other facts about fatherhood access\visitation programs:
- In FY 2008 about 85,000 individuals received services. This is an enormous number of contested custody cases being funded by welfare!
- The most common services were parent education, mediation, parenting plans and supervised visits. Individuals were referred to services by the courts, child support enforcement or welfare agencies.
- Services were both mandatory and voluntary, as determined by the State. In truth, services are mandatory for mothers, which means a judge orders you to go to them or face contempt – jail and/or money fines. Father's want these services as they help them coercively control the family.

The access/visitation program is most heavily used by high income fathers hooked-up by their lawyers who work with support and family court officials to get orders to fatherhood practitioners who will operate under a pro-abuse, pro-father mandate. These are massively litigated cases that continue until the mother is completely eliminated, runs out of money (highly likely because the high-income father can outspend on lawyers and other services), or until the children turn 18.

An Access/Visitation Jurisdictional Profile report confirms that this is a father-only custody program: *"In FY 2005, approximately 32,174 fathers received access and visitation services, 21,874 got more custody."* This report confirms that States contract with court service providers for delivery of custody services. The MHPs and lawyers are being paid at every angle: first, by a court contract, second by the parents, and/or by parents' health insurance. Nobody knows that payment for the same service is coming from several sources. For instance, Dr. Ring would charge mother and father a full rate for counseling for the same session, automatically billing two separate health carriers in addition to receiving a retainer from the County Domestic Relations office, without disclosing that he receives a retainer for providing fatherhood services.

These fathers are not having access/visitation problems. They are being divorced, often because they are abusive. Many get immediate orders giving them custody every other weekend and a day during the week. Because his salary is traditionally higher than the mothers (often mom stayed-at-home), he is expected to pay support. Because he is abusive, he doesn't want to give money to mom without being able to control everyone so he pursues full custody.

Access\visitation funds are training judges that women's claims of domestic violence are merely false allegations and to forbid proof of abuse (physical, emotional, sexual) of mother and children into the court record. Court employees are told that women file PFAs in order to gain the advantage, in order to retain the home and primary custody. Court employees are not trained that abuse increases when she attempts to leave and, in fact, this is the most dangerous time for mothers. Access\visitation funds promote the bogus theory of Parental Alienation Syndrome (PAS) which is used against mothers who leave incestuous fathers. These mothers, who have merely tried to stop the sexual abuse of their children, are ordered to supervised visitation; they have to permit fathers incest in order to see their children!

Access/visitation programs that create corrupt litigation are highly successful in court jurisdictions that operate "The Ferguson Model" that is, where wealthy, privileged, power-elite prey and profit from the underclass. Fathers, lawyers, mental health practitioners, court appointees, and judges are the haves. Mothers and children are the have-nots. The haves must deplete all resources from mothers (and family and friends who contribute to the litigation struggle) in order that they may continue to have; the system works only for those at the top.

Added after 1st printing - the most egregious proof of the intentional ignoring of all forms of abuse in order to forcibly increase custody is the the federal reporting form entitled "State Child Access Program Survey: Guidance (AV Guidance)." This form confirms that states are keeping records of family court cases affected by the intentional custody mandate. Page 4, "Counseling" confirms mental health practitioners ignore (not focus on) abuse including sexual abuse of children, domestic violence, battering, anger, alcoholism and drug addiction in order to increase custody for the non-custodial parent who is usually the father. This mandate is never disclosed to litigants. I know of no lawyer who has disclosed the mandate of the program to litigants. Counseling services are mandated and counselors use other positions of appointment to get themselves these counseling assignments..

Page 6 of the Guidance form, Visitation Compliance

Monitoring, confirms Parenting Coordinators are appointed to positions of high-priced decision-maker for the family. AV contract permits PAS, a nefarious therapy which blames abuse on the victims.

Chapter 10, "Players and Their Methods," further describes how court appointees use their services to act on behalf of abusive fathers. The connection between support and custody is covered below, under Funding, Office of Child Support Enforcement.

Case Profiles (names have been changed)

Chloe & Dale have two sons. When the boys are three and four, they show signs of anal penetration, tearing and bleeding. They act sexualized. Children and Youth are called and they take the boys from Chloe & Dale for several months while they investigate. C & Y determines that Dale, the father, has sexually abused his sons. After a juvenile court hearing, Chloe is given full custody of her sons. They move to another State where the boys begin to recover. Dale is listed as a sexual predator. Dale hires a lawyer, who appeals the sexual predator listing, not to a higher court, but to a lateral court; the case is in Schuykill County, Pennsylvania; Dale appeals to Berks County, PA. Dale's attorney argues that he should not be listed as a sexual predator, not the findings of fact, or the ruling that he sexually molested his children. Berks rules in Dale's favor. Dale returns to Schuykill County and files an emergency custody petition. After two years of safety, Chloe receives by mail, an order that she must return the boys to Schuykill County immediately so that full custody can be given to Dale or face imprisonment. Chloe has a new relationship and has just given birth to a daughter. At the hearing, the boys are given to their father. Chloe is given no visitation and told she must file for a new custody hearing. It takes a full year for a new hearing to occur. During the hearing the court refuses to consider, or permit into evidence, the previous finding of sexual abuse by father. Dale is given full custody with no visitation by mother. Chloe appeals to the PA Superior Court, who rule that the lower court did not have to consider previous findings of sexual abuse. To this day, the boys remain in the full custody of their abusive father.

Ann & Hank are not married and have a son who since birth lives with Ann and two older siblings who have a different father. Hank has a history of drug abuse and violence. Hank lives with his mother in a Section 8 apartment. Ann does not want to marry Hank. She prefers Hank be involved with his son only when he is clean, not on drugs. Hank's mother is disgruntled because the child resides with Ann, so she calls Children and Youth. C & Y counsel Hank to file for custody so he can receive welfare payments and Section 8 housing. Hank tells Ann to give him custody so that he may receive these promised government services. The court orders shared custody. For two years Ann & Hank split the child, Monday to Wednesday, Thursday to Sunday, alternating weeks. Hank still takes drugs, Ann tells the court that splitting the child is not appropriate, the child is confused and suffering. Ann refuses to permit a custody evaluation because she felt the evaluator was "nuts." So Children and Youth return (they are more and more frequently being used successfully by fathers as a method of making false claims) and claim Ann gave her son drugs, without taking a blood test, having no proof. Ann and siblings are eliminated. Hank collects welfare under fatherhood rules. His mother dies and he resides permanently in her low-income apartment. His son is told Ann is dead just like Grandma.

Eve got pregnant right out of high school by Bob who had already fathered a daughter whom he was not providing for. Eve signs up for welfare and receives cash assistance, food stamps, housing (Section 8), and financial aid for community college training in medical billing. After five years together, with Bob not reporting that he lives with Eve, and still no marriage, Eve gets pregnant again. Two months before the birth of the second child, Bob is arrested for stealing razor blades from high-end grocery stores. He and his friends would drive hundreds of miles to rob Wegmans by putting razors into Igloo coolers and leaving, having paid only for the coolers. This is Bob's second offense, he has already served time for stealing from Walmart's stockroom, putting items into friends cars and selling the goods on-line. Bob is 32 years old. Because 25 year-old Eve is willing to marry, Bob is offered the fatherhood option for early release. After six months in prison, he is sent to the fatherhood halfway program and is released after the infants first birthday. Eve & Bob marry in several months. Eve collects welfare and does not work while Bob is in prison. Eve refuses to work a 40 hour week, holding to the 20 hour welfare requirement, working part-time at the hospital as a filing clerk. A full-time job would provide medical benefits for the family and would double her salary, but she writes on facebook that she wants to be a mom and does not feel that either her or Bob should have to work full-time since she wants him to have time to play softball and go to the gym and spend with his kids. The children get early intervention and free health insurance from the State. Eve and Bob still receive Section 8 and other welfare subsidies. Bob works part-time, low pay jobs, because he will not work with his father who has a construction business, he will not work a factory job which are abundant locally, he posts on facebook, he would "rather punch a face than a time clock."

After the prison release Eve & Bob attend the Family Center where they are given free and reduced tickets to amusement parks, museums, zoos, and other subsidies for family activities.

Even though Eve & Bob could make a livable wage if they would work full-time, they prefer to live a welfare-subsidized lifestyle, with the difference being the subsidies are fatherhood provided. The children are still observing a "living-off-the-system" lifestyle. Four years into the marriage, Bob moves out because he is having sex with another teenager.

FUNDING
Fatherhood is Funded by Federal Welfare State Block Grants, TANF, MOE, OCSE & Social Services Block Grants

CRS Report "Fatherhood Initiatives: Connecting Fathers to Their Children" explains the myriad of funding sources for forcing fatherhood (excerpts from this CRS report are italicized and indented from hereon).

> *"Sources of federal funding for fatherhood programs include the Temporary Assistance for Needy Families (TANF) programs, TANF state Maintenance of Effort (MOE) funding, Child Support Enforcement (CSE) funds and Social Services Block Grant (Title XX) funds."*

Fatherhood money comes from many sources. The true amount is hidden. States do not disclose what percentage of TANF, MOE, and OCSE budgets are targeted to fatherhood programs. Fatherhood programs have no accountability. Payments to court service providers are not recorded. They are not audited for proper use of funds because their mandate is already the improper use of government money to force marriage and, if women refuse marriage, rig custody cases for father. An October, 2002, HHS Office of Inspector General audit called "Effectiveness of Access and Visitation Grant Programs" was conducted solely to confirm that fatherhood programs increased fathers custody with the aid of mediators. Not mentioned in this audit is the mathematical truth that increasing father's custody, decreases mother's custody.

Grants

Fatherhood as sold to Congress for government funding, had two objectives: First, to get women, single mothers, off of welfare, by making fathers responsible for the children. Fathers would have jobs, bring home the bacon, become the "Provider" for mom and kids. Since welfare mothers were not married to the child's father, grants would be given to encourage marriage. That would automatically raise the new family out of poverty and get them off welfare. If mothers did not marry, fathers would be given primary custody, and welfare supports like subsidized housing, food stamps, early intervention, would go to dad. Children would turn out better because of this shift in parenting from moms to dads. Punishing moms would force them to get, or stay, married. Government forcing of husbands and dads would give women and children "personal responsibility."

The second objective came about as a backlash to support laws that required automatic payroll deductions. Men claimed they did not pay support because mothers were not letting them see the children. Therefore, Congress would fund programs that gave men custody, called access/visitation. Grants were given to religious groups that would encourage marriage. Grants were given to fatherhood groups that organized to get dads custody. Grants were given to fatherhood groups that opened supervised visit and mediation centers under the premise that violent men could be reformed, and that there should be forced visits between the child and the abusive father in a supervised setting. Grants would be given to mental health practitioners to mediate custody for divorcing or never-married parents; forcing women to capitulate to father.

The federal government is currently giving $75million for Fatherhood Initiatives and $75 million for Marriage Promotion programs yearly through ACF grants. Fatherhood and Marriage Promotion programs often work in conjunction because the ultimate program goal is forced marriage, what government calls "formation of 2 parent families." Fatherhood programs are designed to punish mothers who refuse marriage by giving dad control of the kids through custody orders that limit mother's time and ability to parent. These grants are given directly to state courts, to fatherhood groups who meet and give workshops on parenting and how to get custody, religious organizations that teach marriage skills, and psychological organizations that offer counseling for non-married parents. Grant recipients are not required to be knowledgeable about abuse and how it plays out in a family environment.

TANF & MOE

The Department of Health and Human Services (HHS) has not widely publicized the fact that it has permitted the diversion of funding from direct poverty alleviation to non-assistance programs of marriage promotion and fatherhood, jointly accounted for under the category of "formation of 2 parent families." Over twenty years, States have increasingly moved TANF grants and state matching funds (MOE) towards fatherhood custody programs.

> ."According to HHS about half of all States use some TANF funds for fatherhood programs. TANF received $16.5 billion in 2013 with 75% matched by States for an additional $10.4 billion annually."

The amount of TANF and state matching funds (MOE) dedicated to formation of 2 parent families (fatherhood and marriage) has increased, more than doubling from a total of $119 million in 2001 to a high of $306 million in 2009, to $283 million in 2012.

2001	TANF & MOE combined	$ 119,071,832
2005	TANF & MOE combined	$ 144,802,587
2008	TANF & MOE combined	$ 188,499,683
2009	TANF & MOE combined	$ 305,884,782
2010	TANF & MOE combined	$ 293,469,520
2011	TANF & MOE combined	$ 299,885,407
2012	TANF & MOE combined	$ 282,936,196

While most states diverted less than $10 million, several states diverted extremely large amounts to fatherhood. In 2012, states with high levels include: Connecticut ($22,926,619); Georgia ($12,382,614); Maryland ($35,760,351); Michigan ($27,939,513); Virginia ($48,438,723); Wisconsin ($12,948,772); and, the highest, Louisiana ($99,026,204).

Office of Child Support Enforcement (OCSE)

Fatherhood access/visitation has become an implicit goal of OCSE programs. Twenty years of government funding of fatherhood access/visitation has resulted in OCSE normalizing the promotion and preference of custody to fathers over mothers. Since fatherhood programs are aimed at reducing fathers support obligation by increasing custody, states are permitted to use large portions of Child Support Enforcement funds for payment of fatherhood practitioners; mental health and legal professionals who act to increase dads custody and punish mothers and children who do not bow down to dads authority.

Inclusion of the fatherhood access/visitation mandate in Child Support administration was pure genius for the fatherhood movement! Paying practitioners to become involved in custody litigation with support office funds facilitated the sabotage of state custody laws which offered the protection from abuse that women had won: laws that required courts to consider abusive behavior as detrimental when determining custody; laws that forbid orders to attend counseling with your abuser; laws that put children's needs above parents desires. The OCSE access/visitation mandate obliterated due process: all those involved in custody litigation were required to create false evidence and hide true evidence of father's unfitness to parent. Simple professional ethical standards have to be purposely disregarded in order to increase father's custody. The OCSE access/visitation mandate has grown a family court industry that thrives on abuse!

OCSE's first duty is that of a collection agency operating at the state level to collect and distribute child support payments. While most support is taken directly from payroll deductions, support can also be mailed to state processing offices and walk-in payments are taken at each jurisdictional child support office. However, Child Support offices, often called Domestic Relations, operate as an arm of family court. Child Support offices write court orders for custody and support at office conferences and mid-level hearings. Lawyers are paid to be Masters or Hearing Officers, to make legally binding support and custody determinations. Lawyers employed by support offices write judicial orders and claim judicial immunity from lawsuit. Office clerks and masters order parents to mental health practitioners for custody evaluations, co-parenting, mediation, or other court services. Clerks and lawyers assign lawyers for the children (GALs). These court service providers often act under fatherhood contracts and receive payment from the support office for the purpose of increasing father's access/visitation (custody).

Two reports affirm that support offices operate the fatherhood custody program. Congressional Research Service

Report RS22380, *"Child Support Enforcement: Program Basics,"* by Carmen Solomon-Fears, confirms that although historically, visitation and child support were legally separate, *"in recognition of the negative long-term consequences for children associated with the absence of their father,"* welfare reform legislation provided $10 million/year for grants to states to develop access/visitation programs (custody) which would include mediation, counseling, education, and supervised visitation. These grants have been funding program expansion as featured in the HHS report "A Collaboration and Strategic Planning Guide for States: Child Access and Visitation Programs." States are told to convene judges, court administration, support office administrators, lawyers, mental health practitioners, father's rights groups, domestic violence groups, to work collusively to increase father's custody. Support officers are told to inform fathers who complain about paying support that filing for custody will reduce their support. Divorcing parents are ordered to mediators and other counselors who encourage fatherhood over protection from abuse. States are encouraged to hire consultants (such as AFCC trade association) to form commissions to write and implement the plan (Pennsylvania's commission created "Changing the Culture of Custody in Pennsylvania"). States are encouraged to find other sources for funding such as DOJ grants for visitation centers, and legislative implementation of state fees (for example on traffic tickets, marriage licenses, sin taxes) for court-ordered services.

Annie E. Casey Foundation's "Making Fathers Count" history of the fatherhood movement, lists "Broadening The Mission of Child Support Policy" as an accomplishment.

> *"It was not until the passage of the Personal Responsibility and Work Opportunity Reconciliation Act (PRWORA) in 1996, which overhauled the welfare system,*

that federal efforts aimed at fathers broadened to include several new goals: helping low-income fathers develop the tools they need to find jobs, become better parents, and improve their relationships with their children's mothers.

Judge David Gray Ross served as OCSE commissioner for the duration of the Clinton administration was responsible for implementing much of this shift. "Before I came," he says, "this office was just not a father-friendly place. The mission was to collect child support. Now, it's more to provide for financial and emotional support of children."

Ross drew on his experiences as a circuit court judge from Prince George's County, Maryland. From Ross's point of view, it was important not only to identify fathers and explain their responsibilities for their children, but also to tell them about their rights to see their children—and to help ensure those rights."

Judge David Gray Ross has helped the fatherhood movement so much that the National Partnership for Community Leadership (NPCL) dedicates an annual award in his name, given at their yearly fatherhood conference.

There is no income requirement for fatherhood access/visitation; fathers with average and above average incomes benefit from OCSE custody help, as much as low-income fathers.

The Office of Child Support Enforcement began in 1975 as a vehicle for states to recover welfare payments made to mothers and children by collecting support from fathers who did not live with them. States are permitted to keep support money collected on behalf of welfare recipients. This money does not go back to welfare, it goes to support administration or state general budgets. The federal government reimburses states at 66% of support office administration costs.

In 1979, the federal government paid $117,610,123 to operate child support offices. States made $672,352,454 (welfare payback over administration costs). Due to its 66% reimbursement to states for their costs of administration, federal contributions steadily increased while state profits stayed relatively stable. In 1997, when custody was included in support administration, the federal government was paying $1,707,946,256 in cost reimbursement. States still profited $657,819,774. Ironically, since support administration started paying for mental health practitioners and lawyers to become involved in custody litigation, profits have steadily decreased, quickly becoming a liability for most states. In 1999, overall state support profits were only $112,431,735. The following year, 2000, states lost $47,031,803; in 2001, states lost $225,335,921; in 2002, states lost $418,618,129. By 2009, the federal government was paying $2,942,262,883 (Table 3) and states were losing $718,262,504 on support court administration. While some loss can be blamed on welfare work requirements which decreased cash assistance, the growth of administrative costs can surely be attributed to increased litigation within the support office.

In addition to the federal 66% administration reimbursement, states receive incentive payments for meeting OCSE requirements. While incentive payments are based on six measures, including amount of support collected over amount owed, the CRS report admits the bottom line is *"States that collect large amounts of support receive the largest incentive payment."* Since the welfare rolls decreased, accounting for less than 10% of the support population, 95% of States now lose money on child support administration. For instance, in 2009, Texas received

$202,012,482 in a 66% match, $53,403,514 in incentive payments, it kept $24,448,538 from welfare recovery, yet it spent $286,966,470 to administer its support program. Texas lost $7,101,936.

Overall, for 2009, states paid $5,850,306,362 to administer support offices. States recovered $740,652,294 from welfare, the federal government reimbursed states $3,887,391,564 (Table A-2), and paid an additional $504,000,000 in incentive payments. States lost $718,262,504.

> (Support data from the Congressional Research Reports "Analysis of Federal-State Financing of the Child Support Enforcement Program", July, 2012, - table 3 and table a-2 use differing total amounts for federal CSE costs/share; and, "Child Support Enforcement Program Incentive Payments: Background and Policy Issues," May 2, 2013, both written by Carmen Solomon-Fears.)

Another chart contained in the CRS report lists the average monthly support payment for each state. Poorer states, like Louisiana and Mississippi, have average support payments under $200. Most states average payment in 2009 hovers around $249 with very few states having averages over $300. New Jersey had the highest average payment at $378. It would seem reasonable to assume that a person with an average income would pay support within the state average, someone with a low income would pay less, higher incomes would pay more. Yet, that is far from true. Support amounts are discretionary and open to multiple manipulations. Incomes are not determined by IRS tax records. Instead, support can be based on what a judge or lawyer "thinks" you are capable of earning. Hearing officers can deduct union dues, made-up child care costs, and they can average income based on one week of low earnings. Income amounts are all subject to the concept of who gets to be the winner and who the loser.

Each state gets to write their own Support Guidelines; how much will be paid for various incomes. The incomes of two parents are added together, say dad makes $80,000 and mom makes $20,000, total income would be $100,000. Stay-at-home moms are usually assessed an income, even though they have not worked, sometimes for many years. The state determines that children of parents with higher incomes receive a greater share of that money, therefore, support for one child of a couple jointly earning $100,000 would be $18,000/year, or $1,500/month. The parent with primary custody receives the support payment. Primary custody is determined by overnight visits; the parent with more overnights, has primary custody. By giving fathers increasing amounts of overnight visitation, support courts have made mothers subject to support payments. If mother had primary custody, under the $20,000/$80,000 income, father would pay mother 80%, $1,200/month. When father is given primary custody, mother pays $300 (20%) to him. If mother's income is assessed at $40,000 and fathers is $60,000, and he is given custody, she will pay $600 per month (40%); rather than father paying her $900 to raise the child. If there are two children, support doubles with a slight reduction, for instance, child support would be set at $2,500/month. Paying 20%, mom would owe dad $500/month; $1,000 at 40%; rather than dad paying mom $2,000 or $1,500. Higher income parents pay more. Attaining custody is extremely profitable for higher income fathers.

The parent who has primary custody is permitted to take the child tax exemption, an additional financial incentive. Each child is a yearly tax write-off, $3,950 in 2014! Money paid in support is not tax-deductible, yet alimony payments are a line-item tax deduction. This makes it financially advantageous for a well-off man to obtain primary custody and to prolong, or break-up, a divorce settlement by paying off mother through alimony, instead of a one-time settlement and support payments. Rather than be financially punished by letting mother parent the children, men prefer to obtain primary custody and then defer parenting to their mothers, new girlfriends or wives, or even strangers.

In order to achieve this financial advantage for fathers, especially men with higher incomes, the access/visitation mandate does not require courts to adhere to state custody laws that require abusive behavior, and even friendly-parent provisions, to be considered. Courts are not required to adhere to the rules of evidence or due process. Court service providers are not required to adhere to any ethical standard. Some states, like Pennsylvania, have even passed laws that forbid the filing of ethical complaints against court appointees. When custody is increased for fathers, it is decreased for mothers, a fact never mentioned in any government literature. Nowhere in the HHS report "A Collaboration and Strategic Planning Guide for States: Child Access and Visitation Programs" is there any mention that the entire program is entrenched in litigation; that families are extorted to pay exorbitant legal fees in order to have any standing in the court system. In fact, litigants without representation are routinely punished and ruled-against. Women usually have lower incomes than men so they quickly become disadvantaged. Abusive men frequently control the family assets. Many mothers who do receive support have to spend that money paying lawyers to fight to maintain custody. Nowhere in that same HHS report is it mentioned that mediators, co-parenting coordinators, and all other ordered court service providers become heavily involved in litigation and even, make judicial determinations, often, solely to ensure themselves continued court-ordered clients. Again, the

HHS report never mentions adherence to state laws, guaranteeing due process protections, ethical standards and oversight, the current child care arrangement and future needs of the children or assessing the cause of the family break-up in the first place.

HHS reports often substitute the word "noncustodial" parent for father. It is merely a euphemism, in the same manner that custody has been changed to access/visitation or parenting time. A thorough reading of documents makes it clear that the program runs solely to benefit fathers. When mom is made non-custodial, she is not offered services to get her increased custody; when she is eliminated, she is not offered reunification, a service that is frequently offered to dads released from prison. While counted as participants, mothers are merely mandated to cooperate and they are punished by complete loss of their children, jailing, financial impoverishment and psychological devastation when they attempt to protect their children from an abusive male. Abuse is called conflict or mutual. Fighting and prolonged litigation is sustained and encouraged. Recovery from abuse, self-help and empowerment are denied under this perpetual system. Because of OCSE's fatherhood access/visitation mandate, the litigation and court service provider industry flourishes.

Private Foundations Fund Fatherhood

"In addition, many private foundations are providing financial support for fatherhood programs. These are the largest sources of funding for fatherhood." CRS Fatherhood Initiatives

Groups like the Ford Foundation and Annie E. Casey Foundation give to groups that develop positive-to-father research, leaving out research into the effects of negative father traits such as control, violence, alcoholism, criminal behavior, chronic unemployment, or pedophilia (incest). Casey also funds groups that lobby state and federal governments for laws that benefit the fatherhood movement. The Casey Foundation has paid to write and disseminate reports such as "Promoting Responsible Fatherhood" which advise states to use TANF and MOE (matching funds) for fatherhood custody.

Annie E. Casey Foundation was endowed to improve children's welfare. From its roots of funding camps for developmentally disabled, literacy programs, foster care, what it calls "community support," this large endowment is being used to further the fatherhood movement agenda of male control under the guise of pretending that a father makes life better for kids. Ranked 25th highest endowment in the United States, Casey has assets of $2,933,059,949.

The Ford Foundation funded Mathematica's analysis of fatherhood programs. The Ford Foundation funded Young Unwed Fathers and Partners for Fragile Families along with OCSE. The Ford Foundation had assets of $12,259,961,589 in 2013, and is ranked 2nd highest endowment in the United States.

Social Security Block Grants

OCSE is funded under Title IV-D, Social Security Block Grant. Amounts equal to TANF distributions are disbursed to states under SSBG Title IV-B under the auspices of child welfare. These monies fund Children & Youth, Child Protective Services, Foster Care. This money funds marriage promotion and fatherhood programs under the "preservation of the family unit as the foundation for success for children" goal. Including the marriage/fatherhood goal has shifted these programs to prefer fathers over mothers.

In Pennsylvania, these funds are allocated to state "Family Centers." Family centers operate the fatherhood program for released prisoners. Incarcerated fathers can receive reduced sentences through fatherhood programs, upon release, they are aided by family centers, where they are allegedly taught to be good dads.

FATHERHOOD INSTEAD OF CASH ASSISTANCE

"The 63% reduction in cash welfare caseload, together with the fixed block grant funding, means funds that otherwise would have been spent for cash assistance are now available for other purposes. These other purposes could include fatherhood initiatives which are allowable uses of TANF and State MOE funds. Moreover, fatherhood initiatives are not subject to the requirements that apply to spending for ongoing cash assistance such as work requirements and time limits. The cash welfare caseload declined from a peak of 5.1 million Aid to Families with Dependent Children (AFCD) in 1994 to 1.8 million TANF families in December 2012." Fatherhood Initiatives Congressional Research Report

Since government shifted welfare poverty supports from the poor to fathers, 3.3 million less families receive cash assistance. That money has been shifted to marriage and fatherhood programs. Yet, fathers do not have to adhere to welfare work requirements (mothers must work 20 hours per week to receive welfare), time (there is a limit of five lifetime years for mothers to collect), or even income requirements (fathers are permitted to have incomes of 400% of the poverty rate to receive services).

To anyone attuned to poverty rates, conditions and prevalence, this shift from cash assistance to fatherhood is an alarming disclosure! No longer are women with children permitted the smallest of monthly cash stipends in order to purchase things like toilet paper, toothpaste, deodorant, sanitary products, laundry and cleaning supplies, transportation, etc. Welfare is telling these women and children to find a father to supply their needs!

In Pennsylvania, a paltry $200 monthly cash welfare stipend was taken away from the disabled waiting for Social Security Insurance (SSI) to process paperwork which can take years. The poor disabled must rely on family, friends, and charity to supply all their needs. At the same time, the conservative Governor Tom Corbett increased Pennsylvania's already bloated fatherhood and marriage programs.

Fatherhood Permeates Government Programs

All government social service and private social service groups receiving federal funding are geared towards promoting fatherhood, shifting the focus of their service delivery away from women and children towards fathers, offering fathers preferential treatment. Head Start, job placement, Children and Youth, Public Defenders and Probation offices have a large fatherhood program focus. See https://www.fatherhood.gov/for-programs for a list of government offices offering services for fathers. This site also lists programs by state, but I found links didn't pan out when clicked.

WELFARE PROGRAMS ARE FOR FATHERS ONLY

The claim is that fatherhood programs are gender neutral and their underlying goal is participation of the non-custodial parent in the lives of their child. Several facts prove otherwise.

Non-custodial defined as fathers

The CRS Report "Fatherhood Initiatives" contains an Appendix listing federal funding of fatherhood programs. The first entry, 106th Congress (1999-2000) contains proof that programs were designed for fathers under the pretense that they were the non-custodial parents. An early program was called "Fathers Work/Families Win." The report states "the Fathers Work component would have been limited to non-custodial parents (mostly fathers)." From this point forward, non-custodial has been synonymous with fathers. Reference to non-custodial parents being fathers is made throughout welfare reports.

100% Male

The HHS report "Catalog of Research: Programs for Low-Income Fathers," written by Mathematica Policy Research, December 2011, lists "gender" in its analysis. Ninety-seven percent of programs list participants as "100% male."

Mothers Experience

Mothers are never offered any job training, mentoring, peer support, or help in obtaining custody to reduce support. However, courts do require mothers to participate in mediation, parenting education, supervised visitation and other welfare-paid-for services. Mothers get ordered to participate, but they are treated as a problem, a barrier to fathers, unless they agree to marry him.

Mothers are made noncustodial by the fatherhood system, yet they are not then offered help getting access and visitation. Even eliminated mothers are not offered access and visitation services in order to spend more time with their children. Giving services to the noncustodial parent would only create a back and forth system unless there is shared custody.

Fatherhood Development Literature

A simple fact is: the literature is focused solely on fathers.

For a comprehensive history of the fatherhood movement and the ideology and network behind it, see "Making Fathers Count: Assessing the Progress of Responsible Fatherhood Efforts" Annie E. Casey Foundation 2002
http://www.aecf.org/KnowledgeCenter/Publications.aspx?pubguid={5931A803-4E1C-421B-844C-65644D6968E6}

Program Name

Programs are called Fatherhood, not Parenthood, as was proposed by Rep. Patsy Mink. Changing to Parenthood programs would have negated the gender-specific nature of these custody and forced marriage programs and it did not happen.

Program Reports

Several welfare reports written by Jessica Pearson (who worked with CRC, the father's rights custody network), make it clear that these government programs are for fathers. One such report "Access & Visitation Programs: Promising Practices" looks at state programs run during 2001/2002. This report encourages states to use TANF funds for fatherhood custody. The report mentions four states using TANF for custody: Indiana, Georgia, Iowa, and New York. At the time, Nebraska was unable to get its state legislature to approve the use of TANF funds for litigation. Indiana refers fathers to services at its social services website www.in.gov/fssa/fathers/providers.html

"Promising Practices" mentions that many states are offering fathers legal help to increase access/visitation (custody). Parents Fair Share was an early program mentioned in the Congressional Report that concluded that fathers should be provided legal services to help them gain visitation rights (custody). Casey Foundation fatherhood reports mention that fathers need legal help to gain access/visitation (custody). Many mothers and NOW chapters have petitioned legislators and HHS regarding this gender-specific program; they have repeatedly, and falsely, been told that these programs do not include custody.

Government Website

The U.S. government has a website which hooks up dads with programs. The website is changed frequently and seems to be currently managed by the National Responsible Fatherhood Clearinghouse funded by a separate federal fatherhood grant. Clicking on "about us" makes it clear that services are for fathers only. "The Claims Resolution Act of 2010 (CRA) re-authorized funding for the National Responsible Fatherhood Clearinghouse (NRFC). The NRFC was initially funded through the Deficit Reduction Act (2005) for "the development, promotion, and distribution of a media campaign to encourage the appropriate involvement of parents in the life of any child and <u>specifically the issue of responsible fatherhood</u>, and the development of a national clearinghouse to assist states and communities in efforts to promote and support marriage and responsible fatherhood." https://www.fatherhood.gov/ There is no motherhood.gov website nor is there a parenthood.gov website. The government website is exists solely for fathers. A link to Connecticut's fatherhood resources lists two known father's rights groups: ACFC and CRC.

On October 2, 2015, after the 1st publication of this book, I, Doreen Ludwig, attended an AFCC Conference held at the Capital Hilton. Fatherhood.gov had a table. Two employees confirmed on tape that the programs are for fathers only and that they were attending a court trade group event in order to increase fatherhood programs within legal and mental health professions.

<u>ABUSE LEFT OUT OF FATHERHOOD INITIATIVES</u>

Protection from abuse was never part of Welfare Fatherhood and Marriage Promotion programs. Instead of building these programs with a domestic violence component, protection for mothers and children was purposely left out.

The Annie E. Casey Foundation history of the fatherhood movement "Making Fathers Count," pays lip service to concerns of domestic violence:

> "Oliver Williams of the University of Minnesota School of Social Work's Center on Domestic Violence in the African-American Community, who has been researching domestic violence for years, says the subject is one that most of the fatherhood field resists addressing. "People want to rehabilitate fathers so they can be with their children . . . [but] it's easier for them to talk about substance abuse and joblessness than about domestic violence," says Williams. "And they'd rather talk about mutual violence rather than male responsibility." Williams suggests that it is time "to deconstruct the issue of mutual violence—it's misleading. The level of abuse that women initiate is clearly different than the violence that men initiate. Women and men may hit each other as much, but it's not the same. Women are hurt more—and more often."

The fatherhood movement does not want to talk about abuse!

The long history of ignoring abuse and its effects on women and children is noted in CRS Report "Fatherhood Initiatives:"

> "In the late 1990s when interest in federally funding responsible fatherhood programs first gained national attention, some women's rights groups, such as the national Women's Law Center and the National Organization for Women (NOW) were concerned that an

> *emphasis on the importance of fathers could lead to undervaluing single parent families maintained by mothers, that services for fathers might be at the expense of services for mothers; and that the "profatherhood" discourse could give father's rights groups more leverage in challenging child custody, child support and visitation arrangements. Although that underlying tension has not disappeared completely, then and now, it was thought that the policy debate on responsible fatherhood initiatives had to be based on the view that the welfare of fathers, mothers and children were intertwined and interdependent. Many analysts asserted that otherwise the debate would be very divisive and unproductive."*

Concern about abuse is divisive and unproductive!

In fact, a NOW newsletter did sound the alarm and all of their predictions have come true!

> *"Although backers of H.R. 3073 [Fathers Count bill] would have us think that the bill was meant to help poor non-custodial fathers, NOW and many other women's rights and domestic violence program advocacy organizations know better. The measure is especially tailored to send millions of taxpayer dollars to groups that undermine child support enforcement systems, provide biased child visitation/access programs and counsel non-custodial dads on how to avoid paying child support altogether by switching custody. NOW activists have monitored for years those groups and their extremist leaders because we hear from thousands of women each year who have lost custody of children to abusive ex-spouses due to their tactics. Many of these same groups are pushing state legislatures to adopt forced joint custody laws.*

Those include the _Children's Rights Council_ (CRC, in actuality a men's custody organization), the _National Fatherhood Institute_, _Institute for American Values_ and National Institute for Responsible Fatherhood and Family Development. Men's custody advocates have helped to shape a backlash against tougher enforcement of child support orders. Angry dads groups have a strong advocate in a House Ways and Means staff member, Ron Haskins, who promoted earlier programs in demonstration projects on child visitation and access and who was reported in a 1998 CRC newsletter to be working with Rep. Clay Shaw (R-FL) to get $2 billion in funding for their programs. Haskins is a former board member of CRC and got credit for defeating protections for battered women on welfare in final conference committee (after both the House and Senate had approved).

The ostensible goals of H.R. 3073 are to teach parenting skills to poor non-custodial fathers and to enhance their employability so that they may obtain jobs in order to meet child support obligations. Other services may be anger management training, family planning information, tips on relationship skills and money management. Religious groups are eligible for funding, and right wing groups may get a disproportionate share since they may be more willing to "promote marriage" as a goal, without regard to the situation.

In a letter to House members, NOW questioned the bill's approach calling attention to the dangers of domestic violence, the greater needs of custodial parents on welfare (whose services are constantly in fiscal jeopardy), and the legislation's unconstitutional gender discriminatory language. NOW suggested that funds would be better *utilized by custodial parents, especially those who are in the welfare-to-work process. Another part of the bill provided funds for vocational training and other services for welfare recipients, but restricted custodial parents (mostly women) to a small eligibility pool with increased qualifying requirements. That part of H.R. 3073 was attached to the Omnibus appropriations measure and was adopted in the Senate.*

It is noteworthy that in the mid-1990's a series of demonstration projects that were nearly identical to the programs proposed in the Fathers Count Act were conducted in seven urban areas, with both private and government funding. Known as the Parents Fair Share Demonstration, the projects were later evaluated and, for five sites, were found to NOT result in a significant increase in child support compliance.

Prior to the vote, NOW pointed out to House members that the promotion of marriage is not an appropriate government policy and will not solve the complicated problems of poverty. Numerous studies have shown that family violence is a major factor in divorce and in keeping women poor; five major recent studies have documented that up to one-third of welfare recipients are currently experiencing abuse and a much higher proportion of poor women report experiencing domestic violence and sexual assault at some point in their lives.

H.R. 3073 would provide three grants of national significance that appear designed especially for Wade Horn's <u>National Father Institute</u> and David Blankenhorn's <u>Institute for American Values</u>. Wade Horn, a columnist on family issues in conservative newspapers, relies on discredited fatherlessness research to "prove" that father-

absence alone causes social ills such as teen suicide, poverty, high crime rates, low SAT scores, juvenile delinquency and recently wrote an article about "malicious moms." David Blankenhorn endorses marriage as a cure for domestic violence!

All of these organizations, together with the Children's Rights Council, have encouraged courtroom use of the "parental alienation syndrome," a phony "condition" that has been used against custodial moms. PAS says that women who report abuse are mentally ill and brainwash children against the father -- and therefore judges may conclude that custody should be switched to the father. Biased judges who have little understanding of domestic violence or child abuse often doubt evidence provided about abusive behavior by the husband and award custody to the father. This unjust practice has become a growing trend in family courts all across the country.

Rep. Patsy Mink (D-HI) worked closely with NOW, NOW/LDEF and battered women's advocates to offer several key amendments to H.R. 3073. The amendments would have changed "fatherhood" to "parenting" programs, removed the gender discrimination and deleted the marriage promotion aspect. The amendment did garner 172 votes, but not enough for adoption. "

President Obama's 2009-2010 and 2011-2012 budgets included funding for fatherhood but included addressing domestic violence in programming. However, this inclusion was never included. Legislators still cannot protect abused women and children from the Fatherhood/Marriage Promotion welfare program agenda.

Mothers were questioning this gender specific system and

identifying severe flaws in family court for some time. In August 2006, California NOW wrote a 2-page letter to their congressional representatives requesting an investigation because CA support offices offered pamphlets sending dads to father's rights groups for legal help getting custody; because mothers were denied fair trials; and they believed Wade Horn had a conflict-of-interest because he was awarding large fatherhood grants to NFI. Congress never investigated the program.

The Battered Mothers Custody Conference was begun by Professor Mo Hannah. During an early conference, mothers and professionals wrote the "Truth Commission" report because mothers were seeing an increased incidence of abusers gaining custody and protective mothers being eliminated or ordered to supervised visits. The report identifies problems in family court with judges and service providers such as no knowledge of abuse, denying evidence, denying facts, made-up custody reports, bias against women, etc. Most of these problems have been identified in other chapters of this book.

Added after 1st publication: *the most egregious proof of the intentional ignoring of all forms of abuse in order to forcibly increase custody is the the federal reporting form entitled "State Child Access Program Survey: Guidance (AV Guidance)." This form confirms that states are keeping records of family court cases affected by the intentional custody mandate. Page 4, "Counseling" confirms mental health practitioners ignore (not focus on) abuse including sexual abuse of children, domestic violence, battering, anger, alcoholism and drug addiction in order to* increase *custody for the non-custodial parent who is usually the father.*

Leaving abuse out of the welfare fatherhood custody program has resulted in severe harm to mothers and children!

INSTITUTIONALIZING THE PROGRAM

Access/Visitation Promising Practices report go a long way towards telling states how to institutionalize a fatherhood custody program. One report was written, again by Jessica Pearson's Center for Policy Research in 2006, specifically for the purpose of telling states how to work collusively to systemize the custody scam. "A Collaboration and Strategic Planning Guide for States: Child Access and Visitation Grant Programs" tells states to assemble a group of senior executives in child support and court administration, judges, lawyers and mental health practitioners (MHPs), and to include fatherhood advocacy groups. The report calls abuse "high conflict" which gives parity to abuser and abusee, it tells states to train judges (in fatherhood access/visitation); to have support personnel help and advice fathers to file for custody to reduce support.

Pennsylvania convened such a group (called The Committee for Justice Initiatives) to come up with a plan it called "Changing the Culture of Custody in Pennsylvania." Ironically, this commission was organized in 2005 and published its results in 2007, the years I was embroiled in a custody case with my abuser waiting for the system to correct the fictitious evaluation of MHP Ring. I was challenging an unethical business court service provider not realizing that welfare, and trade association members were actively working to increase unethical business in the courts.

Members of Pennsylvania's Committee for Justice Initiatives include Judge Kaplan, who has a history of CRC involvement. Kaplan is a past President of AFCC (court trade association) and worked with OCSE in setting up access/visitation programs. Judge Kaplan was working on the family court bench out of Pittsburgh, but currently is working as a lawyer and consultant, an example of the judicial revolving door.

The Pennsylvania Plan is an active Plan to get litigants into mediation, especially in cases of domestic violence which, again, is not understood. PA's Plan is based on Connecticut's Plan, another state with strong AFCC and fatherhood roots. While Changing the Culture of Custody in Pennsylvania claims to be offering Best Practices and The Model Gold Standard, it leaves out oversight and accountability of the court system itself, judges and court employees, and court appointed for-profit service providers, lawyers and mental health practitioners. There is no complaint process if a mother feels threatened by her abuser during court proceedings, or does not want to be housed in the same waiting room as her abuser, there is no process for her to follow to request protection. Many clerical and security guards assist abusers in intimidating and threatening their prey; the Plan offers no formal procedure for complaining about staff maltreatment and misbehavior.

PA's Plan offers no ethical requirements, there is no guarantee that ethical standards will be adhered to, and no quick, efficient process for addressing violations of ethical standards by mental health appointees or legal professionals. Indeed, ethical controls have already been written out of the law in PA.

PA's Plan offers no guarantee of the right to appeal. It does not guarantee oversight of judicial conduct; nor does the Gold Standard forbid judges from acting collusively to create a false court record by permitting false evidence and witness, and denying true evidence and witness. When a judge and his cohorts have purposely permitted false allegations, Pennsylvania's Plan contains no guaranteed avenue of correction.

The Plan does not tell court appointees and judges that they must disclose any conflict-of-interest, or personal and financial connections to each other which would call into question their impartiality and ability to measure the credibility of court appointees. The Plan does not inform appointees working under fatherhood access/visitation contracts of their duty to disclose their bias.

The Plan does not require judges, court employees and appointees to have any experience or even knowledge of abuse, its effects on the family, and the probability of an abuser treating the children in the same, or worse manner.

A complete analysis of PA's Plan would take time, immersion in the system, and the ability to read between the lines of positivity to fully understand the hidden agenda of profiting off abuse. "Motherless America" hints at the minutia of everyday court processes, it's overall objective is to explain the structure of welfare money being diverted to family court operations.

Chapter 10

The Players and Their Methods

This chapter explains the Players: the people who get involved in custody cases, how they operate, and use their positions to help abusive men. All of these family court players can be members of the trade association, AFCC. They can have individual membership or be part of an institutional AFCC membership. They often work collusively to enact a for-profit, father-centered court, what I call a Fatherhood Court.

<u>Judges</u>
A judge is a government employee. There are three branches of government: executive, legislative and judicial. The executive branch is administrative. It includes the President, Governors, Mayors, they run the day-to-day operations, including law enforcement. The legislative branch consists of federal and state representatives in the House and Senate. The representatives enact (write and pass) the laws. No law can be enacted without legislative approval. The judicial branch of government is endowed with the authority to implement the law at the state and federal level. Judges do not make laws! They have the right to interpret law, which they do when they write opinions, an explanation of their decision-making process. There are two types

of law and courts: criminal and civil. In order to have a case in criminal court, you must be charged with a crime under the State or Federal Crimes Code. Civil court is where you go when you sue. Civil court is also where you wind up when you file for divorce or want to receive support. This particular specialty of civil court has traditionally been called Family Court. Family court judges are beholden to the laws of the State where they are appointed. Family court judges operate under the requirements of due process and the rules of evidence. Family court judges have legal degrees, they have gone to law school. Family court judges are elected or appointed.

Some couples decide together to divorce. There may be hurt feelings, but these couples are generally amicable and papers get processed easily, the couple might never even see a judge, whose only job becomes to sign final paperwork. A man might decide he wants a divorce. He'll tell his wife and settle money issues quickly and fairly. Sometimes a woman makes the decision to divorce, yet the male, will accept her decision and will, in turn, settle money and child issues quickly and fairly. These agreements permit the family to spend as little as possible of the family resources on litigation.

Some men want to leave the women without losing assets they consider their property. They will hire lawyers to hide money before notifying the wife that they are filing for divorce. They will use manipulative tricks learned in business to win in court. They know that custody of the children will give them a financial upper hand. These men have become abusers. Lawyers love them! Lawyers will charge by the hour and they will encourage these men that paying legal fees is better than paying the wife. Eventually, many of these men tire of paying legal fees and they settle, wanting to move forward with their lives. These couples go before the judge infrequently. However, a small percentage of these men continue to use the court system to abuse the mate they are leaving mainly motivated by their need to control assets and children.

The last type is the abusive male whose target, the wife, has finally decided to protect herself and the children by filing for divorce. She has finally said "I am not going to take this anymore" and "This is not good for the children." The trigger may be that the father has turned his abuse towards the children, whether physical, emotional or even, sexual. Wives and mothers will often file for Protection or Restraining Orders. Men become more violent when the target has chosen to leave! When trying to leave, women and children are at the greatest threat from death and violence! These women believe that a judge will protect them. But for the women whose husband has money, nothing could be further from the truth. Family court is a business and abuse is a boon to business. If there is money, lawyers will be looking to get some of it, and judges, being lawyers, will be more than happy to oblige.

These last two types of cases are what AFCC and its members have named: high conflict. A judge will be heavily involved in these cases. The judge may get angry because these cases demand a lot of his time. The judge may be abusive in his own relationships. The judge may hate women and feel that they are all out to get men. Most likely, the judge will not understand abuse, he will have been coached that abuse is merely physical and can be cured. The judge most likely will be trained to minimize male abuse and believe that fathers are the preferable parent due to welfare's fatherhood program and the influence of CRC member father's rights groups in state politics. The judge will appoint his friends to do his work due to the influence of AFCC trade association; abdicating his judicial responsibility to mental health practitioners working for-profit.

Judges can become consumed with their power, their ability to solely determine the course of other people's lives. An advocate for court reform explained to me "to judges, power is a drug, and the more they get, the more they need." Power corrupts. Absolute power corrupts absolutely.

Judges can use their powers to dictate evidence. Family court judges frequently forbid real evidence such as medical examinations proving sexual abuse of a child. In my case, the judge forbade any evidence of father's pattern of perjury, abuse, or proof of the falsity of the custody evaluation. The judge forbade the witness of the MHP intern, who could testify that father admitted hitting me because I deserved it. On the other hand, a judge will permit evidence he knows to be false. The judge will appoint an MHP for the sole purpose of providing false evidence. Judges fully understand that allowing false evidence and witnesses, and forbidding true evidence and witnesses, creates a false record. Judges know how to manipulate these factors to justify giving custody to abusers.

Judges will use their powers of contempt (jailing and money fines) to punish mothers who persist in attempting to get a fair hearing or trial. Judges will threaten lawyers who attempt to properly represent clients with contempt.

Judges have little oversight. The premise is that you can appeal. But, judges and lawyers are expert at manipulating the record through denied and made-up evidence. If they are not confident in their made-up record, they will make a case for denial of the right to appeal. Appellate judges are inclined to protect their counterparts. The cost of appealing is exorbitant. Custody determinations can take years to overturn on appeal. If an appellate court determines the lower court judge erred, they often just send the case back to that original Judge where he is free to manipulate the record again. The preference is to keep custody cases in the trial, or lower, court where they can be litigated ad infinitum.

In Pennsylvania, when the higher courts protect the lower court they call their Opinions "Non-Precedential." Law books do not print these opinions and lawyers know not to repeat that particular case law. All of the higher court opinions in my case are listed as non-precedential (no precedent in that opinion), even the opinion stating that it was my fault I did not get a fair hearing when Ring submitted an unethical report.

Most states have some type of judicial conduct board where litigants are told to file complaints if a Judge is behaving unethically. These boards usually run out of the higher courts. They are not independent from the court, members are appointed by State Supreme Court Judges. Collusion between judges, lawyers, and MHPs is not investigated. It is rare for a judge to be disciplined or taken from the bench.

Court Administration

Courts have large administrative units. Every trial and appellate court has an administrative division. A Prothonotary is responsible for recording documents, date stamping, and maintaining records. A Clerk of Court is also responsible for maintenance of court records. Judges have law clerks to write opinions. The sheriff's department is present in every family courtroom in case the parents get unruly and need to get jailed, and to process parents who are being jailed for owing support.

States also have administrative offices for administering the function of the entire state court system. This office sets the standards for how state courts will conduct business. Fatherhood training is frequently run out of this office.

Administrators will claim to have no authority, yet they oversee the hiring and payment of court appointed mental health and legal business people. Administrators staff and oversee court procedure committees, called Rules Committees. Courts are supposed to follow state legislative laws, called Statutes or Codes. Courts are permitted to write rules, which are supposed to make processing consistent and simple. But, court administrators write rules to override state laws and enact profit-motivated systems, such as the handing-over of judicial duties to MHPs.

Similarly, using court rules, administration has the ability to provide oversight of court-appointed businesspeople. Yet, to my knowledge, no court has implemented a review process for evaluations and reports submitted as evidence and testimony to ensure adherence to standards and truth. Likewise, no court administration has implemented a complaint and review process for unethical, or biased mediators, counselors, co-parenters, GALs, etc. Administration does not audit, review, analyze, or publish outcomes, or percentages of any court appointed businessperson.

Child Support often called Domestic Relations is an administrative unit, yet many judicial functions are run out of this office including determining support amounts, appointing for-profit court service providers, and making custody determinations. Fatherhood access/visitation programs are run out of child support offices; by turning fatherhood into an administrative function, adherence to State Statutes protecting abused women and children were overridden. Fatherhood programs do not provide protection from abuse!

<u>Lawyers</u>

Lawyers are business people. They charge for their work by the hour. Rates differ geographically but lawyers easily charge $200 and more per hour. They will bill at their high rate even if a paralegal or secretary has done the work. They bill for talking on the phone and sitting in court. They even charge for lunch and travel. You can easily spend several hours in court waiting for one meeting. Before you know it you owe several thousand dollars!

Lawyers are often the first person a women contacts when she decides to leave an abuser. A women leaving an abuser, hoping to protect her children, is in a very vulnerable state. She is most likely suffering from Post-Traumatic Stress Disorder (PTSD). Lawyers will not explain their limitations. Lawyers will not explain that the courts will more than likely fail to protect her and the children. They will not explain that judges will turn over authority to psychologists who often believe the male is the natural familial authority figure; that, by not bowing to that authority, the women deserved to be hit; that she "asked for it." Lawyers will not explain the bogus theory of PAS being used to cover-up father's sexual abuse by claiming that mother made-up the abuse and forced the child to hate father.

A women's only option is to pay the lawyer whatever they ask for as long as the litigation continues, or, learn the law and represent herself. In cases of abuse, litigation will continue until the last child turns eighteen. Fees easily reach into the hundreds of thousands of dollars.

Welfare will pay fathers legal fees and give fathers free legal help. Welfare does not assist mothers. As long as they hold to the fatherhood agenda of giving custody to dad and ignoring his abuse, welfare will pay lawyers, appointed by a judge, to purportedly act for the children, called Guardian Ad Litem's (GALs).

Legal Aid does not represent mothers who are in extended litigation with an abusive wealthy father.

There is very little pro bono (lawyers volunteering free work) legal help for mothers. Pro bono lawyers often act in conjunction with the judge's wishes. If the court has decided to give custody to an abusive father, your free, pro bono, lawyer may be working against you.

Lawyers do not want to make the judge angry. That makes it difficult for them to adequately represent an abused mother.

Lawyers representing abusers will coach their client to counter-file for protection orders. They will help their client make-up false accusations. They work with MHPs to get the results necessary to win in court. In Pennsylvania, lawyers are permitted to lie for their clients, no matter how false or malicious the accusation.

Domestic Violence Groups

Women may contact the local domestic violence group believing they will provide help in leaving. This is a fallacy! Domestic violence groups do not assist women with children who are trying to divorce an abusive husband! They may offer a 30-day respite from physical violence but, after that, you will be out on the street. If you have left your home to be safe, you may never get back in the house unless you go back to the abuser. Domestic violence groups do not keep lists of lawyers who understand abuse, how it affects women and children and who can competently advocate for recognition of the abuse and protection from the abuser. DV groups may offer counseling, but that counseling will tell mothers that the children need their father, that supervised visits or a co-parenting coordinator will cure the abuse. DV groups do not recognize that men who abuse wives have a high potential for abuse of children, especially when mother is eliminated and not available to divert the abuse (see situational pedophile below).

DV employees are members of AFCC. Currently, DV staff are working to get appointed to "classify" abuse, as described in Chapter 7, Abuse. DV groups advocate for the appointment of parenting coordinators in cases of abuse. DV groups that align themselves with the trade association merely assist in propping up the industry. This trend is very dangerous as it does not support women and children's right to self-identify as prey, and their right to a future of security, safety, autonomy, and empowerment.

Guardian Ad Litem (GAL)

GALs are lawyers who are appointed by the court to represent the children. Parents are ordered to pay their fee. Some courts have GALs on staff, with parents ordered to pay additional fees. GALs have no training in abuse, instead, by virtue of their legal training, they are trained in manipulative tactics. GALS can be paid with welfare fatherhood funds. Fatherhood GALs will be trained that because father's are necessary, abuse must be ignored and mother's trying to protect the child by limiting father's access, are to be eliminated. GALs have no standards to follow, no ethical review, and no administrative oversight. In Scranton, PA, the court-appointed GAL, working under contract with the court and billing parents, was found to be billing multiple parents for the same time block. Parents are not permitted to have a say on how much time the lawyer spends with the child (billing for services); approve what the GAL does for the child; nor do parents have a right to fire a GAL if they feel the GAL is not properly representing the child.

Mental Health Practitioners (MHPs)

MHPs have degrees in psychology, social work or psychiatry. The United States graduates more MHPs then there are jobs. So, MHPs have worked very hard to find employment in family law, getting paid to intrude on other people's divorces and child rearing. United States colleges and universities graduate more psychologists than computer scientists, mathematicians, statisticians and chemical engineers combined. Over 90,000 psychology bachelor degrees are awarded per year! Clearly, there is a need to create a lot of sick people for all these MHPs to treat. Divorcing families have created that growth market!

The MHPs who found careers in telling other people how to parent, use a wide range of job titles. They are used interchangeably and there is overlap of duties, with MHPs acting in many relationships to the divorcing parents. I refer to MHPs as psychologists because they hold the majority of court appointments, since social workers and psychiatrists have greater access to work in their field of study and have less need to create a specialty. Another curiosity is that males constitute the majority of court appointed MHPs, yet women dominate the field of study.

MHPs do not understand abuse. Sam Vaknin who studies narcissists and abuse recognizes few psychology and psychopathology textbooks dedicate an entire chapter to abuse and violence. Even the most egregious manifestations – such as child sexual abuse – merit a fleeting mention, usually as a sub-chapter in a larger section dedicated to paraphilias (sexual deviations) or personality disorders. Abusive behavior did not make it into the diagnostic criteria of mental health (DSM) disorders, nor were its psychodynamic, cultural and social roots explored in depth. As a result of this deficient education and lacking awareness, most law enforcement officers, judges, counselors, guardians, and mediators are worryingly ignorant about the phenomenon. The study of human behavior is in its infancy and is not an advanced science. For all we know mental illness is a condition of brain construction.

MHPs who work in the divorce/fatherhood industry do not work with the truly mentally ill. Federal money that is paying for counselors, psychologists and social workers for fathers, and the mothers and children who must obey, could be much better spent on monitoring the truly mentally ill. People like Adam Lanza, the Newtown school shooter, who was not able to get needed help or oversight from a broken mental health industry.

Court affiliated MHPs have no limitation on what they charge, and, they collect from multiple sources. They have no motivation to work with the truly mentally ill, since reimbursement would be limited to market rates. Divorce is much more lucrative than charging by the hour. Court mandated counseling is much more lucrative than client-initiated sessions.

Custody Evaluators

The custody evaluator is often the first outside, business affiliate assigned by the judge. Custody Evaluator's have marketed themselves to the court as being qualified to determine which parent should be given custody and how much. Taking the question of who makes the better parent out of the courtroom and into the psychologists office denies your legal right to due process; your right to dispute all accusations with a complete hearing and evidence. Custody Evaluators are not legally trained. They do not understand the concept of due process and Rules of Evidence, and State and Federal Statutes (also known as codes or laws). They cannot distinguish hearsay and allegations from fact. They do not understand abuse and may even be perpetrators themselves. Anything that occurs at the custody evaluator's office is kept off-the-record, that means that unlike the courtroom, there is no transcriptionist writing every word down. The psychologist is permitted to interpret events according to their own biases and opinions in order to determine who should take care of the children.

The CEs opinion is then submitted to the court as if it is evidence. Judges will then make their decision based exclusively on the custody evaluator. This is a fact known by lawyers and court administrators which is rarely disclosed to parents. The close relationship results in a highly collusive court environment.

States have no regulations for the custody evaluator. Courts have no standards or oversight. By law, the Rules of Evidence, litigants have a right to have what is called a Frye Hearing to determine if the custody evaluator is qualified and if the methods used are proper and accepted as a standard amongst their peers. Judges are not obeying the law because they do not conduct Frye hearings. Courts and judges appoint evaluators they have single-handedly determined to be qualified and using appropriate methods, merely by virtue of having a personal relationship.

Most CEs call themselves Forensic Psychologists. The term "forensic" implies scientific, but, there is no science to determine who will be a better parent. Psychology is a "soft science." Scientific fields are rated based on methodological rigor, measureable criteria, and legitimacy. Hard sciences are evidentiary and measureable, other scientists will arrive at the same conclusion. Psychology, being based heavily on conjecture, conclusions from incomplete evidence, guess and inference, falls at the bottom of the scale. No two custody evaluators will arrive at the same conclusion.

The science used by custody evaluators leans heavily on tests designed to diagnose the mentally ill. While psychiatric wards rarely administer MMPI's to their patients, parents are routinely given MMPIs, a test developed to classify those who are already acting mentally ill. The MMPI was never designed to classify parenting ability. The MMPI cannot determine if a parent is an abuser or the target of abuse. An MMPI is not designed to test victims of abuse suffering from PTSD or even ADHD. In fact, those conditions are used against mothers to imply mental illness. Sociopaths perform very well on the MMPI.

These psychologists may give parents IQ tests to determine who the better parent is. I guess they try to make the case that a higher IQ equals better parenting and conversely, a lower IQ equals bad parenting. They like to give Rorschach tests, the ink blot test. This test is favored by psychologists who want to label mothers with PAS. The psychologist wants the mother to say an ink blot looks like a vagina so that the psychologist can then say the mother has a fixation on sex, that, the Rorschach test proves mother made up her claim of fathers sexual abuse.

The Bricklin Perceptual Scale is a test favored by fatherhood MHPs. These tests, one for parents and one for children, were designed by Dr. Barry Bricklin, whom I profile in depth under Parenting Coordinators.

The Bricklin test given to children of divorcing parents, asks the child "How much patience would your mother have when helping you learn a boring poem?" (taken from Bricklin website). The child is asked 35 additional questions and then the questions are asked about dad. The child makes a mark on a line to indicate their answer. Bricklin claims that children as old as four can answer these questions appropriately. These questions are not about real situations; they create hypothetical (suppose) situations where the child is asked to judge or guess a parents reaction. To most people, children do not have the ability to predict the future, but, Bricklin and his slew of custody evaluators are using these tests to determine parenting ability.

The legal standard is to assess the child's ability to tell truth from fiction and judge supposition before allowing them to become witnesses, the standard being no younger than age nine. Yet, Bricklin's test is routinely given to very young children under the strain of adjusting to divorce, being forced to choose one parent over another, even if one parent is abusive or very threatening. Abused children may still love their abusive parent and have been known to act out of fear by protecting that parent. The Bricklin tests do not address abuse, a child's reaction to, or fear of, abuse or, ability to understand and communicate abuse and its many dynamics.

Custody evaluators can use their reports to get judges to appoint them as lords over the family; getting the judge to appoint them as counselors, mediators or parenting coordinators/educators. All these positions are interchangeable, and since there is no oversight or standards, MHPs conduct themselves however they see fit, again, all off-the-record, occurring out of the courtroom with no parental recourse for dissatisfaction. Instead, dissatisfied parents will be punished, as the counselor, mediator, parenting coordinator/educator uses the court to enforce their rule.

<u>Parenting Coordinators/Educators</u>

Welfare fatherhood means judges prefer to award fathers primary or, minimally, shared custody, regardless of his habits of abuse. Since abusers are bullies, unable to control anger and resolve conflicts, judges appoint a mediator or Parenting Coordinator (PC), or Educator. Such an appointment is a financial bonanza for these psychologists. Parenting Coordinators have no specific training. Psychologists have built a network for getting these lucrative jobs, convincing judges and court administrators that their psychological training qualifies them to make parental decisions. Lawyers, social workers, and anyone else could feasibly be a parenting coordinator since there are no requirements besides getting the judge to issue an order.

The psychologists who act as judges over parents often call themselves Behavioral Scientists. They study the cause and effect of behavior, in that, you can force a person's behavior; reactions are predictable to stimuli or situations. The psychologists who implemented Guantanimo torture routines of waterboarding, stress positions, sleep deprivation, did so under the guise of being behavioral scientists. They claimed that because they were behavioral scientists they could torture and not be held accountable to ethical rules of causing no harm. Parenting Coordinators mimic torture techniques against mothers and children who are not abiding by fatherhood rules of male control. A favorite technique is threatening to take away mothers if the children do not recant claims of father's abuse.

The idea that a third party can force parents to get along is almost ludicrous, especially when you acknowledge that most divorces are occurring because parents are not getting along. Most married couples have tried, and at least one parent has come to the conclusion that reconciliation is not possible and divorce is the only option. While leaving is a difficult decision for anyone, it is especially difficult for women leaving abusive men. Mothers know that they have been protecting the children and when they are not there the children will be on their own with an abusive man. Mothers have a great amount of fear and that fear can be perceived as histrionic (excessively emotional) and irrational to those not privy to the abuse that occurred behind closed doors.

Parenting coordination sessions may begin as an attempt to mediate, that is: come to a mutual agreement. They quickly deteriorate because the abuser has to control; he has to have things his way! Father will demand his way just to prove that he has the power to force mom and children to obey and acknowledge his authority. We already know that our society views male assertion as appropriate and female assertion as aggressive, bitchy, and even, mental.

Parenting coordination is not counseling even if the Judicial Order calls it counseling. It will be called counseling merely so that health care can be billed. Parents do not work on personal, ingrained, negative behaviors, resentments, or patterns learned in childhood. Parents are not ordered to these psychologists in order to work towards healing themselves. Parents are merely under order to pay the PC to tell them what they can and cannot do with, and for, their child. If you fail to obey, you will be punished. You have to go to the office where you, your health care provider, or both, are billed at an hourly rate which is often double and triple the regional market rate for counseling. PCs do not disclose that they have been groomed by the fatherhood industry, that they have attended fatherhood conferences, that they are AFCC members, or members of groups that endorse fatherhood defenses of PAS for sexual abuse.

The trade association AFCC acknowledges that PCs do not fit "statutory privileges" like state laws and constitutional protections of due process, right to fair trial; "rules of evidence" the basis of law; and professional codes of ethics. According to AFCC the PC must be empowered, by court order, to operate freely and effectively in the role of expeditious dispute resolver, thus all these legal protections must be waived. The PC has a significant self-interest in prohibiting parents from filing ethical complaints. In contrast to the United States, where judges are ordering parents to a PC who adheres to no law or ethics, in Canada a PC may function with the parents' consent only. In Canada, parents are still the decision-makers for their children. In the U.S., suddenly an MHP or lawyer becomes the high-priced parental decision-maker.

AFCC PC guidelines acknowledge that it takes 18 months to 2 years to become familiar with a family and develop a working relationship. Appointment of a PC is a long-term proposition. The AFCC task force guidelines state that the decisions a PC may be required to make include when, how, and who performs services for the child, such as haircuts and doctor's visits. The guidelines pay lip service to domestic violence, even acknowledging that abuse such as threats and coercive control need to be identified. Yet, in reality abusers thrive in this heavy-handed, male-dominated situation, especially when the PC has received training and payment from the fatherhood movement. PCs are not at all qualified to identify the nuances of abuse. In fact, as the AFCC confirms, PCs are strictly for "high conflict" cases. High conflict cases are almost exclusively abuse cases. It is in the PCs financial interest to ignore indications of male control as some states have laws that protect victims from court-ordered counseling with their abuser. If abuse was acknowledged and the prey was protected, the PC would not have a job.

Welfare fatherhood will pay for parenting coordinators who classify their services as mediation, counseling or education. Welfare payment assures the PC works for daddy and is required to ignore or minimize abuse, and blame-the-victim. Acknowledging abuse would result in a loss of custody to dad and that is in conflict with the program mandate of custody-for-father.

In addition to ignoring abuse and not treating the perpetrator or the subject of the abuse, prioritizing fatherhood results in sessions that do not give moms parity to dads. Moms are used as stand-in parents, babysitters for the hours dad has to work, or wants personal time. Judicial orders will accommodate dad's work schedule without a thought to mother's work schedule. Conversely, if a mother's schedule accommodates the children, yet awarding her custody would result in dad not getting overnights reducing his support obligation, the children will be forced to sleep over dad's and get themselves off to school, or be with a babysitter, grandparent, or dad's new woman.

This happened to Elizabeth and Kathleen. At no point in the hours of testing by Dr. Ring, did anyone ask about the hours of fathers work. He has to be at work by 7 a.m. and he travels over an hour, so he leaves the home before 6 a.m. I began work at 9 a.m. and could be home by 4 p.m. The funny thing is that for the time before the custody trial, when father picked up the children from school two days a week and dropped them off every other monday morning, he was fudging his time cards. To prove it, I subpoenaed his time cards. The judge sent me an order that I was not allowed to talk to his work again or I would go to jail. When I raised the issue at the trial, Chet claimed he was working from home, but he is a mechanic, and cannot bring the factory, or airport conveyor system, home with him, but Judge Keller said he explained himself. One would think that availability and work schedule would be of major importance when assigning hours of parenting (custody), but it is of very low priority and often not even considered. Another time, Chet told the court that he was going to hire a teenager to watch the children during the summer or someone who advertised in the newspaper. I was ignored when I said I did not think a teenager was an appropriate babysitter and the children should be in an enrichment program. His thinking that an unknown stranger was an appropriate sitter was also ignored and kept off-the-record.

In the Dietrick case, Melissa was a teacher and had the same hours of work as the three children, yet father, who worked second shift, was given custody and Melissa was ordered to leave the house in ten days. The kids spent afternoons and evenings being watched by their grandmother who they did not particularly like. When grandma couldn't be there on school holidays, the kids spent the day with perfect strangers who father had met at the local bar.

In a fatherhood court, the children and their needs are never considered, examined, or made part of the record. The entire system is set-up to accommodate the whims of an abusive man.

The parenting coordinator is merely another agent to achieve the objective of male control.

Dr. Barry Bricklin

Bricklin is, first and foremost, a profiteer, a con man who will do anything for money. He is not a psychologist treating people with mental problems. He is a business person using the field of psychology for personal profit.

We see from his resume that Bricklin bounced around until finding his niche in child custody. Bricklin appears to be a native of Philadelphia, having studied psychology at Temple University and the Medical College of Pennsylvania.

He spent the '60s and '70s working in local hospitals. During the '60s Bricklin and his wife, Patricia, also a psychologist, hosted a call-in radio program giving psychological advice. Bricklin revived the show with himself as host during the late '70s and early '80's. Giving psychological advice over the radio is totally unethical. Psychologists use observation in diagnosis; body language, mannerisms, eye contact. Yet, Bricklin for years told people how to solve their call-in problems in five, ten, fifteen minute sound bites.

During the same time, Bricklin was marketing himself as a psychological dieting expert. Using the radio program, he could market vitamins and wafers for the rotation diet, claiming that one could eat the prescribed restricted diet (starve yourself) one day and eat anything the next and lose between eight to twenty-five pounds. Bricklin settled with the Federal Trade Commission for making fraudulent claims, and stopped being a psychological diet expert.

Shortly after his radio career ended, Bricklin found an area where he could use his unethical psychological proclivity without any supervision, oversight, or accountability. From radio star solving call-in dilemma's, to diet expert, to custody expert, Bricklin finally landed in a field of pretend expertise where he could apply his zeal for personal wealth and notoriety. Without any legal training, or any experience in child rearing, or divorce, Bricklin quickly developed his Child Perception of Parents test. This test would form the base of Bricklin's self-marketing custody empire.

Psychology uses tests to answer questions; for instance, the IQ test. The Welscher IQ test has been developed over time. It has been analyzed by other doctors working in the same field, it has been outcome tested. It has been tested on many before being used in a mass market and becoming an industry standard. Likewise, the Minnesota Multiplastic Personality Index (MMPI) has been widely peer reviewed and validated for assessing people already exhibiting patterns of mental illness. Both of these tests have fields of study where their use is appropriate. Neither an IQ, or MMPI test, has been designed to identify positive or negative parenting traits, yet psychologists who make their money from divorcing parents, make heavy use of these tests to make subjective conclusions about parenting ability.

Bricklin did not create his test for peer review or scientific validation; he created it for personal wealth using his own system of marketing, Village Publishing. Creators of tests sell the test protocols (forms); they can make millions of dollars a year selling their test forms. Bricklin is proficient at creating tests: coming up with questions, creating answers and scoring, and rating these answers. For instance, one question of Bricklin's parent test is: "What would you do if you found your child had stolen?" If a parent answers: "Make them return it and apologize" the parent would be deemed to be "authoritative." If a parent answers: "Punish child." Bricklin's test labels the parent "punitive." Spend a few minutes making up your own questions and labeling the answers and you can get a feel for the arbitrary nature of the

Bricklin test. Just make sure your questions have nothing to do with the mundane tasks of everyday childrearing. Make your questions fantastical situations like babies that cry all day, teenagers who have rubbers under their bed, young adults who, on the first day of college, don't want to go.

The Bricklin tests have never been analyzed in full by any judicial panel for adherence to fact, rule of law or the rules of evidence. The use of these tests has never been put before voters or legislators. There has never been debate about the appropriateness of using these tests for determining the futures of children of divorce. In truth, for-profit court psychologists, hide the content of the tests they are using to claim parenting ability. They write reports with conclusions without ever mentioning they used hypothetical questions to arrive at their conclusions. Bricklin tests are not fact-based. Facts, or evidence, are the basis of law, so since the psychologists conclusions are not fact-based, they are completely illegal and would never be permitted in a legitimate court of law. Bricklin tests are used by fatherhood practitioners in fatherhood courts for the sole purpose of providing false evidence.

Barry Bricklin has been one of the top marketers of his hypothetical tests; books for parents (mostly fathers) on winning custody; and training for psychologists on getting court-appointed jobs; all under the auspices of having some secret ability to determine who will make the better parent. Bricklin uses the internet to sell his books and market his credentialing. Bricklin calls one of his credentialing vehicles The Professional Academy of Custody Evaluators (PACE). He has advertised that he will give a psychologist a credential simply by their filling out a form. He requests the psychologist provide a letter from a judge stating their willingness to work with that psychologist.

Bricklin has a myriad network of websites linking to his list of

MHPs working under his tutelage including: http://pacehelp.org/ http://pace411.com/ ; and, http://www.academyregister.com/. He sells his books on sites like: http://www.mychildcustody.com/; http://www.custody911.com/; and, http://childcustodycenter.com/, most of these sites are connected to fathers' rights groups and advocates.

In selling his books, Bricklin brags that his help "is available only because Bricklin and [his associate] Dr. Gail Elliot have been given access to those private "inner circles" of the judicial process that ultimately decide the fate of your children." In another on-line brag Bricklin states "when he married his wife he gained political access in Pennsylvania and DC." Bricklin's wife headed the Pennsylvania Psychological Association for many years and was instrumental in deterring any ethical complaints filed against Bricklin and his associates.

Another of Bricklin's hat's is as a facilitator for the cover-up of father's sexual abuse, expanding the bogus claim of PAS, administering threat therapy and training others to do the same.

Parental Alienation Syndrome (PAS)

Many children resent being abused and they tell their mothers. The mom may see sexualized behavior, and take the child to a counselor capable of ferreting out the sex abuse. There may be urinary tract infections, vaginal or anal bleeding, that results in mom taking the child to a medical doctor who recognizes sex abuse. Father's sexual abuse is devastating news for mother! Mother becomes very upset, frantic even. These normal reactions will be used against mother by fatherhood courts and mental health practitioners. Many mothers immediately go to court for a protective order and divorce. If mother can't get father out of the home, she will leave herself with the children, not knowing that the court may charge her with kidnapping. These mothers know that father cannot be trusted and should not be alone with the child.

Mothers wrongly think the court will help her stop father's abuse. Instead, the fatherhood is geared to letting daddy have his way with the child. In that vein, the court, the trade group, for-profit affiliates, those behind the welfare fatherhood program (CRC and fathers rights groups), have latched on to the writings of Dr. Richard Gardner, the inventor of Parental Alienation Syndrome (PAS).

Gardner was another psychological freak who spent his life protecting men who sexually abused their children. Gardner actually believed that fathers having sex with their child was normal, yet, because it is not acceptable in our culture, men must be taught not to do it. Children who resisted the abuse and hated their attacker were labeled with Parental Alienation Syndrome (PAS). Gardner blamed the mother for the child not wanting to be around the abusing father! Gardner sold himself as an expert to testify in court for abusive fathers. Judges permitted Gardner to testify that the mother was "alienating" the child, that it was the mothers' reaction to the abuse that made the child hate their father, and that the mother had been able to brainwash the child, so the child needed to be forced to be with the father completely, the mother needed to be eliminated from the child's life, and the child needed to receive special therapy, called reunification, re-education, or threat therapy.

PAS and its use in child custody is an unbelievable study in how these completely fraudulent psychologists have been able to come into court, claim to have an area of expertise, make the most outrageous assessments, and be believed and have judges making orders that sentence children to years of abuse and loss of the parent who was trying to protect them. PAS and its promoters have formed the basis for how abused mothers and children are treated by family court judges, administrators, and their mental health business associates. PAS is pro-abuse. It blames the victims for the abuse and excuses the abuser. This mindset forms the framework for court-ordered mental health services.

Gardner and his pro-abuse theories and therapies were celebrated by the fatherhood movement. Gardner was a frequent speaker at CRC conferences during the years of welfare fatherhood program development. Gardner's books were frequently advertised in CRC newsletters. The Leadership Council, an anti-child-abuse nonprofit, has done the best work of highlighting the pro-pedophilia thinking of Richard Gardner. Using excerpts from Gardner's writings, they show the curious thinking of the maker of PAS, which include telling mothers to be more sexually responsive to father so that he will then stop having to have sex with his daughter; telling children that sex abuse by fathers is normal and no parent is perfect; telling an upset mother that her denigration of the abusing father causes the child to wrongly see the abuse as a crime; and, telling therapists it is their job to "sober up" mother. Anyone wanting to read more about this nonsense can go to http://leadershipcouncil.org/1/res/dallam/2.html and http://leadershipcouncil.or/1/pas/RAG.html (retrieved 2/1/14).

Gardner's bizarre-to-those-who-think-there-is-something-wrong-with-incest theories and therapies have been taken up by several others, including Dr. Richard Warshak author of the PAS book "Divorce Poison" which outlines for fathers this method of custody litigation. Warshak has been a board member of the fatherhood group ACFC, American Coalition for Families and Children (ACFC), which lobbies state and federal legislators for increased funding for welfare fatherhood court programs; diversion of TANF and Child Support Enforcement funds to pay fatherhood court practitioners; and, passage of state laws that support fatherhood such as forced shared parenting, appointment of parenting coordinators, and minimization of abuse.

Bricklin is another MHP who carries on the Gardner tradition of approving of fathers abuse and treating children of abuse by threat therapy. Bricklin loves to bully children! Most of Bricklin's time is spent spreading PAS quackery. But, occasionally, he takes on a therapy case personally. A New Jersey family is one such case.

I first spoke with the mother of two NJ girls in 2007. Ring, the fraudulent evaluator in my case, was proclaiming himself to be a member of the Professional Academy of Custody Evaluators (PACE). Ring would put this under his name when signing letters and cover pages of his evaluation. The counselor at RAISE, a battering man program, told me Ring gets away with it because he "has credentials." In researching Ring's PACE credential, I discovered Bricklin, which I shared with Liz Richards who first alerted me of the fatherhood welfare case rigging incentive. Liz Richards referred me to NJ mom. NJ mom told me an incredible story of Bricklin's abuse of her children. On top of losing my own children to my abuser, I had to comprehend the enormity of the nightmare that these two girls had to endure solely because they didn't want to be abused by their father!

Hearing their story let me understand Ring's true motivation when he wrote the fraudulent report was to get court-ordered counseling sessions where he could help father continue to control me, Elizabeth and Kathleen. The fact that Ring is part of a group that believes father has the right to abuse me and the children explains why Ring ignored Chet admitting he hit me but I deserved it. Ring agreed that I did indeed deserve it, he even wrote that he believed any abuse was mutual!

NJ mom told me about the Gardner, Warshak, Bricklin, and

PAS court litigation protocol for abusive men, all spelled out in their books. NJ mom explained threat therapy sessions where her children were told to love their father, that his abuse was OK and normal. When the eldest girl refused, Bricklin told her "I can usually break someone down in 24 hours" and "I believe in the Hitler method." When the girls told Bricklin that they were repulsed and frightened by the child pornography found on their fathers computer, Bricklin responded "All men do it, I have done it myself." Then he told father to get rid of the computer. The girls found emails from Bricklin telling their Dad to "use physical force to assert his authority" over the children and that "we are working with the Judge."

Bricklin never personally appeared in court. That means, he was never sworn in to "tell the truth and nothing but the truth so help me God;" never got cross-examined, questioned by mothers lawyer; the judge never got to observe Bricklin's rather freakish, facial tic and mannerisms which make him frightening to children.

Yet, custody was given to dad. Mom was termed an "alienator" and ordered to supervised visits at Bricklin's office. It did not matter that Bricklin's office was located in another state, Pennsylvania. It did not occur to this New Jersey judge that there could be someone closer to home instead of requiring mother and children an hour-plus drive up the treacherous Schuykill Expressway, through heavily populated Philadelphia, in heavy traffic.

When the girls still refused to love their father and his abuse, Bricklin contacted the judge over the phone without a hearing, without notifying mother or her lawyer, got an order to take the girls out of school, put them on an airplane, fly them to Texas and institute them in a trailer owned by the Rachel Foundation for reprogramming. The Rachel Foundation received a $50,000 grant from the Department of Justice for its program to reunite children with fathers.

At the trailer, the girls were locked up with their father. They were told to sit on his lap and hug and kiss him. Their food was limited and meals were a reward. The girls were made to walk a mile to go fetch eggs for breakfast. One girl was attacked by a vicious dog. A doctor was flown in from India. The girls told mom later that a second staff looked like a drug addict.

Miraculously, NJ Mom was able to find her children with the help of an international lawyer. The girls faked loving dad in order to get released. NJ mom was told that most children are never seen again once they have been sent to this program. When the girls returned to NJ they still had to endure living with their father and seeing their mother only when they were inconvenient for dad, with all time arranged through Bricklin and his associate, Gail Elliott. Each week, the girls schedule would change in order to accommodate father and his dating. As they aged, the girls got left alone more and more as father became less interested in his maturing girls. This dad preferred pre-pubescent girls, yet he would still make a habit of coming into the bathroom and looking while the girls were showering.

Like Gardner, Bricklin is a huge proponent of collusion between Judges and MHPs. A letter to MHPs telling them how to work with the Judge in order to get court appointed threat therapy was retrieved on 2/5/08 at http:/www.drbarrybricklin.com/pastherapy.html. At the time I retrieved this letter, which NJ mom had told me about, I was stunned when I first read this Bricklin piece because it clearly outlines collusion and unethical psychology.

In the letter, Bricklin tells the MHP to get *"special and strong"* Judicial orders, become the court's *"favorite witness"* and *"appreciate the politics of how to approach members of the court."* Bricklin tells the MHP to form alliances with attorney's to get the order. The judge and lawyers are to be told that "traditional" therapists cannot be assigned because they will believe the child's claims of father's abuse resulting in the therapist becoming an advocate for the child. *"The child must rapidly see that he or she is NOT going to be the major (or even minor) decision-maker of importance as to who attends the therapeutic sessions or for how long. This "tail-wagging-the-dog" phenomenon in which a child gets to exercise control over parents will ultimately not only ensure that an out-patient reunification process fails, but is also ultimately harmful to the child as he or she grows up."* (Remember: the goal of PAS therapy is to force the child to love the abuser.) A common psychological practice is to threaten the child that the therapist (and court) will "take away the mother" and/or "institutionalize them."

Bricklin's letter states: *"Even if a parent has a (mildly) "negative" style, a child who interacts with this parent has the opportunity to learn how to deal with it, increasing that child's available coping and resource-styles throughout life."* This "abuse is good for the children" philosophy is frequently espoused by fatherhood advocates.

Bricklin admits PAS therapy forces an unwanted parent on a child. *"It is the intention of the Court that the involved child therapeutically learn how to sustain interactions with the estranged parent. (Note that we do not say "come to love" or "get along perfectly with." For us, the ability for a child to sustain interactions with a parent without any credible signs of harm, is a more realistic match with what is attainable even in intact families.)"*

When mothers have been eliminated by the PAS method, or by another method perpetrated by an unethical lawyer, Judge, MHP or, more likely, all of them working collusively, mothers are NEVER given "reunification" therapy. The child does not need it because the child wants to be with their mother. This is a therapy used solely for the benefit of abusive fathers!

Dads can search the internet and easily find the fathers' rights networks that will get them custody (the government funded website fatherhood.gov contains referrals to father's rights groups including ACFC and CRC). NJ dad found Dr. Barry Bricklin, who advertises on-line that he can "win fathers custody." Bricklin told dad to wait for a specific judge (NJ changes Judges every two years). When that judge was assigned, dad won custody and Bricklin was assigned to be the families parenting coordinator.

Pedophiles & Incest

There are several types of pedophiles. Some are called preferential child molesters because they have a sexual preference for children. The majority are called situational offenders, falling into four categories: repressed, morally indiscriminate, sexually indiscriminate and inadequate. A repressed situational pedophile will molest his own child because it is safe. The morally indiscriminate will rape anyone. He has no conscience, will rape his own child, and may have children just so he can use them for sex. A sexually indiscriminate pedophile will prey on anyone, including his children, because he is bored, or likes the risk and sense of adventure. To the situational pedophile incest can be an outgrowth of other forms of abuse in his life; a continuation of his mistreatment of spouse and family members. He views sex with his children as a way to prolong the violence that is already an active part of his existence. His main criterion for selecting his child is availability.

When protective mothers are eliminated, the situational pedophile has been given permission to rape their child as frequently, and in any manner, that he chooses. Even if there was no previous sexual abuse, eliminating mother, increases the likelihood that the abusive father will escalate his feelings of entitlement and ownership by starting an incestuous relationship with his child. Father's perform incest on both genders; boys and girls, and on all ages. Acts include looking, touching, fellatio, and vaginal and anal penetration. Filming and posting on-line is becoming more prevalent.

Supervised Visits

    When mothers began to receive greater protections from abusers, laws were enacted to consider abuse when awarding custody. Highly abusive men were thought too dangerous for custody. Those men began complaining, especially when they were still ordered to pay support, and payroll deductions made it difficult to avoid payment. The creative solution became The Supervised Visit Center. These were to be places where abusive men could go to visit their children while being watched, supposedly providing a safe environment for father/child positive interaction. Supervised visits would cure abusive men, usually, in just a few months. Abusive men could quickly be awarded unsupervised visits and, ultimately, full custody. The government began to fund these start-ups through a grant process. Father's Rights group members were awarded many of the grants. Judges and court-affiliated MHPs secretly and openly invested in "Mediation" Centers. A lawyer or MHP can also be paid to hold supervised visits in their office. The parent being supervised pays for time by the hour. Rates vary, but can range from hundreds to thousands of dollars. Welfare will fund supervised visits under the fatherhood access/visitation program.

    According to a GAO report, staff at these centers have minimal training in abuse. At best, they believe abuse is a physical act and easily cured. Since father's rights groups are heavily invested in visitation and mediation centers, the fatherhood philosophy permeates these centers. Center staff work in conjunction with lawyers, judges and courts. Staff testify and send reports that the abuser is not abusive anymore and can be trusted alone with the child.

An effect of the fatherhood permeation is that the supervised visit/mediation center is frequently a place for mothers to be placed because they have reported the abuse, and are not willing to permit it; because they mistakenly expect the court to stop the abuse, especially sexual abuse. When a court determines mother is a parental alienator, she will be eliminated. The only way mother can see her child is by supervised visits, where she and the child are not permitted to speak of father's abuse.

Supervised visits can also be called reunification. Reunification, where a child is told an abusive father is good, is conducted during the visit. Imprisoned fathers being released and on a path to receiving full custody will begin with the reunification process; they are reintroduced into the child's life, and eventually receive custody.

Reunification centers can also be long-term, overnight institutions, such as the Rachel Foundation, as described in Bricklin and PAS above.

Conferences

The American Psychological Association (APA) works with the American Bar Association (ABA), nationally and in the states, to increase business for psychologists in law. Conferences are held where lawyers and MHPs get together to devise ways of increasing business, using MHP services to "win" litigation and extend cases.

The trade association AFCC also works to mine business between the legal community and the mental health profession with a yearly conference.

Fatherhood organizations hold yearly conferences where they can promote the importance of fathers and network with those who win fathers custody.

Conclusion

From Wikipedia: *"A racket is a service that is fraudulently offered to solve a problem, such as for a problem that does not actually exist, will not be affected, or would not otherwise exist. Conducting a racket is racketeering. Particularly, the potential problem may be caused by the same party that offers to solve it, although that fact may be concealed, with the specific intent to engender continual patronage for this party."* Family courts operate a racketeering industry. The problem they claim to solve is conflict among divorcing, or never-married parents. The service they fraudulently sell is the assignment of a wealth of service providers. Family courts encourage "fighting to win" by prolonged litigation. They use terms such as conciliation and mediation to portray the illusion that they are solving the conflict problem, all the while, they do nothing but foster disagreement and protect abuse.

Conflict is defused by quick resolution. Extended litigation does not resolve conflict, it increases it! Conflict is defused by addressing the cause. Appointment of a decision-maker merely adds to conflict. Family court and AFCC trade members do not mitigate conflict. Instead, lawyers and MHPs identify and feed the predator; they encourage and add to the oppression of the prey.

Once you step into family court's racket you cannot be a parent if you do not pay the extortion fees exacted by family court players.

This chapter lists some of the methods used against women and children who have merely tried to leave abuse and the abuser behind. As old methods are discovered, the trade group and its profit-oriented members have steadily developed new methods and have worked diligently to increase their influence over legislators and court institutional judicial rules, procedures and operations. This chapter presented an overview of the people who work in family court. Each individual case uses its own particular meld of methods. As the use of custody evaluators is slowed, the use of attorney's for the children (GALs) increases. Instead of assigning a custody evaluator, courts order automatic joint custody with appointment of a parenting coordinator or educator. The best way to document all the methods used and which methods are preferred by certain judges, courts and states, is accountability, analysis of current and previous cases, and forensic audits.

PART THREE

A BETTER WAY

A BETTER WAY

Motherless America confronts the government program which was designed to punish women who leave abusive men. Motherless America confronts a government program that endorses the unaccountable, for-profit court industry, resulting in extreme harm to children.

Our founding fathers created three branches of government so that no one branch could operate individually, without the oversight of the other two branches. When one branch, in this case the judiciary, acts corruptly, it is the responsibility of the other two branches of government to intervene. Motherless America explains how custody courts use federal money to operate fatherhood courts which do not adhere to state custody statutes requiring abuse to be a factor, and instead deem a father to be the only important factor when considering best interests of the children. Motherless America has proven by personal story and research that the judiciary has no accountability, or internal oversight – the appeal process merely endorses due process violations. Therefore, the United States Constitution mandates that the legislative and executive branches immediately act to stop the corruption of the judicial branch.

Legislative Branch
- Stop funding custody as outlined in Chapter 9, Best Interests of Father
- Reform Welfare (see separate heading below)
- Reform OCSE (see separate heading below)

- Require Accountability
- Create a Task Force or Commission to investigate and propose solutions
- Appoint a Special Investigator

Executive Branch
- Create a department within the FBI to investigate judicial "color-of-law crimes" prevalent in fatherhood custody cases
- Appoint a Special Investigator
- GAO Investigation of access/visitation
- Forensic audit state support access/visitation practitioners

Once government has a larger picture of the enormity of the collusion, there must be a complete overhaul of the system. I believe the optimal solution is a complete reform of custody determinations for divorcing and never-married parents from a legal forum to an administrative process. Fatherhood programs have already converted custody determinations from legal decisions based on fact and law to mandates requiring a plethora of for-profit service providers hiding behind constitutional judicial protection from suit for intentional unethical behavior, malpractice and denial of due process rights. The legal and mental health community has already proven itself unable to fairly determine children's futures. Therefore, custody determinations must be taken out of the legal system and into an administrative environment that has accountability, oversight and correction of mistakes as its first priority.

DATA, PROBABILITY, ANALYSIS

I propose the development of computerized templates for assessing the many factors contributing to custody determinations. The forms would use data gathered from questionnaires of parents, education and child care providers, family, friends and neighbors. The amount of non-family questioned would be specific to each case based of level of conflicting answers. Because discrepancies would be addressed neither party would be able to make false claims about their level of care. A parent's inability to put the children's needs first would become apparent. These computerized forms would negate the ability of abusers to manipulate the system; a standard computerized process would immediately stop abuse by proxy of family court.

Standardized forms of assessment for abuse, potential for abuse of children, existing caregiving duties and future caregiving qualifications would also be developed. Computerized forms would create a factual record which could be disputed and verified, what is legally termed "on the record." The computer program would integrate and analyze all data. The computer program would make more accurate custody determinations which would include probability factors. Probability would be a developing field of knowledge and adaptations of the computerized formula would have to be made as the field of knowledge develops and outcomes are assessed.

Assessing Abuse

Child Abuse Solutions, Inc., a California non-profit (http://childabusesolutions.com/), offers templates for assessing families, especially in cases of abuse. CASI's templates first outline the law, the legal requirements for proof, making it clear that any evaluator, mediator, or other MHP is going to be held to a high legal standard. California law is written on each form so it cannot be ignored by the MHP. Research about abuse and its effect on children is included in the template so the MHP cannot claim to have no knowledge or understanding. Checklists are prevalent. The MHP is asked throughout to verify their qualifications and methods. Facts are stressed and the MHP is required to ascertain the veracity of these facts. CASI templates are investigative reports, not fictitious stories of dad and mom's ability to parent, or a vehicle for the denigration of mothers through the use of false theories (PAS) or manipulated psychological tests. CASI templates are a good example of a standard investigative outline for contested custody assessment of existing abuse against partners and children.

Cause for the deterioration of the parent's relationship must be stated – abuse, alcoholism, drug abuse, criminal actions, and other negative behaviors must be a factor in custody determinations. When negative behaviors are the cause, parental completion of computerized templates modeled after CASI templates, would be required. Probability for abuse of the child would be assessed and factored into outcomes. Those who have treated battering men are the best candidates for assessing the potential to abuse the children.

Assessing Current and Future Caregiving

A computerized template for assessing current primary caretaking duties would be developed. Each parent would write how often they do laundry; cook; shop for groceries and children's items; clean the home; drive children to, and attend, school events, extra-curricular and enrichment activities, friends' homes; each parent's relationship with the child's friends parents; the child's current schedule and activities; friends, family members and amount of time spent with each; each parent's current method of discipline. Answers to these types of questions and more would be factored into determining the current primary caretaker. Custody would coincide with the current level of caretaking involvement.

A computerized template for assessing future caretaking duties should be developed factoring in age of the child. Each parent would provide their work schedule and plans for future changes to that schedule; living situation and plans for future changes; child care needs and solutions; preferred method of discipline; goals for the child's education and enrichment; parent's caretaking needs; plans for working with other parent; etc. While second to current primary caretaker, answers to these questions would also be factored into determining custody.

The best people to develop questions and analysis of caregiving duties are educators, researchers and hands-on childcare workers. Published research such as "How to Raise an Adult" by Julie Lythcott-Haims, former dean of freshman and undergraduate advising at Stanford University, could be incorporated into the knowledge.

Protect the Family

The administrative unit would treat abuse like the highly dysfunctional, detrimental, behavior that it is. If abuse is the cause for divorce then it would be treated seriously. Allegations of abuse would not be discounted but given a full and thorough investigation.

Every employee and affiliate of the administrative unit would focus solely on creating stability for the child, helping the family adjust, rebuild and move on from the trauma of divorce.

The most efficient way to determine custody is for the children to stay with the parent who has been the primary caretaker.

Shared custody would only be an option for parents who shared household and child care responsibilities previous to filing for divorce.

Services would be family-oriented, not profit-motivated.

The administrative unit would be forbidden from ordering counseling, mediation or coparenting, of any kind, but especially untraditional therapy, such as PAS therapy. Counseling can be offered, or recommended, but only for self, not for instituting of a businessperson into the family relationship to be the decision-maker. The unit could offer battering man therapy. Therapeutic services would be low-cost, not above-market value, which is the current norm.

REFORM WELFARE
<u>Combat Poverty Instead of Funding Litigation</u>

Welfare should never pay for one gender (father) to get custody (access/visitation). Temporary Aid to Needy Families (TANF), Office of Child Support Enforcement (OCSE) and Maintenance of Effort (MOE) funds should never be used for paying mental health practitioners and lawyers to favor a specific gender.

Welfare funds should be used for both parents to improve their economic situation and parenting capabilities. No gender is more important than the other. Children need one good caregiver. An abusive, dysfunctional caregiver is detrimental to a child, no matter what their gender. Fathers do not ensure a child grows up to commit less crime.

Replace welfare funding court service providers with economic improvement services that HELP families. For instance: education and skill training for higher wages.

Welfare should ensure both parents have the tools to adequately provide for their children. That means welfare should support education leading to living wage jobs, safe housing, good education for the children, preschool and after-school care, and summer programs for children. It is a reality that both parents need to work and the government should be supporting both parents, not merely forcing a father in the hopes that he will provide an income.

There must be greater access to birth control, especially to teens, since many of the fatherhood programs have been designed to force men on young mothers who are incapable of providing for themselves. Young parents need to be taught that they must be able to care for their children financially and that requires a living wage job which is only available to those with marketable skills and education. Instead of teaching abstinence, government should fund responsible birth control and teach the economic advantages of waiting to parent. Disadvantaged youth should be given greater opportunity for self-fulfillment and importance, instead of learning that importance comes from having a child. Pregnancy is not a way to get a man, and welfare should not be another mechanism for forcing marriage. Welfare should help both parents become financially stable, not just fathers.

Instead of forcing fatherhood, welfare should fund programs that truly help children achieve. Programs such as The Children's Zone, run in New York City's Harlem, replicated in Cleveland under the name The Promise Neighborhood, prove that virtually all kids, no matter what their birth circumstances, will achieve at similar levels throughout their lives if they are given enriched educational environments, stability and nurturing from day-one of life, regardless of whether they are living with their father, a single mother, or grandparents. By guiding kids from birth to adulthood, The Children's Zone has proven outcomes: 93% of Children's Zone charter school 9th-graders and 100% of 3rd graders tested at, or above, grade level on the State math exam. The program begins at birth with a nine-week parenting workshop called Baby College, encouraging reading to children and verbal discipline over corporal punishment. Welfare can require participation in this type of program for parents receiving subsidies (housing, food stamps, medical). Welfare money should support educational and enrichment opportunity for poor children, instead of assuming that a father cures poverty.

One of the most important ways our government can improve the state of the family is to increase the minimum wage to a level that permits women (and men) to adequately provide for a family without having to subsidize their incomes with welfare and support payments. Since older women, mothers, hold the majority of low-wage, service jobs, elevating their income would positively impact children. A low minimum wage supports a highly abusive system, where owners profit at the expense of the underpaid worker. Owners who claim they would not profit themselves if they paid their workers more money are similar to abusive husbands; owners feel they are more important than their slave-wage workers.

Providing quality, low-cost, year-long, education and child care services would improve outcomes for the child and decrease the financial burden of parents. The burden of child care is often added to support obligations. Low-wage workers cannot afford the costs of quality child care. Government subsidies should elevate the entire family, not one gender.

REFORM OFFICE OF CHILD SUPPORT ENFORCEMENT (OCSE)

There MUST be separation of custody and support. Support should not a reward for custody, nor should custody be given to reduce support. Support and custody must not be tied to each other. Support should never be a motivation for fighting for custody. Nor should any federal program be geared to reducing one gender's support obligation by giving them custody as is currently the unstated goal of welfare Fatherhood Access/Visitation. Child Support Enforcement should be an administrative unit only. Child Support Office's or any other government department, should never advice parents to fight for custody in order to reduce support. The federal Office of Child Support Enforcement needs to immediately end incentive payments to States for the goal of increasing non-custodial custody.

OCSE must rely on technology and tax records to determine income; income and income potential can be computer-generated based on data, analysis and income history. Certainly, the technology exists to average several years of income using tax records to arrive at credible income potential.

Support should not be a lucrative source of income for one parent. If the parent paying support requests, it would seem reasonable to require an accounting of expenses to ensure that support payments are necessary and benefitting the children instead of elevating already adequate income levels, without becoming overly dictatorial.

Any parent who is unemployable and needs great amounts of support to provide for themselves and their children should be given a specific amount of time to become self-supporting, for example: three to five years. Support payments should never leave either parent below the poverty line, especially parents who are at, or just above it. If a parent wants custody, they must assume the financial responsibility of child rearing. No parent should rely on support for basic needs. If a parent makes only $20,000 per year, they cannot maintain a support obligation of 25-40% of income before taxes, meaning, they cannot pay $5,000 to $8,000 for support.

High-income parents would be free to support their families at higher levels if they prefer to willingly elevate the income level of the primary caretaker without having a judicial order to do so.

Incentive payments to states should not be correlated to the amount of support collected. This has led to a system of manufactured incomes and high support obligations. Higher obligations lead to higher collections leading to higher federal OCSE awards to states.

REQUIRE ACCOUNTABILITY

The federal government must require States to institute accountability, oversight and overhaul custody determinations within three years or forfeit the 66% reimbursement of OCSE costs.

OTHER VIEWS FOR IMPROVEMENT

Others have considered the problems in custody court and have proposed solutions. Any lasting reform should consider a vast array of ideas, so I have listed other views below.

The Quincy Solution

Barry Goldstein is a lawyer who understands abuse. In representing a mother charged with Parental Alienation (PAS), he ran up against an industry set on giving custody to the abusive father. Since Barry did his best to represent the abused mother, he was singled out for retaliation and was disbarred. Barry is a founding member of the Battered Mothers Custody Conference. Barry has authored and co-authored numerous books including "Representing The Domestic Violence Survivor;" "Domestic Violence, Abuse and Child Custody;" "Scared To Leave, Afraid to Stay: Paths from Family Violence to Safety." His most recent book "The Quincy Solution: Stop Domestic Violence and Save $500 Billion" confirms that properly addressing abuse against women and children will save health care costs and prevent a host of illnesses, many of which contribute to premature death.

To make his case, Barry cites the Adverse Childhood Experiences (ACE) study conducted by Drs. Felitte and Anda for the Centers for Disease Control and Prevention. The research confirmed that children exposed to domestic violence, abuse and childhood trauma suffer more illnesses and injuries throughout their lives and they are likely to have shortened lifespans. Children who live with a father who assaults their mother; children who are targets of their fathers abuse whether verbal, physical, emotional, or sexual; children who live in homes with alcoholics; children who live in severe poverty (an inherently abusive condition); children who suffer from years of abusive litigation and custody-related mental health services; children who have their life-time primary caretaker eliminated and forbidden from stopping the abuse are going to suffer long-term, perpetual, negative reactions. Some of these children will go on to repeat the cycle of abuse.

A second consequence of abuse highlighted in "The Quincy Solution," is the foundation for the implementation of the Quincy Solution itself: the majority of the prison population has suffered from childhood abuse! While fatherhood promoters have successfully claimed fatherlessness is the cause for crime, the true cause of negative outcomes stems from abuse – in all its forms – societal and familial. Barry is right: confronting abuse and treating the perpetrators, protecting the prey from further abuse is the only way to reverse the damaging aftermath.

Child at Risk Classification Office (CARCO)

Leora Rosen recently authored "Beyond the Hostage Child: Towards Empowering Protective Parents." It contains an excellent history of legislation meant to address abuse of women and children; a historical look at custody determinations, an assessment of the problems in the current system; fatherhood funding and its effect on custody; and it proposes several solutions including the creation of new judicial units which would have jurisdiction for children at risk of abuse.

Divorce Corporation

The movie and book, "Divorce Corporation" was released in the spring of 2014. Its premise is that family court is a business which operates collusively to prolong resolution and increase conflict amongst litigants, in order to operate for the profit of all affiliates. http://www.divorcecorp.com/

Divorce Corp. highlights economic facts like the high cost of operating family court and the devastation to families in extended cases. It interviews several parties with outlandish litigation. Divorce Corp. ignores issues of abuse; abuse is not addressed or even mentioned. Divorce Corp. makes the point that government is paying large amounts for the administering of family court, yet, the movie does not mention that welfare is paying for family court through access/visitation, formation of 2 parent families, TANF, MOE, OSCE, and direct grants. Nonetheless, the movie informs the public of the myriad of problems of family court and begins a discussion about change.

Divorce Corp. contrasts divorce and custody in the country of Sweden where cases are not endlessly litigated in family court. Accountants are used to settle distribution of marital financial assets. Sweden rarely issues support orders. If support is awarded, it is short-term. In Sweden, divorcing parents amicably work out mutually-satisfactory child care arrangements. The problem with that comparison is that the United States is not Sweden. The US does not provide the social service supports available to Swedish parents. Over 70% of Swedes work under union collective bargaining agreements, they are not low-wage workers. College education is 100% free and the government provides low-interest (3.8%) loans for living expenses that can be paid back over 30 years. Child care is free in Sweden. Family leave is exceedingly generous (up to 18 months paid leave). Health care is free, provided by a government tax. Housing subsidies are available for lower-wage workers. 71.8% of females are employed. Therefore, divorcing parents do not fall into an economic abyss, which is especially true for US women.

Joint Custody/Shared Parenting

Father's Rights groups and Divorce Corp. endorse "shared parenting" as a solution. Shared parenting means the child lives with mother half the time and dad for the other half. Children can be put on an every other week schedule, an every other day during the week and alternating weekends, or a more selective arrangement with one parent picking days and the other parent working around that schedule. Unfortunately, this is not always best for children. The constant moving is destabilizing as it takes an enormous amount of emotional stamina for children to constantly adjust to a perpetually changing environment. Having a primary home and every other weekend visits, supplemented by several hours during the week, creates less upheaval and gives children a greater sense of security. It also gives them a greater sense of ownership of their physical environment. They can keep personal possessions in one home without having to constantly transfer belongings from house to house.

Shared custody can be a vehicle for abusive males to maintain control over the family. Therefore, shared custody often results in the appointment of an MHP to mediate or co-parent. MHP services are expensive, prolong litigation and cause extreme family stress. This is what I call Solomon's Choice. Because parents cannot decide who is the primary parent, the Judge will decide to split the child in half. I decided my children were better off with their father, where they had continuity of home and school, than in a constant state of instability dictated by family court and its affiliates. Having to go to JR's office, Keller's chambers, and counseling, gave the children anxiety and upset stomachs. Threat therapy counseling sessions are merely an opportunity to discount children's dislike of abuse, extending their trauma, and cutting off any opportunity to recover from the divorce.

Grants to DV Groups

The Office of Violence Against Women supports giving grants to domestic violence groups to train judges and court service providers, and to represent abused women in custody. They endorse court's hiring DV trained staff to classify abuse. These solutions are questionably practical as I have discussed in Chapter 7, Abuse. In most cases, these solutions merely prolong litigation. Government cannot possibly provide equal amounts of funding to both sides, fatherhood and DV groups, to argue it out in court. Instead of focusing on father's abuse of mother, custody determinations must focus on parenting and treatment of the children.

CONCLUSION

Some men who have participated in family courts get-even, need-to-win, racket, have come to realize that, in the long run, no one wins; everyone loses but the businessperson. Some of these men will support my solutions because they realize courts that operate the profit motive do not serve the family. But, there is still a large group of abusive men who feel entitled to control the family even after divorce. These men will always cry that dads are disadvantaged in family court because moms are making up allegations of abuse.

In the long-run, false allegations will prove to be fiction. If abuse is occurring, there will be evidence. True abuse is not spoken of with vengeance. It is spoken of in horror, shock, shame, and fear.

Relying on data, analysis and probability to determine custody discourages false allegations and abuse by proxy. Lies and manipulation cannot gain momentum in a factually based, verifiable record. Verifying the current distribution of parenting responsibilities, and basing custody determinations on that history, what has already been established, would prevent an unqualified parent obtaining primary care. If he did not participate in child care, a record of his parenting ability does not exist. Abuse is sometimes only noticed after an original custody determination because that parent has never been alone and in charge of the child. Abused women rarely leave their children in the sole care of their abuser. When he finally gets alone with the child, he targets his inappropriate behavior toward the child, instead of the mother. Family courts and the fatherhood custody mandate create situational pedophiles.

In ending, I will steal from Martin Luther King, Jr., by writing "I look forward to the day a parent will be judged by their character, not their gender."

Research Citation

Page 149 - "Report From The Wingspread Conference on Domestic Violence and Family Courts" written by Nancy Ver Steegh and Claire Dalton

Page 149-160, 165-166 - "Differentiating Types of Domestic Violence: Implications for Child Custody" Nancy Ver Steegh, 2005

Page 161 - "Domestic Violence Practice in Louisiana" Mark Moreau, 2005

Page 235 – "Access/Visitation Programs: Promising Practices," Pearson, 2001/2002

Page 223, 228 – "A Collaboration and Strategic Planning Guide for States: Child Access and Visitation Programs," Pearson, 2006

Chapter 9 – "Fatherhood Initiatives: Connecting Fathers to Their Children," Solomon-Fears, 2013, Congressional Research Service (CRS) report

Pages 222-230 – "Analysis of Federal-State Financing of the Child Support Enforcement Program," July, 2012

Page 226 - "Child Support Enforcement Program Incentive Payments: Background and Policy Issues," May 2, 2013

Page 223 – "Child Support Enforcement: Program Basics," CRS Report RS22380

Page 181,182, 224, 234, 236 –" Making Fathers Count: Assessing the Progress of Responsible Fatherhood Efforts" Annie E. Casey Foundation, Sylvester, Reich, 2002
http://www.aecf.org/KnowledgeCenter/Publications.aspx?pubguid={5931A803-4E1C-421B-844C-65644D696

Page 203-211, 233 – "Catalog of Research: Programs for Low-Income Fathers," Mathematica Policy Research, December 2011. Often referred to as "Strengthening Families Evidence Review (SFER)

Page 214 - OCSE, Access/Visitation, "Jurisdictional Profiles" 2005, 2007, 2008. http://www.acf.hhs.gov/programs/css/resource/child-access-and-visitation-grants-state-jurisdiction-profiles-for-fy-2008 and http://www.maccabuse.org/research.php

Page 164, 242-244 - "Changing the Culture of Custody in Pennsylvania," Commission for Justice Initiatives, 2007 https://www.pabar.org/public/committees/CJI/cjiabout.asp

About the Author

Doreen Ludwig grew up in a family of three generations of Philadelphia firemen. Doreen worked as a secretary for non-profits focusing on helping the disadvantaged until resigning to become a full-time mother.

Doreen Ludwig founded Mothers Against Court Custody Abuse, www.MACCAbuse.org to publicize and combat family court and fatherhood funding corruption.

Made in the USA
Middletown, DE
19 April 2016